THE BLACK PRINCE AND THE CAPTURE OF A KING, POITIERS 1356

THE BLACK PRINCE AND THE CAPTURE OF A KING, POITIERS 1356

Morgen Witzel and Marilyn Livingstone

CASEMATE

Oxford & Philadelphia

Published in Great Britain and the United States of America in 2018 by
CASEMATE PUBLISHERS
The Old Music Hall, 106–108 Cowley Road, Oxford OX4 1JE, UK
and
1950 Lawrence Road, Havertown, PA 19083, US

Hardcover Edition: ISBN 978-1-61200-451-8
Digital Edition: ISBN 978-1-61200-452-5

A CIP record for this book is available from the British Library

Printed and bound in the UK by TJ International

For a complete list of Casemate titles, please contact:

CASEMATE PUBLISHERS (UK)
Telephone (01865) 241249
Email: casemate-uk@casematepublishers.co.uk
www.casematepublishers.co.uk

CASEMATE PUBLISHERS (US)
Telephone (610) 853-9131
Fax (610) 853-9146
Email: casemate@casematepublishers.com
www.casematepublishers.com

Contents

Acknowledgements

Many people contributed to this book, and without them it would never have seen the light of day. We want first to thank our agents, Heather Adams and Mike Bryan of HMA Literary Agency, who believed in this project right from the start and made it happen. Thanks too to our many friends and followers on social media, who contributed their own helpful thoughts; especial thanks to Michael Jecks for so generously letting us use his photo of the monument at Poitiers. We still owe you that pint.

Our warmest thanks also to everyone at Casemate who worked with us. Clare Litt has been an extremely patient editor, and Isobel Nettleton has done a superb job of production. Thanks also to Julie Frederick for her meticulous copy-editing and for saving us from the worst of our errors. Needless to say, any mistakes which remain are entirely our own responsibility.

CHAPTER I

'Terrible is God Towards the Sons of Men'

On the afternoon of 26 August 1346, a tired, footsore and hungry English army stood on a low ridge near the town of Crécy-en-Ponthieu in northwestern France, waiting for the French to attack. King Edward III, the English commander, had invaded Normandy six weeks earlier with about 15,000 men, but battle and the natural wastage of a campaign had thinned their ranks until only about 10,000 remained.[1]

For the past two weeks the English had been retreating steadily, marching sometimes as much as 30 miles a day, driven north by a powerful French and allied force that outnumbered the English by five to one. Only two days earlier Edward and his army had narrowly escaped a French trap, fighting their way across a defended ford on the river Somme before making their way to the edge of the woodlands of the Forêt de Crécy. There, on the hot, humid afternoon of the 26th, the retreat ended and the English turned to stand and fight.

The French, advancing to attack, were supremely confident. Their army included not only the cream of the nobility of France but many great and famous names from across Europe: the blind Jean of Luxembourg, King of Bohemia and one of the greatest war leaders of his day; his son Charles, King of the Romans, elected but not yet crowned Holy Roman Emperor; Jaume, King of Majorca; the Genoese mercenary captains Ottone Doria and Carlo Grimaldi who had brought 5,000 crossbowmen to swell the French ranks. As they rode to battle, Edward's adversary King Philippe VI ordered the royal standard of France, the Oriflamme, to be unfurled. This was to be a glorious day for French arms, the day when the upstart English king – who had the impudence to claim the crown of France for himself – would be finally crushed and England forced to sue for peace.

Six hours later, the English still stood on the ridge – but the ground in front of their lines was thick with the bodies of French men and horses. Among the several thousand dead was Jean of Bohemia (also known as Jean of Luxembourg). The blind king had tied the reins of his horse to those of two of his companions so that they could guide him to the fighting, but all three men were shot down together by English archers before they could reach the enemy line. Among the many hundreds of wounded were King Philippe himself, shot – some say twice – as he advanced with his knights. The standard bearer who carried the Oriflamme was killed by the king's side. Philippe's brother, the Comte d'Alençon, lay dead on the field.

Shattered and bloodied, the French army retreated; and still it was not over. The following morning English horsemen and archers advanced through thick fog and fell on the remaining French detachments as they slept, killing many more and routing the rest. The Archbishop of Sens and the Grand Prior of the Knights of St John in France were killed, and Charles, King of the Romans very nearly went the way of his father. He was shot and wounded by an English archer while he and his followers fought their way clear of the wreckage of their army, and lived with the pain of that wound for years to come.

By any standards, Crécy was a stunning victory for King Edward. Almost overnight it became the stuff of myth – myth, it should be added, which was very skilfully created and exploited by Edward and his propagandists. One star, King Jean of Bohemia, had fallen, but a new one was rising: the king's 16-year-old son Edward of Woodstock, Prince of Wales, famous to later generations as the Black Prince.

Knighted at the beginning of the campaign in July, the prince was in nominal command of the vanguard division of the English army. It was his division which bore the brunt of the French attack at Crécy. At one point during the battle he was knocked to the ground by a French knight and saved only by the gallantry of his own standard bearer, who stood over the prostrate prince and defended him until help arrived. In one of the most famous events of the battle – another event which English propagandists exploited to the full – one of the prince's knights, Sir Thomas Norwich, left his post and ran back to the king, standing at the head of his own division which was being held in reserve. Norwich pleaded for reinforcements, but the king refused. *'Laissié l'enfant gaegnier ses esperons,'* he said ('let the boy win his spurs').[2] And indeed, no aid from the king was needed; the prince and his men were able to drive the French back without assistance.[3]

Yet it could be argued that Crécy was not so much won by the English, as lost by the French. True, the English army was well led and well disciplined, and it had a tried and proven tactical system based around a powerful weapon which it had recently introduced into continental warfare: the longbow. The French had attempted to counter the English archers by hiring thousands of

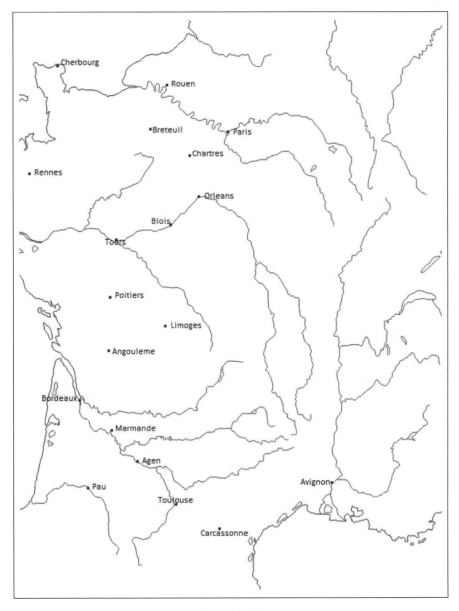

France 1356

mercenary Genoese crossbowmen, but to no avail. At Crécy, assisted by the elevation and perhaps also by the weather, the English and Welsh archers had shredded the Genoese crossbowmen with massed volleys of arrows before the latter could make effective reply.

Philippe and his commanders had failed to learn the lessons of earlier encounters in Brittany, at Morlaix in 1342 and St-Pol-de-Léon earlier in the summer of 1346, where the longbow had brought the English victory. The French also lacked the discipline of the English, and they failed to capitalise on their huge advantage of numbers. The French knights and nobles were glory-hungry and believed in their own invincibility.

Instead of halting and forming up for battle, each French contingent attacked as soon as it came in sight of the enemy. Thus, instead of a single mass assault which might have stood a chance of rolling over the English by sheer weight of numbers (despite the power of the archers), the French launched a series of uncoordinated attacks, most of which were beaten back with relative ease. According to one contemporary account, there were 15 separate attacks lasting from late afternoon until well after dark.[4] It is hard to escape the conclusion that the French were beaten by their own pride and lack of discipline as much as by the English archers. One contemporary chronicler, the French monk Jean le Bel, castigated the defeated French along very much these lines. Through their pride and envy, he said, all was destroyed.[5]

A hollow victory

But, when the dust was settled and the dead were buried, what had King Edward and the English army really achieved?

French losses had been heavy, between 2,500 and 4,000 dead with an unknown number of injured,[6] but there were still many thousands of French and allied troops in the field. Reinforcements were arriving too, including a large contingent from an important ally, the Count of Savoy, and 20,000 fresh troops from the southwest of France led by Philippe's son Jean, Duc de Normandie.[7] The French army was still formidable.

And although Edward of England had won a victory, he was still no closer to achieving any of his war aims. He had gone to war in 1337 with two objectives in mind. He had challenged Philippe for the crown of France, which he believed was his by right. He had also hoped to halt the continuous French encroachments on the English province of Guienne, in southwestern France. Nine years later, both goals remained elusive.

There was nothing spurious about Edward's claim to be King of France. His mother Isabella was the daughter of King Philippe IV of France. Her three brothers were all dead, and none had living male children. Edward was Philippe IV's only surviving grandson, and thus had a clear legal claim to the throne. But the French nobility disliked both Edward and his mother, and believed – quite rightly, as events in the following century would demonstrate[8] – that it would be impossible for a single ruler to govern both England and France. They conducted a quick legal sleight of hand and came up with Salic Law, said to be an ancient Frankish custom but more likely to have been invented on the spot. According to Salic Law, the offspring of the daughter of a king could not inherit the French crown. Succession could only be through the male line. This 'law' gave the French nobility the pretext for offering the throne to Philippe IV's nephew, Philippe Comte de Valois, who duly took the throne as King Philippe VI in 1328.[9]

Edward had objected to this and made public his own claim to the French throne. Predictably, he had been ignored by the French nobles. In 1337 he declared war on France with the stated intention of enforcing his claim. For this reason historians have generally considered Edward to be the aggressor, although the alacrity with which the French responded, even preparing to invade England in 1338, suggests that Philippe and his nobles were not exactly unhappy at having this war forced on them. The outbreak of war gave France an opportunity too.

Edward had inherited the great estates in southwestern France that Alienor (Eleanor) of Aquitaine had brought with her when she married Edward's great-great-great grandfather, Henry II. The lands of Aquitaine, which the English often called Guienne or Gascony, were of vital economic importance to England. Then, as now, this was one of the major wine-growing regions of Europe and revenues from the wine trade were important to the English treasury. France had always coveted those lands, and those revenues. In the century and a half since the marriage of Henry and Alienor, French kings and their lieutenants had slowly nibbled away at this patrimony, sometimes using the law courts to contest inheritance cases in order to get pro-French heirs into key towns and manors, sometimes using bribery and coercion to win over important local nobles to the French cause. Philippe VI had made it clear to his young antagonist that he regarded the whole of Guienne as rightfully French, and that Edward only held Guienne in the capacity of a French vassal. Edward III, who had his own fair share of arrogance, refused to acknowledge this.

The outbreak of war meant that Philippe no longer had to use subterfuge to gain control of Guienne. He could now use armed force and attempt to seize the territory by right of conquest. He did just that, driving the English back and seizing town after town; at one point his armies were almost within sight of the walls of Bordeaux, the English capital of Guienne. Edward, campaigning in northern France and the Low Countries, was forced to respond. Troops under his cousin Henry, Earl of Derby – later promoted to be Earl, then Duke, of Lancaster – arrived in Bordeaux in 1345 and drove the French back up the valley of the Dordogne as far as the town of Bergerac, 60 miles from the capital. The withdrawal of the Duc de Normandie's army to the north in 1346 after the disaster at Crécy allowed Derby to win back more territory and launch raids as far north as the city of Poitiers, 140 miles from Bordeaux. These successes in the southwest eased the pressure on Guienne, but they did not remove it.

Bloodied though they were, the French were far from beaten. Twice in the summer of 1346, Philippe VI had been gifted chances to trap and destroy the English army, once against the Seine west of Paris and once below the Somme west of Abbeville.[10] Both times the English had managed to wriggle free. At Crécy Philippe lost a third chance to crush his enemy. Had he destroyed the English army and killed or captured King Edward or his son, the Prince of Wales, he would have been in a position to dictate peace terms to his enemy. That chance too had been lost. But the French army was still powerful; the losses suffered at Crécy could be made good. Despite the damage caused by Derby's raids, France had lost little in the way of territory or possessions. From the English victory at Crécy, only one thing followed with any certainty: the war would go on and one day, at some unknown point in the future, there would be another battle in which the French would seek to wipe out the humiliation suffered at Crécy.

Calais and Neville's Cross

In the immediate aftermath of Crécy, while the wounded King Philippe struggled to regroup his army, the English marched north to the Channel coast. In September they settled down to lay siege to the important seaport of Calais. The town was well defended with strong walls and a quantity of artillery, mostly heavy catapults but also including another new weapon just beginning to make its appearance: cannon firing projectiles propelled by gunpowder. (The English army also had several cannon of their own which had been used at Crécy, possibly the first use of gunpowder weapons on a battlefield in Europe.) French ships could also run supplies into Calais harbour by sea.

In October 1346 Philippe made his first attempt to relieve the town, coordinating his own advance with an invasion of England from the north conducted by his ally King David II of Scotland. Philippe hoped that the Scots advance would force Edward to withdraw troops from the siege of Calais, making his own task easier. Once again the French king was doomed to disappointment. Although a few northern barons and knights did return home to help protect their lands, on the whole local English forces already in the north proved to be more than capable of dealing with the Scots without further assistance. At Neville's Cross, within sight of the walls of Durham, the Scots charged into a barrage of English arrows and, like the French at Crécy, withdrew shattered and defeated. Two wings of the Scots army broke and ran; the third, commanded by King David, was surrounded by the advancing English and forced to submit. David himself fought valiantly; disarmed, he still managed to knock out the front teeth of his captor, the Northumberland esquire John Coupland, with a blow of his fist before being forced to surrender. David was carried off in triumph to the Tower of London, where peace terms were dictated to him. The Scots threat was removed.

Calais continued to hold out. In the end Edward deployed more than 30,000 troops against the city, a colossal effort and the largest English army to see service on the continent during the entire Hundred Years War.[11] Another French attempt to break the siege failed in July 1347, but by now English ships had finally taken control of the Narrow Sea and prevented French provision ships from entering the harbour. The French garrison, cut off from all sources of food and other supplies, was now doomed. The besieging troops suffered too, with sickness thinning their ranks, but they held their positions. On 3 August 1347, Calais sent word to the English camp that it was ready to surrender.

In another carefully stage-managed scene, Edward instructed that the six most prominent citizens of Calais should come out to deliver the keys of the city dressed only in their shirts and with nooses around their necks, ready to be hung. When the keys had been delivered, Edward then ordered the six to be executed as punishment for the obduracy of their defence. His captains (and reportedly his wife, Queen Philippa) remonstrated with him, appealing to his better nature and telling him that such an act would be a terrible stain on his honour. Edward allowed himself to be persuaded to pardon the six men. It was cleverly done; thanks to chroniclers such as Jean le Bel the tale spread quickly around western Europe. The story had a long currency too; centuries later, the scene was painted by Benjamin West and then immortalised in bronze by the sculptor Auguste Rodin. Edward's self-created reputation as a ruthless but ultimately honourable man was further enhanced.

Historians have been divided over the wisdom of the English capture of Calais, some seeing the siege as a distraction from the main English war aims, others regarding it as a strategic masterstroke. There seems little doubt that Edward himself regarded Calais as important. Over the past 10 years, its port had often been used as a base by French raiders attacking English shipping and coastal towns. Possession of Calais also gave England a toehold on the continent close to the wool markets of Flanders, one of the English kingdom's principal sources of revenue. Finally, Calais became England's permanent beachhead, a base from which invasions and raids across northern France could be launched. While Edward may have theatrically pardoned the six burghers, they were left with little but their lives; one of his first acts after the town was taken was to evict the French inhabitants and repopulate the town with English settlers. A few years later in 1351 the nearby castle of Guînes was captured from the French in a daring piece of private enterprise by some English soldiers of the Calais garrison, and this further strengthened the English beachhead. Calais would continue to be a thorn in the side of France for the next two centuries.

Edward was not the only one to appreciate the value of theatrics and symbolism. A similar piece of theatre had taken place early in 1347 at the French court. The Norman baron Godefroi d'Harcourt had rebelled against Philippe VI in 1343 and been declared a traitor and an outlaw. Harcourt sought asylum in England, where Edward received him with honour and promoted him to the office of marshal in the English army. Harcourt became one of Edward's most important officers. It was almost certainly he who had advised the king to land in Normandy in the summer of 1346, in the hope that the invasion would provoke another rebellion against Philippe.[12] That hope proved illusory. Only a handful of Normans came forward to join the invaders, and once the English army moved on the country was quickly re-occupied by the French; a few small garrisons left behind by the English at Caen and other places were promptly wiped out. Harcourt, however, continued to fight valiantly for the English. At Crécy he had stood on the ridge beside the Prince of Wales and watched as his own brother, the Comte d'Harcourt, was killed leading his Norman knights against the English position.

Then, abruptly, at the end of 1346 Harcourt left the English army. Taking refuge with friends in the County of Brabant, he opened negotiations with the French court with a view to seeking a pardon and restoration of his lands and property. Philippe saw a chance for a propaganda coup of his own, to draw a line under the unfortunate affair of Harcourt's rebellion and to restore relationships with the Norman nobility. A few months later Harcourt appeared at the French court, also with a noose around his neck, humbly begging clemency.[13] This was duly granted, and Harcourt was restored to his lands in the Cotentin peninsula. To all appearances, he was once more a dutiful subject of King Philippe.

But was he? There is much about this affair that is suspicious. For one thing, Edward III seems to have made no attempt to detain his friend and officer when he left the siege of Calais (though according to one French source, the king did issue letters confiscating Harcourt's lands in England on 5 March 1347).[14] Harcourt has been presented as a disappointed man, deserting the English when they failed to help him start a revolt in Normandy. But it is equally possible that the strategy of inciting rebellion in Normandy was still very much alive, and that Harcourt's secret purpose in returning home was to help lay the groundwork for just such a rebellion. Either way, the result was much the same. Even if Edward did not deliberately plant Harcourt as his agent in Normandy, the effect was very much the same as if he had.

The fruits of victory

The fall of Calais left both belligerents exhausted, financially if not physically. At the end of the summer of 1348 a truce was arranged and both kings withdrew from the field, at least for the moment. The defeat at Crécy and the failure to save Calais had dampened French morale. Philippe needed to regroup and plan how he might resume the offensive.

For the English, on the other hand, this was a time of celebration. Along with Crécy, Neville's Cross and Calais, there had been a fourth victory, this time in Brittany.

Since 1341 France and England had been fighting a war by proxy in Brittany. The Duchy of Brittany, although owing allegiance to France, had always been semi-independent. The state was small but wealthy, its revenues bolstered by exports of salt, an important commodity which the country had in large supply.[15] All of this made Brittany a valuable prize. The death of the reigning duke, Jean III, in 1341 led to a disputed succession. One claimant appealed to France for support, the other to England. Both larger powers intervened enthusiastically, in all likelihood with a view to seizing advantage for themselves rather than any deep concern for seeing justice done.

Despite several English victories in the field, the tide ran strongly in favour of the French until June 1347, when an English expeditionary force under Sir Thomas Dagworth collided with a much larger French army led by the French-supported claimant, Charles, Comte de Blois, who also happened to be a nephew of King Philippe of France. The French laid siege to the town of

La Roche-Derrien in northern Brittany, hoping that Dagworth would march to its relief. Dagworth duly obliged.

Unlike many French military commanders during the early part of the Hundred Years War, Charles de Blois was intelligent and competent. A pious ascetic in his late twenties who was canonised soon after his death in 1364, Charles tied knotted ropes around his arms and legs so tightly that the knots bit into his flesh, and is also reputed to have put stones in his shoes to make walking more painful.[16] But his soldiers respected him, and he had led from the front throughout the war in Brittany so far. He had seen his forces beaten by the English in the field, at Morlaix and St-Pol-de-Léon, but each time he had rallied his followers and fought on.

Once again, unlike his contemporaries, Charles had learned lessons from the disaster of Crécy. He knew very well what had happened at Crécy; his older brother Louis had been killed there, shot down by English archers while charging towards the enemy line. Instead of waiting to meet Dagworth's men in the open and suffering a similar fate, Blois built field fortifications, wooden palisades that gave cover to his crossbowmen and men-at-arms and were proof against English arrows. Dagworth's small army, lured into attacking these wooden forts, found itself trapped between two enemy forces and cut off. Dagworth had little alternative but to surrender.

At this point, Blois made an uncharacteristic mistake. Thinking that the day was his, he moved his men out from behind their palisades to round up the defeated English. As he did so, the garrison of the besieged town, mostly militiamen with makeshift weapons, made a sudden sortie. Blois turned to deal with this new threat, whereupon Dagworth and his men picked up their weapons and rejoined the fight. It was Blois's turn to be caught between two fires, and in the end it was he who was forced to surrender, along with many of his knights. It had been a lucky victory; but it was a victory nonetheless, one which the English were only too happy to claim. Blois himself, talented but unlucky, spent the next nine years in captivity.

Edward III's stock was now riding very high and the English people, formerly lukewarm about the war with France, were enthusiastic supporters. Edward was determined to maintain that mood and popular support. He had learned a great deal in the 20 years of his reign, and one important lesson was how to get people on his side. His biographer Professor Mark Ormrod describes him as 'one of the most image-conscious kings of the Middle Ages'.[17] During the Crécy campaign, he had even used small incidents to build popular myths around himself and his son. In the course of that campaign, the king's officers and even the king himself had written letters home, letters which were then read out in public in London and other major centres.[18]

Edward also knew the value of symbols. He made deliberate attempts to associate himself with the legendary hero King Arthur, who was very much in fashion after a series of epic poems had popularised his cult in the previous century. (Edward was not the first to do so; his great-uncle Richard of Cornwall had also tapped into the Arthurian legends to lend support to his bid to become Holy Roman Emperor, and among other things had rebuilt the castle of Tintagel in Cornwall, Arthur's reputed birthplace.) Arthur and his knights were also very popular figures of romance in French literature, so the Arthurian association may have been an attempt to appeal to the French popular imagination as well. In January 1344, as preparations began for a renewed English offensive in France, Edward held a tournament at Windsor. One of the prominent features of the tournament was a replica of King Arthur's Round Table. Edward also ordered the construction of a round building, possibly to hold the table.[19]

In 1348, even before the fall of Calais, Edward decided to recreate the fellowship of Arthur's knights of the Round Table on a more permanent (and exclusive) basis. This was the foundation of the Order of the Garter, which took place at Windsor on 23 April, St George's Day (thus also reinforcing the connection between King Arthur and England's patron saint).[20] Twenty-six knights of England were named as members. They were divided into two 'colleges' of 13, with the king at the head of one college and the Prince of Wales at the head of the other. Some of the members were high nobles, such as the king's cousin the Earl of Lancaster, or William Montecute, Earl of Salisbury, the son of one of his closest friends. Some were important foreigners, such as Jean de Grailly, Captal de Buch, an English ally in Gascony whom the king was keen to keep sweet. But many others such as Miles Stapleton and John de Lisle were ordinary knights who had distinguished themselves in battle.

Significantly, more than half were veterans of Crécy (although William Bohun, Earl of Northampton and arguably one of the architects of that victory, was strangely omitted and not appointed until the following year). Thomas Beauchamp, Earl of Warwick, had been de facto commander of the Prince of Wales's division during the campaign; John Chandos had been at his side during the battle itself; Richard Fitz-Simon was the standard-bearer who stood over the prince when he had been knocked off his feet by the French attack and defended him until he could rise again. And even those men who had not been at Crécy had illustrious reputations. Henry of Lancaster and the Captal de Buch had won a string of sparkling victories in 1345 and 1346, removing the threat to Bordeaux and driving the French almost back to their pre-war start-line.

The name of the order and its device, a blue garter with the legend *Honi soit qui mal y pense* – 'shame upon him who thinks evil of it' – has prompted speculation amongst historians for centuries. That the garter was an important emblem right from the beginning is attested to by the royal wardrobe accounts, which record that specially made garters were presented to each of the founder members of the order.[21] Why an item of apparel should have become a symbol of knighthood has puzzled many. A popular myth arose that Edward had been inspired by an incident during a court festival, when he was dancing with a lady whose garter happened to slip and fall to floor. The king himself reportedly knelt, collected the garter and handed it back to her. *Honi soit qui mal y pense* is said to have been his rebuke to those who had laughed at the incident. This story is obviously fairly thin, and other inventive minds began to embellish it; according to some accounts, the lady was the Countess of Salisbury, with whom the king was also having an affair. (According to others, inspired by a libel by the French chronicler Jean le Bel, a passionate hater of Edward and all he stood for, the king had already raped the countess; this was his threat to any who might dare to make the matter public.)

There is, however, a problem with all of these accounts: garters, in 1348, were not used as garments in this way. The historian Richard Barber has made a detailed study of women's legs in the Middle Ages, or more precisely, the methods they used to hold up their stockings – who says academic research is dull? – and found only one example of garters being used before the 15th century. This was by a group of prostitutes in Toulouse in 1389, more than 40 years later, and as Barber says, they were probably only doing so as a way of mocking the English.[22] Indeed, the word 'garter' itself is rare and only occurs once in English glossaries before 1348. The story of the dancing countess is thus holed below the waterline. Barber's suggestion is that the 'garter' was in fact a reference to the belts worn by knights, and that both the badge and the motto were intended to support Edward's claim to the throne of France. *Honi soit qui mal y pense*: shame to anyone, in other words, who doubts the king and his claim.[23]

This fits better with what we know of Edward and his keen understanding of the value of myths and symbols. The Order of the Garter symbolised the king's determination to prosecute the war. It also showed that those who served him well would receive praise and recognition. It became the inspiration for a whole series of orders of chivalry, including the French Order of the Star in 1351 (see Chapter 3) and thereafter spreading rapidly. By the 18th century every major state and most minor ones had their own orders of chivalry, and the fashion spread to South America, the Middle East and East Asia. Many of these orders, including the Garter, still exist and the British crown has created several new ones over the centuries.

Yet, while all this celebration was taking place many people must have been aware of the shadow hanging over England, a shadow which had nothing to do with the French. The pandemic known today as the Black Death was making its way west. The plague is thought to have first originated as a disease among rats and other rodents in the steppes of Mongolia, and then mutated until it could affect human beings.[24] There is still some debate as to how transmission took place. It is generally thought that fleas living on rats were a primary carrier, but it is possible – and certainly this was the belief at the time – that the disease could also be passed directly between humans. The plague took two forms, as the French physician Guy de Chauliac describes in a chilling first-hand account:

> The mortality began with us in the month of January, and lasted seven months. It had two phases: the first lasted two months, with continuous fever and the spitting of blood, from which victims died within three days; the second lasted for the whole of the remainder of the time, also with continuous fever, and with abscesses and carbuncles in the extremities, principally under the armpits and in the groin, and the death took place within five days. The disease was extremely contagious.[25]

The Mongolian empire, which dominated Asia from the Pacific Ocean to the borders of Europe, was well organised, and travel across Asia was comparatively easy and swift. Trading caravans brought the plague west. By 1346 it had infected the Italian merchant colonies on the coast of the Black Sea; by the spring of 1347 it had reached Constantinople, from whence it spread through Syria, Egypt and North Africa. The plague made landfall in Europe in Sicily in October 1347, brought either from North Africa or by Italian merchants fleeing the stricken cities of the Black Sea littoral. Remorselessly it spread north, reaching Avignon in 1348 where Guy de Chauliac attempted to treat patients and recorded his failure.

By the summer of 1348 it was clear that the plague would reach England. Bishops wrote public letters to their clergy to be read out in church, urging people to pray and repent their sins in order to ward off the catastrophe. King Edward, as alarmed as anyone, urged the Archbishop of Canterbury to arrange for prayers, vigils and processions.[26] But as the historian John Hatcher has written, even the church struggled to come to terms with the looming catastrophe. 'Terrible is God towards the sons of men', wrote the prior of Christchurch, Canterbury, a statement that suggests that even the church had given up hope.[27]

By August the plague was ashore in England. Bristol was among the first centres affected, the plague probably carried by wine-ships coming from Bordeaux. By October it had reached London, and thereafter it spread across the country. Easter 1349 saw the plague at its peak, raging up and down the country. John Hatcher's *The Black Death*, a moving and painstakingly reconstructed account of the impact of the plague in one medieval village, was replicated thousands of times across England. The great and the good were not spared. Thomas Bradwardine, the celebrated mathematician and philosopher who had just become Archbishop of Canterbury, was struck down and died within three days of taking up his post. How many others died is impossible to calculate precisely. The plague was uneven in its impact; some communities were barely touched; others were annihilated. But scholars generally agree that by the time the plague finally ran its course in England at the end of 1349, one-third of its population had died.[28]

The violent peace

France had suffered just as severely as England from the plague. King Philippe's own wife, Queen Jeanne, and his son's wife, Princess Bonne of Luxembourg, were among the dead. It was not just the loss of manpower that affected both kingdoms; the economic and social aftershocks of the plague were considerable. Peasants began to leave the land to seek more lucrative work in the devastated cities. Fewer people to work the fields meant smaller harvests, and prices began to rise. The recovery period of 1350–51 was largely devoted to getting both realms back into some kind of order, replacing officials who had died of plague, sorting out the inheritance of manors whose owners had perished, getting prices under control and ordering the peasants back to the land where – according to the ideals of the medieval establishment – they belonged. The peasants went, but not willingly, and they also began to demand much higher wages. A dangerous reservoir of resentment began to build up, especially in France. As we shall see in a moment, the stock of the French king was beginning to run dangerously low. For the time being, at least, Edward of England was still benefitting from the victories his armies had won and his shrewd manipulation of public opinion.

Throughout this period, neither kingdom was able to conduct major military operations, and the truce arranged in 1348 was renewed annually until 1355;

in 1351, and for several years thereafter, there were half-hearted peace talks between the two sides, exploring whether it might be possible to bring the war to an end. But at heart, neither side really wanted peace. Edward still desired the throne of France; Philippe still wished to bend Edward to his will. So long as their views remained unchanged, the war would go on. The 'peace' that existed from 1348 to 1355 was marked by treachery, double-dealing and violence by both sides.

Even while the plague was raging across both countries, the French made an attempt to take back Calais by stealth. In the autumn of 1349 an approach was made to an Italian mercenary officer in the Calais garrison, Enrico di Pavia (generally known in English accounts as Aimeric of Pavia). Enrico was a turncoat, a former officer in French service who had gone over to the English after the fall of Calais. Now he was offered a bribe of 40,000 florins and a post in French service if he would hand over the town to the French. The plot involved Enrico secretly admitting a party of French knights under the command of Geoffroi de Charny – a veteran soldier who was also an important member of King Philippe's household – who would take the English garrison by surprise.[29]

The plans were duly laid, but what Charny did not know was that Enrico had secretly sent word of the plot to the English court. Receiving Enrico's message, Edward quickly dispatched one of his most trusted lieutenants, Sir Walter Manny, with a small force of men-at-arms and archers. Among the men-at-arms were Edward himself, travelling under the not-very-convincing alias of 'Edward of Windsor', and his son the Prince of Wales, also incognito.

Travelling fast, this little force reached Dover and sailed across the straits to Calais, where Manny and his knights hid in ambush at various points around the main gate. Two days later, a small French party was admitted into the town at night by Enrico di Pavia. One of the French had brought a sack with 20,000 florins, a down-payment on Enrico's fee. He received the money rather casually, telling the French commander that he 'was certain the money was all there, for he had not time to count it'.[30] The French quietly reconnoitred the town, failing to spot the carefully concealed ambush.

On the following night, the French party took possession of the main gate of Calais, opening it and letting down the drawbridge. But as the first of the French men-at-arms came riding over the drawbridge, Manny and his men, including 'Edward of Windsor', leaped from their hiding places and attacked. At the same moment, the ambush party broke down the drawbridge, trapping the French who had already entered the city. These, sensibly, surrendered at once. 'Edward of Windsor' then launched an attack on the rest of the French who, led by Charny, were waiting outside to enter the town once the gate had been seized. Edward's violent attack threw the astonished French back, and Charny retreated for some distance along the causeway leading to the town before realising that Edward had only about 30 men-at-arms and perhaps as many archers.

Realising his advantage, Charny turned and counter-attacked. His knights and crossbowmen pressed back along the causeway, taking heavy losses from the English archers as they did so. But Charny pressed his attack home; desperate hand-to-hand fighting ensued. According to one report, Edward was twice knocked to his knees by the French knight Eustache de Ribeaumont.[31] The king was in real peril, but the day was saved by his son, who came rushing up from Calais with reinforcements, crying the new war cry of 'St George! St George!' and drove the French back. Charny and most of his senior knights were taken prisoner, two of them being killed.

In those dark days of plague and mass death it must have been a relief to report a success, however small. Edward had once again played his hand well, foiling a plot which made the French king look dishonourable – it will be recalled that this incident took place in a time of truce – and showed Edward at his best. Fighting incognito under the command of one of his own knights was a classic piece of theatre – King Arthur himself had once done the same – and while the addition of the war cry of 'St George!' may have been an embellishment by chroniclers, it showed Edward managing once again to bind himself and his son to the emerging English myths, myths that they themselves were of course helping to create. (Edward was rather more circumspect about the efforts of his own men to do the same to the French, such as the failed seizure of Nantes in 1354.)

For all on the English side save one, there was a happy ending. Geoffroi de Charny, quickly ransomed by the French, took revenge on Enrico de Pavia. When Charny's men captured the Italian at an outpost near Calais two years later, they tortured and then beheaded him. All this too, in a time of truce.[32]

The attempted seizure of Calais was just one of many violations of the truce that took place up and down the frontier between French and English, at Calais, in Brittany and in Gascony. One of the most bizarre of these was the fight known as the 'Combat of the Thirty' in 1351. After the English garrison of Ploërmel in southern Brittany raided French outposts near the French fortress of Josselin, the French captain of Josselin, Jehan de Beaumanoir, issued a challenge to his opposite number in Ploërmel, Sir Robert Bramborough.[33] Each side would bring 30 men-at-arms to meet at an appointed time and place. The combatants would be on foot, heavily armoured, and were allowed lances, swords, maces and axes but, significantly, no bows or crossbows. Victory would go to the side with the last man standing.

This exhibition of organised mayhem duly took place on 26 March 1351 at a place called the 'Midway Oak' (*la chêne de mi-voie*) halfway between Josselin and Ploërmel. Boredom, rather than any idea of gaining military advantage, seems to have been the motive of those involved. These men-at-arms were trained to fight, they probably enjoyed fighting, and the truce had denied them the chance to do any fighting. Now, with every appearance of eagerness, they rode to the Midway Oak, dismounted and arrayed themselves in full armour. After a few polite preliminaries and the setting out of the ground rules, they proceeded to hammer each other, quite literally, to death. Every man on either side was seriously wounded during the skirmish, but they fought on. At one point the French captain, bleeding profusely, asked for some water. 'Drink your blood, Beaumanoir,' one of his companions told him grimly, 'and your thirst will pass.'[34]

The fighting eventually ended when one of the French knights mounted his horse and charged into the remaining English, knocking the exhausted men to the ground. This piece of unsportsmanlike conduct gave the French victory. Four French were killed outright along with eight English, including Bramborough. The story of the Combat of the Thirty circulated around Europe and became the stuff of legend, a source of inspiration to poets and musicians for generations to come. The survivors of the battle, especially Beaumanoir the victorious captain, were popular heroes. Years later, Jean Froissart recalled seeing a survivor of the Combat of the Thirty at the royal dinner table in France, being treated with great honour by all those around him.[35]

More fighting followed in Brittany, culminating in a pitched battle at Mauron in 1352 when a small English force under Sir Walter Bentley inflicted a sharp defeat on a much larger French army. The largest battle during this time of peace, however, took place not on land but at sea. Most of the original French navy had been destroyed by the English at the battle of Sluys in 1340, and Philippe had first turned for help to the Italian republic of Genoa, hiring galleys and other ships there. But relationships with Genoa had cooled after the disaster of 1346 (hundreds of Genoese had been killed at Crécy, many by their own French allies), and the French had turned instead to another ally, the Kingdom of Castille.[36]

In the spring of 1350 a fleet of around 40 Castilian ships under the leadership of a 24-year-old nobleman named Don Carlos de la Cerda – of whom more will be said in a moment – began raiding the coasts of Gascony and attacking wine ships en route from Bordeaux to English ports. Alerted to these incursions, in May Edward began to assemble his own fleet off the south coast of England. His son, the Prince of Wales, and his cousin, the Earl of Lancaster, were among his captains. The Castilians then sailed north, probably with the intention of raiding the English coast, and found Edward waiting for them with a fleet of about 50 ships off the south coast of Sussex near Winchelsea.

The action known as the battle of Winchelsea or, more quaintly, the battle of Les Espagnols sur Mer, began at about five o'clock in the evening of 29 August 1350 and lasted until darkness, though the main fight was probably over within an hour or so. The action was witnessed by onlookers standing on top of the South Downs, though whether they could see anything important is debatable. There was nothing subtle about naval tactics in the Middle Ages; both sides simply sailed straight towards each other. Most of the ships, if not all, would have been fitted with 'castles', wooden fortifications packed with English longbowmen on the one side and Spanish crossbowmen on the other. Once they were within range, the archers began trying to shoot each other down. The ships then rammed, grappled and tried to board each other, with hand-to-hand fighting between opposing troops of men-at-arms surging to and fro across the blood-stained decks. The Spanish had an advantage in that their ships were larger and had higher bulwarks than the English ones, giving more protection from English arrows, while their own crossbowmen could sweep the English decks.

At the outset of the battle Edward's flagship, the *Thomas*, rammed a large Spanish ship but came off rather worse in the encounter, springing a number of leaks. Edward and his men had to fight a desperate action to board and capture the Spanish ship before their own sank beneath their feet. Even more serious was the plight of the Prince of Wales, whose ship was likewise beginning to sink. Several times they tried to board the Spanish ship with which they were engaged, and each time they were beaten back to their own deck. Only the timely intervention of the Earl of Lancaster, sailing up on the Spaniard's opposite side and boarding it, distracted the enemy long enough for the prince and his men to scramble aboard. No sooner had the prince and Lancaster taken the Spanish ship than the prince's ship slipped beneath the waves.

In the end, Carlos de la Cerda signalled a retreat and his surviving ships slipped away into the twilight. The chronicler Jean Froissart estimates that the Spanish lost 14 ships; the English are known to have lost two, including the flagship, but there were probably other losses as well.[37] It was not yet the end for Don Carlos, who was back raiding Gascon wineships that autumn. Fate had other plans for him, however.

Jean le Bon

In January 1350 the widowed Philippe VI of France remarried. He was then 57 and his wife, the beautiful Blanche d'Evreux, daughter of the King of Navarre, was 18, but this was not what shocked contemporaries. Rather, it was the fact that Blanche was the betrothed of Philippe's son and heir, Jean, Duc de Normandie. The marriage came as a complete surprise to Jean. Relations between him and his father, always cool, now became positively glacial. Within two months Jean had also remarried (possibly on the rebound) to Blanche's first cousin Jeanne, Comtesse d'Auvergne.

However, this uncomfortable situation did not last for long. In August 1350 Philippe also died, and his son now ascended the throne as Jean II of France.[38] The widowed Queen Blanche retired discreetly to her family's lands in Normandy.

History has not been terribly kind to Jean of France, possibly with good reason. Some later historians called him Jean le Bon, 'John the Good', but it is difficult to see why. His reign saw misfortunes shower upon the country, and while not all of the tribulations of France could be attributed to him, at least some could. One of his most spectacular mistakes was to take up as a royal favourite and pet the defeated commander at the battle of Winchelsea, Don Carlos de la Cerda, sometimes also known as Charles d'Espagne, or Charles of Spain.

Quite how Jean and Carlos came together is not clear. There may have been a distant kinship between them. According to some accounts Carlos and Jean were childhood friends, but this seems unlikely as there was seven years' difference in their ages. What is clear is that soon after Jean's coronation, and indeed soon after Winchelsea, Carlos appeared at court and rapidly became very close to Jean. Although Jean had fathered 10 children in 11 years with his previous wife Bonne of Luxembourg, according to historian Jean Deviosse there were rumours that the relationship between the two men went beyond mere friendship.

Carlos was young, handsome and had an engaging personality, and there were obvious parallels between his relationship with King Jean and that of the English royal favourite Piers Gaveston with King Edward of England's father, Edward II. That story, and the grisly fate of Gaveston – captured and beheaded by the side of a road, at the orders of a group of rebellious English nobles – were well known in Europe. And, just like Gaveston and every other royal favourite before and since, Carlos soon acquired enemies.

It may have been at Carlos's instigation that Jean opened his reign with a spectacular piece of judicial murder of his own. Raoul de Brienne, Comte d'Eu and Constable of France, had been under a cloud since 1346. In July of that year, during Edward of England's sweep through Normandy in the run-up to the battle of Crécy, Brienne had been defeated and captured by the English at Caen. After his ransom and release, Philippe VI had accused Brienne of treason, alleging that he had deliberately handed over the city of Caen to the enemy.

Jean now revived that accusation, claiming that Brienne was in treasonable correspondence with the English and was planning to hand over his castle of Guînes, near Calais, to the enemy. (As we saw above, Guînes was indeed taken by the English in 1351.) His reasons for doing so are not entirely clear. He may genuinely have suspected a new plot among the Norman nobility, many of whom were in a perpetual state of disaffection with the crown, and may have believed Brienne was planning to lead a revolt. More likely, he was egged on by the ambitious Don Carlos. In November 1350 Brienne was arrested, given a very cursory trial, and executed. His title of Constable, one of the highest offices in the kingdom, was handed over to Carlos de la Cerda.

If Jean had hoped to defuse any budding Norman revolt, he was quite in error. The news of Brienne's execution was greeted with shock and anger. The Briennes were one of the great old families of France, and were particularly influential in their native Normandy. The angry nobles looked for a leader, and found one in King Charles of Navarre.

Known to French historians as Charles le Mal and to English ones as Charles the Bad, he was only 18 in 1350 but was already full of malice and ambition. He had inherited the Kingdom of Navarre in the Pyrenees from his mother, but on his father's side he was also Count of Évreux and an important landowner in Normandy. He was related to both the French royal family – Blanche, widow of Philippe VI and one-time intended bride of King Jean, was his older sister – and many of the Norman nobles. When the Norman nobles began hatching their plot for revenge against Don Carlos, Navarre was only too ready to join them. It is quite likely that he wanted the post of Constable for himself.

Alarmed by the hornet's nest he had stirred up in Normandy, Jean tried to arrange a peace using his former fiancée Queen Blanche as mediator, and in 1352 Navarre married Jean's eldest daughter, Jeanne de Valois. But the bribe did not work. The plotters continued to plot, and early in 1354 they struck. In January of that year, assassins hired by Navarre ambushed Carlos at an inn and hacked him to pieces.

This was a challenge that the king could not ignore. Royal troops invaded Navarre's lands in Normandy. At the same time, Jean could not press matters too far as Navarre was already threatening to call in the English, and the rest of Normandy, led by supporters of the late Raoul de Brienne including the Harcourt family, was now on the brink of revolt. Well might Jean have regretted the pardon offered by his father to Godefroi d'Harcourt, for the latter now stood among the ranks of the rebels. Negotiations ensued, while Navarre remained defiant within his castles and Normandy waited like a powder keg with a burning fuse. Meanwhile, John's lack of decisive action against the killers of Carlos de la Cerda intensified the disgust that many of his other nobles were beginning to feel towards him.

Not all of Jean's appointments were entirely unsuccessful, however. In 1352 the king named a pro-French Gascon nobleman, Jean, Comte d'Armagnac, as his captain-general in the south. Jean resumed the old pre-war policy of nibbling away at the English frontier, bribing or persuading key nobles to go over to the French side, even using the legal process to seize territories to which the French could claim title.[39] Nor did he pay much attention to the truce. In the autumn of 1353 Armagnac's troops raided the area around Agen on the Garonne; early in the new year they moved further north and attacked several pro-English towns in the County of Quercy, and in June 1354 Armagnac briefly laid siege to the important town of Lusignan, south of Poitiers. Those Gascon lords loyal to England such as the Captal de Buch were alarmed by the strength of French forces and the energy of their commander. The English governor of Gascony, the Earl of Stafford, seemed unable to counter the blows that Armagnac was landing.

Early in 1355 the Captal and two other Gascon lords arrived in England and presented themselves at court. The Captal, a Knight of the Garter, made his plea; unless action was taken soon Armagnac and his men would soon reverse all the recent English gains and perhaps even threaten Bordeaux once again. His timing could not have been better. Negotiations for a permanent treaty, brokered by the pope, had finally broken down. England was largely recovered from the ravages of the plague. Gascony was threatened, but France was ruled by an incompetent king who had lost the trust of many of his nobles. Much of Normandy was in *de facto* revolt. All of this could only mean one thing.

It was time to start the war once more.

CHAPTER 2

'The First to Pass Beyond the Sea'

It is easy to be cynical about the medieval papacy, thanks largely to the popes themselves, who sometimes seemed to go out of their way to demonstrate as many vices as possible. Even so, it is hard not to feel a twinge of sympathy for Pope Innocent VI, who had taken over from his spendthrift predecessor Clement VI in 1352. A Frenchman himself, he was – like all popes of the period – under the thumb of the French crown. In 1309, King Philippe IV had used military and diplomatic force to compel the papacy to move from Rome to Avignon on the River Rhône where it could be more easily controlled, and henceforth papal policy on a wide range of political issues had been more or less dictated from Paris.

Innocent did what he could to throw off the French yoke and be his own man.[1] He attempted to reform the administration of the church and cut down the excess spending of his predecessors. He intrigued with the Roman populist leader Cola di Rienzo, helping the latter seize power in Rome in hopes that Rienzo in turn would assist the papacy's return to the holy city, but this came to nothing when Rienzo was killed in a popular revolt in October 1354.[2]

Innocent was well aware that the war between France and England was about to bubble up once more, and he tried – with every appearance of sincerity – to broker a peace between the antagonists. Late in 1354 he offered to mediate between France and England and also between King Jean and his mortal enemy, Charles of Navarre. The offer was accepted by all parties, though with what evidence of sincerity it is difficult to guess; Armagnac's men were on the march in Gascony, Charles was stirring up revolt in Normandy, and the English government was already raising money for a campaign and meditating on its own next strategic moves. But the English negotiators, led by the ever-reliable Lancaster (now raised to the title of Duke) and another veteran diplomat and soldier Richard FitzAlan, Earl of Arundel, arrived in

Avignon around Christmas, to be joined by French envoys led by the Chancellor of France, Pierre de la Fôret, and the Duc de Bourbon. Charles of Navarre himself was lurking on the fringes of the papal court, spying on both parties.[3]

Things did not go well. Lancaster and Fôret eventually agreed to extend the truce to July 1355, partly, one suspects, because both sides needed a little more time to raise their armies and prepare for all-out war. On the issue of French sovereignty, Lancaster refused to concede an inch; King Edward of England, he said, was the rightful King of France and King Jean was an usurper. Not surprisingly, the negotiations broke down and Lancaster, Arundel and their entourage returned to England in March 1355.

Undeterred, Innocent continued to send envoys to both Paris and London urging reconciliation and peace. No one wanted to listen. In Paris, it had become clear that England intended to support – indeed, probably already was supporting – Charles of Navarre and the Norman rebels. King Jean intended to draw off English strength by reinforcing Armagnac's army in the south and encouraging Scotland – quiescent since the disaster at Neville's Cross nine years earlier – to rouse itself and attack England's northern border. In London, King Edward and his diplomats were as always highly suspicious of the papacy, seeing in its every move another attempt by the French to gain the advantage, and the very fact that the French-dominated papacy was asking for peace made them more inclined towards war.

Edward and his councillors believed that the advantage lay with them. Since Winchelsea, England had largely had undisputed control of the sea, meaning English expeditionary forces could land at will around the coastline of France. In Gascony, in Brittany, in rebellious Normandy and, thanks to the capture of Calais, in Picardy, they had friendly ports ready and waiting for them. Jean's armies could not be everywhere at once. Edward also believed – wrongly, as it turned out – that Scotland had no appetite for a resumption of war. King David of Scotland was an English prisoner, in effect a hostage for his country's good behaviour, and negotiations for his ransom were ongoing.[4] As a result, Edward began diverting men from the northern counties, traditionally earmarked for defence against the Scots, to the expeditions already being prepared for France.

By the spring of 1355, two armies were preparing. One would go to Normandy and reinforce Charles of Navarre and the rebels there. The second force would go to Gascony, check the advances of Armagnac and his forces, reassure the loyal Gascons that England was still there to defend them, and if possible draw French royal troops away from Normandy. In effect, both sides were attempting the same strategy; launch a series of campaigns in the peripheries to distract the enemy, while focusing on the main theatre of war in the north of France. England hoped to wrench Normandy away from its allegiance to the French crown; France intended to crush Charles of Navarre and restore French royal control over Normandy. In the end – thanks in large part to the man at the centre of the storm, Charles of Navarre himself – neither side succeeded in reaching their strategic aims.

The question of command of these two armies then arose. Edward seems to have decided early on to remain in England, overseeing the direction of the war and ready to follow with reserve forces if needed. Command of the army destined for Normandy was given to the king's chief lieutenant and trusted advisor, the redoubtable Lancaster. The question then arose as to who should command the second army, bound for Gascony. That honour was begged by the Prince of Wales, who wrote to his father and, in his own words, 'prayed the king to grant him leave to be the first to pass beyond the sea'.[5]

Edward of Woodstock

In fact, the prince may not have had to lobby very hard. He was the obvious choice to receive this, his first independent command.

In 1355, Edward of Woodstock was 25 years old. He was so far unmarried; various diplomatic marriages had been proposed, and ambassadors were sent several times to the Duchy of Brabant with a view to persuading the duke to offer his daughter Margaret as a bride for the prince, but this attempt had floundered in 1347 when Margaret married the pro-French Count of Nevers instead. Since then, no other candidates had offered themselves. The prince seems to have been prepared to wait for the right woman to come along; and in the meantime, enjoy himself with the wrong women. By 1355 he had sired at least three and possibly more illegitimate children, including the future Sir Roger Clarendon, by a young woman named Edith Willesford. It is possible that the affair with Edith continued for some time, even after his marriage in 1360; another son, John Sounders, may also have been born to Edith.

Little reliable information about the prince's character has come down to us. Richard Barber, his principal biographer, comments that most contemporary accounts of the prince were deliberately designed for public consumption. Edward is painted always in a heroic light, possessed of all the knightly and noble virtues: he is generous, honourable, courteous, brave, a lion-hearted fighter, a swift and decisive military commander who yet treats his defeated foes with great chivalry.

At least some of this behaviour, if not actually made up by the chroniclers and other writers such as Chandos Herald, was a façade; the Prince of Wales was heir to the kingdom, and he behaved as the kingdom expected him to behave. In many ways he modelled himself on his father, also famous for his courage, military skill and chivalric behaviour, so much so that in later years contemporaries referred to him as 'Edward the Fourth', a kind of king-in-waiting, all ready to step into his father's shoes when the time came.

There were other aspects to his behaviour as well. The prince was famously extravagant, and his household officials, especially those in charge of his finances, spent much of their time staving off creditors and trying to raise fresh funds to pay for his whims; this state of affairs persisted from the time he was about 10 years old until his death. This aspect of his character he may have inherited from his mother, Queen Philippa, who was also noted for her spending habits; and like both his parents, Edward loved to gamble, and did not always win. He was also fond of parties, and spent vast sums on dinners and celebrations to which he invited not only his household and loyal followers but, apparently, anyone who happened to be in the neighbourhood.

Of course, this extravagance was, at least in part, a calculated effect. Medieval society, especially courtly society, prized generosity, and largesse was one of the most prized traits of a truly chivalric king – or, as above, king in waiting. Giving gifts to friends and followers was a way of demonstrating largess. So too was losing at gambling, especially if one lost deliberately to a friend who might just happen to need money at that point. Barber notes that one of the first appearances of the prince in historical record concerns him losing 12 shillings at gaming to John Chandos, at a time when Chandos was a relatively minor figure from a not particularly well-to-do background.[6]

But not everything was for show. Even more than his father, perhaps even more than his mother, the prince was fond of bling. Barber describes how at his first official public event, meeting two emissaries of the papal court in 1337, the prince appeared 'arrayed in a new robe of purple velvet and a hat made specially for the occasion with a scarlet border sewn with pearls', and how his wardrobe included 'scarlet hats embroidered with silver roses and a broad ribbon belt with 37 enamelled plaques and 234 pearls sewn onto it'.[7] Barber notes further that his rooms were hung with expensive tapestries. The prince was at this point seven years old.

He could be capricious, and he could be cruel. The devastation his army caused in Languedoc (see Chapter 4) rendered thousands of innocent people homeless and destitute. In 1370, after his troops sacked the city of Limoges, the prince was accused of ordering the massacre of the entire population, around 3,000 people. The evidence was largely fabricated by French chroniclers, and the real civilian death toll was likely nearer to 300.[8] Nor were the prince's actions at Limoges anything like unique; other medieval war leaders were similarly ruthless, and even the saintly Charles of Blois had ordered the massacre of rebel Breton civilians in Quimper in 1344; the death toll may have been as high as 2,000. Nevertheless, the fall of Limoges leaves an unpleasant impression in the mind.

Against that, the prince was indeed very generous to his friends, and especially his former servants. He remembered fondly his former wet-nurse, Joan of Oxford, granting her a pension of £10 per annum in later life – enough to enable her to live very comfortably indeed – and sending her a tun of wine in 1357.[9] He gave similar gifts to many serving and former members of his household, and once gave a coat to a minstrel who had played music for him while he was ill, even though he apparently did not know the man's name.[10] His long-serving tailor, Henry Aldrington, who must have been a very hard-working man indeed, was rewarded in 1355 with a knighthood. The fighting men of his household were similarly looked after. John Kentwode, an unknown young esquire in 1355 who shot to prominence during the events of 1356, was rewarded with money, position and ultimately a knighthood of his own.

The prince was also loyal to his friends, and never forgot them. His near contemporary William Montecute, Earl of Salisbury, was one of his close companions during the Crécy campaign and continued by the prince's side throughout most of his career; their friendship even survived Edward's marriage to Salisbury's ex-wife, Princess Joan of Kent, in 1361. John Chandos, James Audley, Bartholomew Burghersh and others who had been in his household in the early days also became close friends and companions. Chandos in particular had an almost avuncular relationship with the prince, who relied on Chandos utterly until the latter's death in battle in 1369.

Apart from stylised portraits in manuscript illustrations, which make Edward look like anyone and everyone else around him, the closest thing we have to a portrait is the effigy from his tomb in Canterbury Cathedral. The effigy is clad in full armour, the head covered by a helm and the face framed by a curtain of chainmail, so we can see only a few features: a square brow, strong cheekbones, a long nose and a drooping moustache above a firm mouth. Whether this is an accurate portrayal or yet more idealising on the part of the sculptor, we shall never know. We do know, however, that his mother Queen Philippa insisted that her face be sculpted from life for her own tomb effigy a few years earlier, in 1369. So, it is possible that we are looking at a lifelike portrait of the prince.

There is a further intriguing possibility about his looks. Long after his death, Edward acquired the nickname by which the world now knows him – the Black Prince. Barber and the prince's other modern biographer, David Green, agree that this nickname is a fabrication, most likely created in the 16th century when a certain amount of mythologising about the earlier Plantagenets was going on (in part, at least, to confer legitimacy on the Tudor dynasty, and discredit the Yorkists whom the Tudors had ousted).[11] One commonly held theory is that the name refers to a tradition of depicting princes in black armour, although it must be said that examples of this practice are not exactly common.

It has been suggested, quite possibly in our view, that the prince's mother Queen Philippa was of mixed race. This is not as far-fetched as it might seem. Philippa was born in the Low Countries, in the County of Hainault, but she had Spanish ancestry. The princes and kings of the Iberian peninsula had for centuries been marrying their Moorish counterparts from southern Spain. Spanish princesses then went on to marry widely across Europe – so widely that most royal houses including that of England could boast of at least some Spanish ancestry. And Spanish, by the 14th century, also meant Moorish.

In 1325 an English ambassador, Walter Stapledon, Bishop of Exeter, visited the court of Hainault and recorded this impression of the young Philippa, then being considered as a bride for the future Edward III:

> The lady whom we saw was not uncomely. The colour of her hair is dark, betwixt blue-black and brown. Her head is clean-shaped; her forehead high and broad, and standing somewhat forward. Her face narrows between the eyes, and the lower part of her face is still more narrow and slender than her forehead. Her eyes are blackish-brown and deep. Her nose is fairly smooth and even, save that it is somewhat broad at the tip and also flattened, and yet it is no snub-nose. Her nostrils are also broad, her mouth fairly wide. Her lips are somewhat full, and especially the lower lip ... Moreover, she is brown of skin all over, and much like her father, and in all things she is pleasant enough, as it seems to us.[12]

The historian Ian Mortimer doubts whether this is in fact a description of Philippa, suggesting the passage refers to her sister Margaret.[13] However, the passage also suggests that her father is similarly dark of skin, meaning Philippa may have been as well. As noted, it is not genetically impossible. Certainly we need to think again about some of the people dubbed 'Black' in medieval Europe – Black Agnes of Dunbar, Countess of Man and Annandale, springs immediately to mind – and reassess whether these appellations were applied to their characters or, much more simply, to their appearance.

As for the Black Prince, the name is indeed of much later origin. But it is just possible that some faint memory of his appearance survived and resulted in the creation of the nickname. Once again, we will never know. But the possibility is there.

Band of brothers

Like many gifted military commanders, the prince had an ability to inspire loyalty in others. The largesse, the gifts and the favours of course had a role to play in this, and there is no doubt that several of the men around the prince owed their high positions and success entirely to his influence. But reading the histories and accounts in the administrative records and chronicles, one senses there was much more to it than self-interest. Like Nelson and his 'band of brothers', like Alexander of Macedon and his captains, the prince gathered around him a coterie of men who respected him, liked him and trusted him, and whom he respected, liked and trusted in turn. On the battlefield, that mutual bond is worth many battalions.

Though he had proven his courage and fighting ability at Crécy and Winchelsea, the prince had never before held an independent command. Now, he was going far from home to southern France, where he would not be able to rely on the advice and guidance of his father. To support his son and give him counsel, Edward III appointed several officers of proven ability to the expedition. Of these men, the one the prince would have been most glad to see was Thomas Beauchamp, Earl of Warwick and marshal of England.

Forty-one years old when the Gascony campaign began, Warwick was one of the rock-hard pillars of Edward III's reign and arguably one of the finest soldiers the Plantagenet kingdom ever produced. A veteran of campaigns in Scotland, France and Brittany, he had been appointed marshal for life in 1343, an indication of the trust the king reposed in him. In 1346, Warwick's hour had come. He had been appointed *de facto* commander of the vanguard division of the English army, nominally led by the prince, and had been at the forefront of every major action on the campaign.

Sent forward during the assault on Caen with orders from the king to break off the fighting and withdraw, Warwick had scented advantage, disobeyed royal orders and sent his men straight into the attack. The outcome was a stunning English victory. He had been one of the first to cross the disputed ford at the Blanchetaque a few days before Crécy, and during the battle itself had directed the vanguard division, which bore the brunt of the fighting, with resolution and skill, suffering only a handful of casualties and causing carnage among the French. The presence of this great soldier at his right hand must have been an immense relief to the prince.

The other three senior nobles were also veterans of Crécy. The oldest, Robert Ufford, Earl of Suffolk, was in his late fifties, a veteran diplomat and military commander on both land and sea.[14] The son of a relatively obscure Suffolk baron, Ufford had first come to prominence during Edward III's revolt against his regents, his mother Queen Isabella and her lover Roger Mortimer. Ufford was one of the men who had followed the young king into Nottingham castle in the dead of night to arrest Mortimer, and had killed two of Mortimer's men who tried to bar their way. His reward was an earldom and a string of official posts, and he went on to become another of the king's most reliable men.

John de Vere, Earl of Oxford, was in his early forties, and had learned his trade as a soldier in the Scottish wars before serving as a captain under the Constable of England, the Earl of Northampton. He was a veteran of both Morlaix and Crécy. Finally, as mentioned, there was the prince's friend William Montecute, Earl of Salisbury, two years older than Edward. Prince Edward had personally knighted Salisbury at the church in Quettehou soon after landing in France in 1346, and they had fought side by side during the campaign and ever since.

Another senior figure was Sir John de Lisle, second Baron Lisle, another Crécy veteran and Knight of the Garter; wealthy and influential, he had fought through most of the key engagements in the war so far, and was also close to the prince's father, King Edward. Sir Reginald Cobham of Sterborough in Surrey was also one of the king's trusted officers, a diplomat and soldier who had served with great distinction in the Crécy campaign, often in the thick of the fighting. It comes as something of a surprise to find that he was overlooked for the foundation of the Order of the Garter; he did not become a Garter Knight until 1352.

Of all the prince's friends and companions, John Chandos was the one whose fame has resounded most loudly, then and since. Born around 1320 in Radbourne, Derbyshire, Chandos was knighted for valour after the battle of Cadzand in 1337, one of the opening skirmishes of the war, and quickly proved himself a brave and reliable soldier. Taken into the king's retinue, he was befriended by the Prince of Wales and served alongside him through the 1346 campaign. Chandos would go on to become a knight banneret and hold many high offices before his death in battle late in 1369. In 1355 his star was still rising, but he was one of the men to whom the prince turned most often for advice.

Chandos was steady and reliable; James Audley seems to have been more mercurial. Born out of wedlock to the knight James Audley of Stratton Audley and the redoubtable Eve Clavering – herself a remarkable character, who had already been widowed twice and would go on to marry again, this time to a much younger man, after Audley senior's death – Audley too had risen through the ranks through sheer fighting spirit and valour. Like Chandos, he was a veteran of Crécy and a founding member of the Order of the Garter. He too was still very much a man on the rise, constantly on the lookout for chances to prove his bravery and worth. Along with Chandos, he was perhaps the prince's closest and most trusted friend.

Richard Stafford was an older man, close to 50 by the time the expedition set sail for Gascony. As well as a veteran soldier – he too had played a prominent role in the Crécy campaign – Stafford was an able administrator who had served as one of the prince's commissioners in the principality of Wales. Bartholomew Burghersh was another wise old head, who had served as one of the young prince's tutors and was now a key advisor. He had also been at Crécy, fighting by the prince's side, and was a founder member of the Garter; so had Nele Loring, the prince's chamberlain, knighted for valour at the battle of Sluys in 1340 and another rising star. Baldwin Botetourt, who served as master of the prince's horses, came from an illustrious fighting family, as did Maurice de Berkeley, the eldest son of Lord Berkeley.

Probably the oldest man in the group, if not the army, was Sir John Sully of Iddesleigh in Devon who, if his own testimony is to be believed, was over 70 years of age but still hale and hearty enough to take the field. A veteran of Halidon Hill, Crécy and Winchelsea, he continued to serve in the field until around 1370, when he finally retired. He was still alive in 1385 when he gave evidence to a commission on heraldry; he claimed then to be 105 years old. In 1361, Sully received an unusual honour: once a year, in any royal forest or park, he might have freely one shot with his bow, one course with his hounds and one chase with his dog, who was called Bercelette.[15]

One of the more unusual members of the company of knights gathered around the Prince of Wales was Matthew Gurney from Somerset. In 1327, Gurney was one of four assassins who murdered the deposed King Edward II in his cell at Berkeley castle, allegedly by inserting a red-hot poker in his rectum (it is more likely that he was strangled). Orders for the murder were supposedly given by Roger Mortimer, the lover of Edward's wife Isabella, who had engineered the king's overthrow. But when Edward III seized power three years later, sending Mortimer to the scaffold, he seemed curiously reluctant to punish his father's killers. After a period in exile, Gurney was allowed to return home, and a few years later he could be found in the Prince of Wales's retinue during the Crécy campaign, where he fought with distinction. Ten years

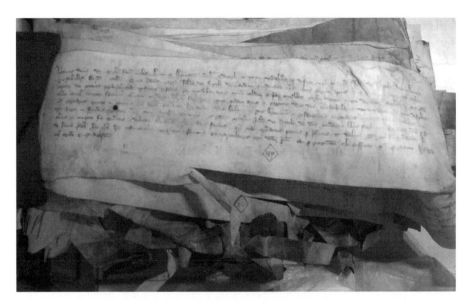

Documents from the Bordeaux administration

later he was still there. Not many men are happy to take their grandfather's murderer into their service, but Prince Edward appears to have held no grudge.

We know too a little about the members of the prince's household who accompanied him on campaign. As well as Loring the chamberlain and Botetourt the master of horse, there were Nicholas Bond, the prince's esquire, and Dietrich Dale, usher of the chamber. Servants included Robert Egremont, who had charge of the royal household's tents, John Henxteworth the financial controller, Geoffrey Hamelyn the keeper of the king's armour, William Bakton the king's butler, Richard Dokesey the baker and Henry Aldrington his tailor. Three ordinary servants are named – William Lenche, John Palington and Henry Berkhampstead – and several clerks are mentioned but not named. Overseeing them all was Sir John Wingfield, the governor of the household.

The lower ranking members of the expedition are sometimes visible, but often only fleetingly. Denys de Morbecque, or Morbeke, was an exile from Artois in northern France; according to legend, he had fled to England to avoid prosecution for a murder committed as a young man and taken service in the English army, probably as a way of making a living. Some chroniclers refer to him as a knight, but this seems highly unlikely. He was a veteran soldier, while the young John Kentwode, son of John Kentwode of Tilehurst in Berkshire, was having his first taste of military service. Another young man, an archer by the name of John Hawkwood, may also have been about to see battle for the first time. It would not be the last; years later, as Sir John Hawkwood, he would become one of the most famous and feared *condottieri*, the mercenary captains of medieval Italy.[16]

The archers, recruited in Cheshire and North Wales, appear occasionally in the records too, and the prince's clerks became so tired of writing the name Llewellyn that they simply abbreviated it to 'Ll' with a flourish underneath. Gronou ap Griffith was the leader of the archers from North Wales, and we know a few other names too.

The Guienne expedition

The force the prince took with him was small, around 1,000 men-at-arms, 1,000 mounted archers with a further 400 archers on foot, and 170 foot soldiers armed with spears who are described simply as 'Welshmen', for a total of just over 2,600 men.[17] Servants, grooms, wagon drivers and other non-combatants are not included in this total. Other forces, garrison troops and Gascon allies, would be waiting for the prince in Bordeaux.

This little army was raised through two methods: the retinue system, and direct recruitment from the prince's own domain lands. Each of the nobles and senior knights who came to join the prince brought their own retainers. The size of the retinue depended on the influence, reputation and wealth of its leader. People could and did switch retinues, and younger men in particular were eager to serve a leader who could promise them action, plunder and fortune. If the leader was also famous for his generosity and largesse towards his followers, he gained still more in popularity.

The prince had his own retinue, and unsurprisingly this was the largest in the force, being composed of 433 men-at-arms – nearly half the total – 400 mounted archers and 300 archers on foot. The other captains – Oxford, Suffolk, Salisbury, Warwick, Lisle and Cobham – also brought their own retinues to the army. These retinues were in effect a method of raising an army through private enterprise. Leaders of retinues – including the prince himself – had written contracts, or indentures, with the crown by which they promised to bring a certain number of troops of various types into the crown's service for a specified period of time. For example, in 1355 Sir John de Lisle engaged to provide 20 knights, 39 esquires and 40 archers.[18] Leaders of retinues were paid for this service, and paid well; providing retinues was one way in which a knight or nobleman could make a tidy profit out of the war.

The knights, esquires and about two-thirds of the archers were recruited through the indenture system. These men would have come from all over the kingdom, along with a few foreign mercenaries like Morbecque. The rest of the archers came from the prince's own lands. As well as Prince of Wales, he was Earl of Chester and Duke of Cornwall, and he used his private lands in Wales and the northwest as a recruiting ground. Cheshire, famous for its archers, was required to provide 300 men from the Hundreds of Macclesfield, Nantwich, Eddisbury, Wirral and Broxton.[19] A captain named Sir John Danyers provided another 200 and received several payments in advance for their services, totalling £16, 13s 4d. Sir Ralph de Mobberley provided a similar number of men, and was probably paid a similar amount.[20] Another hundred archers came from Flintshire, and 140 men, probably a mixture of archers and spearmen, were recruited in a district vaguely defined as 'north Wales'.

Many of the retinues were quite small. John Mohun, for example, recruited just four men-at-arms and nine mounted 'serviens', possibly light cavalry used as scouts, and Thomas Ros had six men-at-arms and nine archers. It is worth noting that the same system was also used by the king's subjects in Gascony, and here again retinue sizes varied. The important nobleman Bertrand de Montferrand had 85 men in his retinue, including 37 men-at-arms, while Jean Galter from Castillon had just nine men-at-arms. The Gascons were paid at exactly the same rates as the English.[21]

Assembling the army was not always easy. During the spring of 1355 the prince and his officials complained bitterly about the poaching of what they regarded as 'theirs' by the king's officers, looking for troops to join Lancaster's expedition. An ordinance was issued ordering that no archer engaged by one of the prince's companies should leave to join any other company without the prince's explicit permission, on pain of forfeiture.[22] Money also had to be found, and although England was a well-organised country with an effective system of taxation, the costs of raising and supplying even a small army were very high. According to one estimate, even before it sailed for France the prince's expedition had incurred expenses of over £22,000.[23] A grant of around £8,000 from the king proved to be nowhere near enough, and the correspondence coming out of the prince's household during the spring and summer of 1355 is full of increasingly desperate requests for money to be begged or borrowed wherever it can be found.

As well as men, horses had to be found, not just the warhorses and ponies for the troops, but sumpter horses and draught animals to pull wagons loaded with supplies. As always, casualties among horses on campaign were likely to be high, so plenty of spares and remounts were needed. All the other paraphernalia of an army on the march had to be assembled: tents and pavilions, baking ovens and farriers' forges and tools, stocks of spare harnesses for horses and, of course, thousands of sheaves of arrows for the archers. Food had to be gathered too; provisions would be waiting for the army in Gascony, but the men still had to be fed while they assembled and waited to sail.

Men-at-arms

The mailed fist of the prince's expeditionary force was the force of 1,000 men-at-arms. This term, 'men-at-arms', was used and continues to be used as a catch-all for any armoured, mounted man who could take his place in the line of battle. We are accustomed, in part thanks to the influence of the novels of Sir Walter Scott and various Hollywood films, to think of all these armoured fighting men as 'knights'. The truth is that most of them were not knights, nor did they have any aspiration to be knights, now or in the future. There were of course knights in the prince's service, men like Chandos and Audley and Richard Stafford described above. They were the leadership cadre of the force, but they were not typical of its rank and file. It is hard to tell just how many actual knights were in the prince's force, but the number is likely to have been comparatively small, a few hundred at most.

Knighthood, in the 14th century, was an honour but it was also a responsibility. The duties of the knight extended far beyond military leadership. In times of war as well as times of peace, knights could be called upon to fulfil a wide range of administrative posts. They could, and did, serve as law enforcement officers, judges, coroners, collectors of taxation and customs, arbiters of local disputes and much else besides. Local government posts such as sheriff and escheator could, in theory, only be filled by knights. Moreover, there was no salary attached to these posts, though sometimes there were perquisites to which the knight could help himself (and for the unscrupulous, there were plenty of opportunities for corruption). The demands in terms of time and money could be onerous indeed, and in addition most knights had their own estates to maintain and run.

Far from being an honour eagerly sought after, knighthood had become a duty that some tried to avoid. The historian Nigel Saul, in his studies of knights in Gloucestershire and Sussex, gives examples of men eligible for knighthood who attempted strenuously to duck this honour, or at least postpone it.[24] Sometimes the crown had to use legal measures to compel them to become knights against their will. However, there were others for whom knighthood was an honour eagerly sought.

These men were usually those trying to make a career close to the royal household or that of the Prince of Wales; for them, knighthood was recognition that led to greater things. Sir Nele Loring, knighted for valour at the naval battle of Sluys in 1340, was an exemplar for many ambitious young men. In 1346 and again in 1355 and 1356, the Prince of Wales often knighted members of his following as a reward for services; among those fortunate enough to be recognised was the prince's tailor, Henry Aldrington.

At the upper end of the scale were the noblemen, like Warwick, and the senior captains like Chandos, Audley and Stafford. Professional fighting men, they were well armed and well mounted. They had the money to afford not only a full hauberk of mail to protect the body, arms, legs and head, but plenty of additional armour to go over top of it. In the mid-14th century we are still some way from the head-to-toe armoured suits that came in during the 15th century – at least, for the wealthy who could afford them – but plate armour was becoming more common.

A well-off knight would have worn additional headgear with face protection; the heavy, squared-off helms of the 13th century were disappearing, replaced by lighter, more rounded bascinets with visors that could be raised and lowered. The visors themselves often had a pointed muzzle to ward off blows to the face, giving rise to the nickname 'dog-faced' bascinet. Additionally, he would have worn a steel breastplate, or cuirass, and matching backplate, along with plates covering the upper and lower arms and legs and the groin.

Much is often made of the weight of this armour and the supposed lack of mobility of armoured men on foot, but in truth all this gear, including the knight's shield and sword, weighed no more than 80–100 pounds; about the same as the gear of a front-line infantryman in a modern army. Most of the metal plates were only a few millimetres thick, and their weight was not substantial; the heaviest item in the inventory of armour was the mail hauberk, composed of thousands of small, tightly interwoven iron rings, worn over top of padded or quilted garments to stop the mail rings from chafing the flesh, but this garment was flexible and followed the contours of the wearer's limbs. Professional men-at-arms were trained to move and fight wearing full armour, and were nowhere near as immobile as we might think.

The less affluent knights wore whatever armour they could afford. A mail hauberk would have been standard for most. These hauberks were expensive and were often handed down from father to son. On top of that they wore whatever plate armour they could afford or scrounge, often as little as a simple cuirass. Standard too was a shield, made of wood and sometimes banded with metal for reinforcement, then brightly painted with the knight's coat of arms so that his followers could see him on the battlefield.

The most important and expensive elements of a knight's equipage were his horses and his sword. Lances, smaller and lighter than those used for jousting, with a wooden shaft 8 to 10 feet long and a sharp-pointed metal head, were used during mounted charges. The maces and axes so beloved of reconstructionists and the props masters of films were perhaps preferred by a few, but the sword was the queen of the battlefield. The sword was not just a weapon; it was the emblem of knighthood, the symbol of chivalry. In the poems and legends of the time, great swords had names, such as Durendal, Excalibur and Joyeuse; in the romances of the Round Table and the court of Charlemagne, swords almost had characters of their own. In the real world, swords were handed down through families, along with stories real or imaginary about battles where the sword had been carried and foes it had faced.[25]

Along with the sword, the horse was one of the symbols of knighthood, though here the impact of new weapons and tactics was beginning to change things. In the mid-14th century, knights still made major investments in horseflesh, and horse breeders – evincing the medieval passion for classifying things – defined several different grades of horse.[26] At the top of the pecking order was the destrier, or 'great horses', the heaviest and most expensive. Probably about 15 or 16 hands in height, they were not especially large in modern terms but they were strong, capable of moving at speed while bearing the weight of a heavily armoured man. Destriers were meant to be ridden in battle; bearing the knight into combat was their primary purpose.

Lighter grades of horse included the courser, or hunter, probably the favoured option of knights who could not afford the heavy destriers, and then the rouncy and the palfrey, both too light to be used in battle and mostly employed for riding while the army was on the march and the rider was not heavily encumbered with armour (armour was not normally worn when marching unless the enemy were believed to be close at hand).

How many and what grade of horses a knight had depended on what he could afford. Wealthy nobles and bannerets might have a string of as many as half a dozen horses of various grades, each with a groom to look after it; a poor knight from the shires might make do with a single courser or rouncy. For horses were extremely expensive. The historian Andrew Ayton calculated that the mean value of all war horses belonging to knights on the 1342 expedition to Brittany was £29. (By way of contrast, the standard rate of pay for an ordinary knight on campaign was 2 shillings per day, meaning that the average horse was worth 290 days' salary.) Some horses were worth less than this, but others were worth a great deal more. Warhorses with a value of £100 – several times the value of some smaller knightly estates – were not unknown.

We know the value of these horses for the simple reason that knights going to war registered them with army administration, so that if the horse died of disease or was killed in battle, the knights could claim compensation. This practice was known as *restauro equorum*, and was an essential part of the arrangements for service between knights and the crown. Without this promise of compensation, knights would have been extremely reluctant to expose their valuable beasts to the hardships of campaign and battle.

It seems clear that in some cases compensation was paid in cash, but in others, especially if a horse died on campaign, the knight would receive a horse of similar value from the crown. The royal stud farms were well organised and run by men with long experience of breeding and training warhorses. As well as the studs belonging to the crown itself, the Prince of Wales's household maintained at least four studs around the country, at Macclesfield, Woking, Princes Risborough and Byfleet.[27] Horses from these studs were often given as gifts to the prince's followers, and we can assume that in at least some cases this was to compensate men for horses they had lost in the prince's service. But the prince also received horses too; a document from June 1355 records the gift of a destrier, three mares and two foals from Sir John Avenel.[28]

And yet, these elaborate arrangements were becoming increasingly out of date. The warhorse itself was becoming dangerously obsolescent as missile weapons, the longbow in particular, came to dominate the battlefield. Crécy, like a long list of battles before it – Morlaix against the French, Neville's Cross (1346) and Halidon Hill (1333) against the Scots – had shown the vulnerability of mounted horsemen to massed volleys of arrows. Much of the chaos at Crécy had been caused by wounded horses falling or turning away from the showers of arrows and disrupting the French line of advance. More than one French man-at-arms had died at Crécy, not killed by arrows but trampled by the horses of his comrades after falling from his own mount.

At La Roche-Derrien, Charles of Blois had refused to mount his men when facing the English archers, and though ultimately unsuccessful, he had shown the way forward. The English themselves were increasingly prone to dismounting their own men-at-arms and using them to bolster and reinforce the formations of archers. The great massed charges of mounted men-at-arms were rapidly becoming a thing of the past. As we shall see, armoured cavalry had not entirely disappeared from the battlefield, but its role was becoming more specialised. Increasingly, the role of the horse was becoming one of transport to and from the battlefield.

Next in importance after the knights, in terms of both wages paid and fighting capability, was the class of soldiers known as esquires, or *escuyers*. Some esquires, like Delves of Doddington and his comrades who served Sir James Audley, filled what we now think of as the classic role of the squire, a kind of servant and fighting lieutenant of the knight, perhaps himself a trainee knight in the making. But, as we have seen, not everyone desired to become a knight. Some esquires were wealthy landowners in their own right, and their armour and equipage might be more elaborate than those of some knights. Their place in the pecking order might well be higher too. Esquires like Denys de Morbecque and John Kentwode came from good families; Kentwode would go on to become a knight. Others, such as Hamo de Mascy and Hugh Goulborn from the Wirral, and Robert Legh from Macclesfield, were reponsible for raising and organising archers in their districts and may have served as captains during the battle as well as joining the line of battle when required.[29]

The average esquire was probably armed and armoured more or less like the poorer knights: that is, sword and lance, mail hauberk, shield and whatever pieces of plate armour he could afford or had inherited. The lowest class of men-at-arms were the serjeants, usually household retainers of knights and wealthy esquires who acted as bodyguards, messengers, general men-of-affairs and auxiliary fighting men. They too ranged in status from the serjeants-at-arms of the Prince of Wales's household to the ordinary fighting men in the retinues of the lords and knights. The latter were paid a shilling a day, half the rate for a knight, and indifferently armoured with a mail coat or a gambeson, a kind of padded leather garment stuffed with animal hair, rags or anything else that would absorb the force of a blow. The least well-off made do with jerkins of stiffened leather. In certain circumstances, these jerkins might stop a sword cut. They offered little defence against the thrust of a lance, or a crossbow bolt.

Archers

The archers from Cheshire and Wales, whether on horse or on foot, were fairly uniformly armed and equipped. Their main weapon was of course the longbow.

Like so many things that are regarded as quintessentially English, the longbow is an import. The early Celtic inhabitants of the British Isles were no great archers – slings and javelins were their preferred missile weapons – and the Norman and early Plantagenet kings of England followed the example of their continental counterparts and relied on contingents of mercenary crossbowmen. Longbows first enter the historical record in the 12th century, when the chronicler Gerald of Wales describes the skill of Welsh archers, but did not impinge on the military mind until the English conquest of Wales in the late 13th century. Edward I, an astute military thinker, recognised the value of this new weapon and began to both recruit Welsh longbowmen in large numbers and train native English archers. By the middle of the 14th century, longbowmen had become the dominant arm of any English army.

It is easy to see why. The longbow is a simple weapon; modern versions are often laminated from several pieces of wood, but the medieval weapons were a single wooden shaft, tapering at either end and notched at the tips to hold the waxed bowstring, usually made of hemp or flax.[30] The length of the longbow depended on the height of the archer – the best archers choose their bows carefully to match their own physique and strength – but bows of up to 6 feet in length were not unknown. The arrows they shot were equally simple, slender shafts of wood anywhere from 27 to 36 inches long, fletched with feathers – the wing feathers of geese were preferred, but other feathers would do at a pinch – that imparted both flight and spin to the arrow and ensured accuracy.

Arrowheads varied, and an archer might have a variety of arrows in his quiver, depending on his quarry. Broadheads, triangular steel points with two swept back wings, were used for soft targets, game such as deer, or unarmoured men and horses. Bodkins, a narrow head with a long point like a needle, were favoured for shooting at men wearing gambesons or chainmail; the narrow point would find its way through mail rings and the arming doublet beneath into flesh and bone. If the target was armoured men, then the archer would switch to a pile, a hard point like a chisel that would simply smash its way through a target's defences.

The longbow had three advantages. The first was its range. Heavy medieval war bows were capable of hitting a target at up to 300 yards, although it is unlikely that they could do much damage to armoured targets at that range. This compares favourably with the range of all but the heaviest contemporary crossbows. The second is their penetrating power, the kinetic energy that they deliver to a target. That energy falls off rapidly at longer ranges, but at close range – 50 yards or less – the power of a longbow arrow is devastating. We have discussed the power of the longbow in detail in our earlier book on Crécy, and so will not rehearse the evidence here.[31] Suffice it to say that the kinetic energy of a longbow arrow shot at close range from a heavy war bow compares very well with a bullet fired from a police revolver. These arrows would carve through chainmail like butter, and could – and did – penetrate plate armour as well.

Again, the heavy crossbows used by Genoese mercenaries on the continent had similar power, but where the longbow dominated was in its rate of fire. A crossbowman might, under ideal conditions, manage four to five aimed shots per minute – and heavier bows took longer to wind and load – whereas a skilled longbowman could shoot 17–18 arrows per minute; even an archer of ordinary ability could manage 12–13. A mass of archers could deliver a withering fire of hundreds or even thousands of arrows a minute onto its target, a withering fire that – as happened at Crécy – can shred even the bravest and most determined opposing army. Over the previous two decades in particular, King Edward of England and his captains had honed their tactics and become very adept at deploying their longbowmen. Rightly, the longbow was the weapon that England's opponents feared most.

Like the horses of the knight, archers prized their bows, and it is likely that most if not all of the longbowmen brought their own bows. But bows too could be lost or damaged, and the army had ordered several thousand bows from the bowyers of Cheshire. Bows are described as 'white', meaning made of untreated wood, or 'painted', i.e. varnished to ward off damp; both types were supplied. The prince's officers also ordered thousands of sheaves of arrows, the indispensable ammunition of the longbowman. Typically, some arrows came with heads and others without, so that arrows could be customised at need; and, of course, the blacksmiths supplied baskets of arrowheads of various types.

The equipment of a longbowman was simple: the bow itself; a quiver of arrows – 24 was the standard issue, but double issues of 48 were sometimes passed to the troops before battle; a knife or some sort of personal weapon, perhaps a sword if the archer had been lucky enough to loot or steal one from a fallen foe; several spare bowstrings sometimes carried coiled up inside the archer's cap to keep them safe; and a kit with glue and thread for repairing damaged fletchings. The Cheshire archers in the prince's army had a uniform, a green and white surcoat.[32] One man, Thomas Brescy, was issued with a uniform but failed to report for duty, and an order was sent out to remind him of his obligations, or arrest him if he failed to show up.[33] The other archers wore their own clothes, probably plain homespun wool tunics, jerkins and hose dyed in simple colours; russet and green were the cheapest and most widely available.

In a practice that was increasingly common, a large proportion of the archers were mounted. Their mounts were not as exotic as those of the knights and other men-at-arms; most were probably Welsh hill ponies, sturdy but small of stature. These men are occasionally described as 'horse archers', but this is misleading; their horses were intended to transport them quickly to and from the battlefield, not for use in combat. The remainder of the archers were on foot. Here again there was a difference in pecking order; mounted archers were paid six pence a day, while those on foot received only three pence. The 'Welshmen' referred to above were armed with spears and lightly armoured; their function was probably that of camp guards. They were at the bottom of the pay scale, receiving just two pence per day.

Final preparations

On 10 July, the formal contracts for service between the crown and the two commanders, the Prince of Wales and the Duke of Lancaster, were drawn up. Lancaster was appointed to command his army for six months, with the king having the option to renew the contract at his pleasure; the prince, on the other hand, was commanded to stay in Gascony 'as lieutenant during the king's pleasure', i.e. indefinitely.[34] The prince was also given supreme power in Gascony, including control over its finances, which must have pleased him greatly. His financial problems continued to grow. His men were gathering around Plymouth, the designated port of embarkation, and the presence of so many extra mouths to feed was driving food prices up. A bill for provisions of over £1,000 was presented, and the prince's staff were struggling to find the money to pay it.

Several men, including the archers William Barker and Howell ap Llewellyn and the esquire Roger Bechington, fell ill and were given leave to return home.[35] Others simply departed without leave. Thomas Brescy was not the only one to fail to show up. A document dated 7 September lists several men who received uniforms and wages and then absconded, and in late August orders went out for the arrest of Richard Wynstanton, who had deserted.[36]

Delays were mounting. There were not enough ships to transport the prince's men; it later transpired that Lancaster's officers had purloined a number of ships meant for the prince's use and taken them to Sandwich, where his own army was assembling. The prince was forced once again to fall back on his own domains and send out warrants to commandeer ships from Devon and Cornwall. Eventually enough shipping was found, but then the weather turned. Strong southwesterly winds blew up the English Channel day after day. Medieval ships, small and unwieldy, could not sail close to the wind, and both fleets were effectively penned up in their ports. Lancaster did finally manage to sail from Sandwich on 15 August, but two weeks later he had progressed no further west than Portsmouth, only about 150 miles away.

Finally, on 9 September the winds changed. The prince boarded his flagship, the *Christopher*, captained by John Clerk (who was also mayor of Southampton), and the rest of the army embarked.[37] Most of the ships could hold no more than 50 or a 100 men, or a few dozen horses, all in cramped conditions. Their names are testimony to the dangers of sea travel at the time. There were at least seven ships named *St Mary*, in honour of the patron saint of seafarers, and at least three named *Christopher* and two named *Nicholas*; *Welfare*, *Saint Esprit* and *Jerusalem* also feature. The names, the sailors hoped, would give them some kind of protection against storms and shoals.

On this occasion, no divine intervention was needed. The weather remained fine, the winds fair. The fleet steered southwest, rounding the point of Brittany, and then turned south for Gascony. On 20 September, the prince's ships sailed up the estuary of the Gironde and reached the harbour at Bordeaux.

CHAPTER 3

'Nothing but What a Loyal Vassal Should Do'

On the far side of the Channel, France too had begun to prepare for war. In the southwest, two royal forces under Jean d'Armagnac, the king's lieutenant-general, and Jean de Clermont, one of the marshals of France, resumed their raids on English territory as early as April 1355. Unfortunately for them, Sir John Cheverston, the Devon knight who had taken over the post of seneschal in Gascony several years earlier, was both highly competent and possessed of a good intelligence service. When Armagnac advanced through the Agenais district south of the Dordogne river, Cheverston's garrisons were waiting for him. After attacking several fortified places without success, Armagnac settled down to besiege the town of Aigullon on the Garonne. But Aigullon too was well fortified – it had successfully resisted several French sieges in the past – and its garrison had been reinforced. Armagnac's advance ground to a halt.

Further north, Clermont's force operating around Angoulême fared little better. Despite the limited resources he had available, Cheverston even went on the offensive in May, capturing the town of Guîtres on the river Isle a dozen miles northeast of Libourne. Guîtres made a very useful bastion to protect the northern flank of English territory from Clermont's raids. Clermont himself was then recalled to Paris to deal with problems in Normandy. By June, it was clear that the French had lost the initiative in the southwest.

King Jean of France seems barely to have noticed. No further aid was sent to Armagnac and Clermont, and warnings from spies that England was planning to send reinforcements to Gascony were ignored. Jean's attention was now focused entirely on the rebels in Normandy, and especially on their leader, Charles of Navarre. Already in January 1355, Jean had summoned Charles to Paris to face an accusation of murder. Charles, safe in his fortress at Pamplona, the capital of Navarre, ignored the summons. When it became clear he did not intend to appear, Jean began to prepare for an all-out invasion of lower

Normandy, where Charles's supporters were concentrated. As a preliminary, ships began to assemble at Rouen and other northern ports still in friendly hands, and orders went out to recruit several thousand crossbowmen from Genoa.

Charles too was preparing for war. In Navarre, he had raised around 2,000 men and was hiring ships to take him to Normandy. Some of these ships were English, provided by the seneschal in Bordeaux.[1] In May 1355, Navarrese envoys visited England, asking for aid. King Edward was only too happy to agree, and as we saw in the previous chapter, an expeditionary force led by the Duke of Lancaster began to make ready.[2] News of the Anglo-Navarrese negotiations soon reached Paris, causing alarm at court. A solid alliance between the English and the Normans was one of France's strategic nightmares. Control of Normandy would not only mean the loss of a large and rich province; it would also give England a fortified base only a few days' march from Paris itself.

On 17 May King Jean went to the abbey of St-Denis north of Paris, and there in the great abbey church, where generations of kings of France lay buried, he received the Oriflamme, the battle standard of France. This symbolic act was in effect a declaration of war. Proclamations were issued, summoning the French army to assemble. Some royal troops had already gathered at Rouen, the capital of Normandy. The commander in Rouen was Jean's eldest son, the 17-year-old Dauphin Charles.

In June 1355, Charles of Navarre marched his little force down from the mountains to the coast of Gascony and his waiting ships. Embarking his army, he sailed north for Normandy. On 5 July he landed in Cherbourg. In England, Lancaster's expedition was mustering at Sandwich. The local rebels, led by the Harcourt family, pledged their support. Everything seemed ready for Normandy to go up in flames.

There was just one problem. Charles of Navarre was playing a double game. Even before he left Navarre, he had sent letters to the French court, offering to negotiate. Now he renewed that offer. Facing the prospect of regaining control of Normandy without the need for a costly and divisive war, Jean paused. The French army continued to muster, but for the moment the king stayed his hand, and opened secret negotiations with Charles.

France divided

Jean was right to hesitate. An all out-war against Charles of Navarre, his men packed into heavily fortified towns and castles across lower Normandy and backed by English arms, would have torn France apart. The costs, politically, militarily and financially, would have been ruinous.

One of the puzzling things about the early part of the Hundred Years War is how England, with a population perhaps a third that of France and far less in the way of military resources, should have defeated France so convincingly and so often. There are several reasons why, including better weapons and tactics on the battlefield and superior leadership, but beyond doubt one of the key reasons was efficiency of administration. Over the past couple of centuries the English had perfected the art of bureaucracy. A small civil service ran an extremely effective tax and revenue gathering system. There had been a serious financial crisis in 1339–40, but lessons had been learned from that event, and since then the system had – just about – been able to cope with the demands of war. In England too, power was largely centralised. The crown's authority was somewhat restricted by Parliament, but sensible kings made a point of getting Parliament on their side, and in fact, king and Parliament working together made a very effective combination. Parliament could help the king find the money he needed, and lend legitimacy to his war aims.

The situation in France was very different. In theory, the King of France was an absolute ruler; in practice, he could not simply give orders and expect them to be obeyed. The great feudal nobles were semi-independent of the crown.[3] Some of the later kings of the previous dynasty, the Capets, had managed to impose themselves on their nobles through strong leadership and force of personality; the saintly Louis IX and the strong-armed Philippe IV, the Fair, are examples.[4] But the Valois dynasty was new and its hold on the throne was not entirely secure; there remained doubts about its legitimacy. The nobles had rarely missed a chance to remind Jean's father, Philippe VI, that he owed his throne to their support.

The nobles knew their rights, and they guarded their privileges jealously. Within their own domains they were autocrats, and unless they committed outright treason, the king had little right to interfere. They could, and did, impose whatever taxes they wished within their own counties and duchies, and the crown had no right to this revenue.[5] The nobles themselves could not be taxed, and tended to react with extreme hostility to even the mildest suggestion that they might wish to contribute to the defence of the realm. This meant that the burden of taxation fell on the nascent middle class – which barely existed outside of Paris and a few other larger cities – but most of all on the peasantry. Thus, the class that could least afford to pay ended up paying the most.

The king was expected to support himself from his own domains, and that included raising the money to pay for wars. By the 14th century, warfare had become so expensive that this was no longer possible. In 1302 Philippe IV had called an assembly of the Estates-General, a representative bodysimilar to the English Parliament (and possibly modelled on it) in an effort to improve cooperation between the crown and the people. The Estates-General could, if its members agreed, consent to extraordinary taxation in time of war. The problem was that the Estates-General usually wanted concessions from the crown in exchange, concessions the crown was usually very reluctant to give.

The power of the French nobles remained unchecked. They were, in some cases quite literally, a law unto themselves. They were not even duty bound to obey the orders of the king on the battlefield. Nobles and knights had what some later historians have called the right of independent withdrawal; that is to say, if they felt they no longer wished to participate in a battle, for whatever reason, they could simply march away. This right was rarely exercised, but its existence was a reminder to the French kings of their lack of real authority.

Nowhere were the privileges of the nobility guarded more jealously than in Normandy. The Duchy of Normandy had only been a French possession for a little over a hundred years, seized by force during the reign of King John of England in the early 13th century. It is doubtful whether many Normans considered themselves to be French at all.[6] They had their own courts, their own legal system and their own administration. They resented attempts to control them from Paris, and in 1315 forced the French crown to recognise their liberties. The Charte aux Normands, or Norman Charter, promulgated that year has been compared to the Magna Carta in England; indeed, the Charter may have been influenced by the English example.[7] Among other provisions, the judgement of Normandy's highest court, the Exchequer, was considered to be final. The crown could not appeal against its decisions, nor could it overturn them.

The Normans were not overly fond of the English either. In 1346, Edward's hopes of raising an anti-French rebellion in Normandy had been dashed; only a few rebels like Godefroi d'Harcourt had joined his cause, and many Norman nobles including Brienne, the Constable, and Harcourt's brother the Comte de Harcourt had fought on the French side. But when France began to encroach on Norman liberties, their enemy's enemy became their friend. By 1355, more than just the Harcourt family were prepared to let the English in. Even the Dauphin, the king's own son, had some sympathy with their cause. Unlike his confrontational father, the young prince had worked hard to build relationships with the more moderate Norman nobles.[8]

Unable to collect taxes anywhere except in his own lands, the king had only one other option for raising money: debasing the coinage. There were various ways in which this could be done, either through clipping silver coins to make them smaller and then using the leftover silver to create new coins, or melting down and reminting coins with a lower proportion of silver. Jean resorted to this tactic no fewer than eight times in 1355, with consequent anger among the middle classes, who saw the value of their money fall.[9] Even this was not enough, and at the end of the summer Jean was forced to suspend payment on all royal debts, in effect declaring bankruptcy. The Estates-General was summoned and agreed to the imposition of taxes, but with conditions; the three Estates, not the crown, would supervise the collection of taxes, and henceforth the Estates also wanted a say in the king's war policy. Jean had little choice but to agree.

All in all, it was a good thing Jean decided to temporise, and to negotiate with Charles of Navarre. The troops he had managed to raise could not be paid, and some had begun looting the villages around Rouen. Others were already deserting.[10] Had a full-scale war erupted that summer, France was in no condition to fight.

Jean le Bon

As we noted in Chapter 1, the king was not entirely the architect of his own misfortunes. He was not responsible for the strangling inefficiency of the royal bureaucracy, nor the laws and customs that allowed his over-mighty subjects to behave pretty much as they pleased. It must be noted, however, that Jean did have a predilection for making bad situations worse.

In the summer of 1355, Jean was 36 years old. Unlike the Prince of Wales, we have a fair idea what he looked like because he was one of the first European monarchs to have his portrait painted from life. The portrait, painted in oil on a wooden panel by an unknown artist, cannot be dated for certain, but one theory is that it was painted around the time of his coronation. That could well be the case, as the portrait is that of a relatively young man.

The portrait shows us a man with a strong jaw and long nose and slightly receding forehead. He has dark eyes and long hair falling to his shoulders. In the portrait today his hair is red, but it is possible that the pigments have changed colour over time and the original colour may have been more of a red-blond. There is a slightly humorous cast to the mouth and eyes; he looks like a man who might enjoy a joke.

Unsurprisingly, what the portrait fails to show is the mass of insecurities and tensions seething beneath the surface. His father, Philippe VI, had been

Jean II de France

suspicious to the point of paranoia, seeing treason everywhere, and this trait Jean seems to have inherited to the full. The brutal execution of the Constable, Raoul de Brienne, which so antagonised the nobles of Normandy, was an early sign of this.

When Jean made enemies, he made them for life. As a matter of expediency, he would sometimes pardon those who offended him, but he rarely forgave them entirely. On the other side of the coin, when he made friends he clung to them, sometimes almost desperately. His friendship with Carlos de la Cerda which raised so many eyebrows shows us a man almost pathetically desperate to be loved by those around him. At court he surrounded himself with a handful of advisors, whom he trusted absolutely and upon whom he heaped lands and wealth. Robert de Lorris, the son of a Paris innkeeper who served as Jean's chamberlain, became rich beyond dreams of avarice in the king's service (which did not apparently stop him from also spying on the royal household on behalf of the King of Navarre).[11] Simon de Bucy, president of the Parlement of Paris and another close advisor, owned a number of houses and palaces in and around Paris. For Jean's friends, nothing was too good; for his enemies, there was a burning resentment that never died.

The historian Jonathan Sumption summarises Jean as 'a man of limited intelligence and mediocre talents'.[12] That is probably too harsh. As other biographers, namely Raymond Cazelles and Jean Deviosse, have pointed out, Jean had plenty of virtues. He was in fact quite intelligent, cultured and well read (at a time when these things were not necessarily considered virtues by the more red-blooded of his noblemen).[13] He had no lack of courage, and he never shirked danger. He had a strong sense of honour and tried to uphold the ideal of a chivalric knight, even if the suspicious portion of his nature sometimes led him to do dishonourable things; indeed, he might have fared better on the throne had he been a touch more machiavellian. His chivalry was of the romantic kind, harking back to the myths and legends of the past. He was fond of music and poetry, particularly the Arthurian legends of poets such as Chrétien de Troyes.

Fascinated by Edward's Order of the Garter, Jean tried to create his own version, the Order of the Star.[14] Originally known as the Company of Our Lady of the Noble House, the order was intended to be rather more religious in character than the Garter, with the Virgin Mary and various military saints at the centre of its philosophy. The history of the order is typical of many of Jean's projects. For a start, most of the nobility who Jean invited to join the order turned up their noses and refused. Enough candidates were eventually scraped together, and 120 knights were installed at the inaugural meeting in

November 1351. One of the French knights, the captain of the fortress of Guînes, near Calais, left his post to attend the ceremony.

Even before the captain's departure, one of his garrison, an English turncoat named John Dancaster, was planning to betray him. According to the chronicler Geoffrey le Baker, Dancaster had 'become acquainted with the lewd embraces of a washerwoman', and through her had learned of a weakness in the defences of Guînes.[15] As soon as the captain departed, Dancaster deserted and rejoined his former colleagues in Calais, informing them of what he had learned. A small party of English sortied from Calais and took Guînes by surprise, capturing the castle and then holding it against desperate attempts by the French under Geoffroi de Charny to retake it. Eventually, King Edward agreed that seizing the castle during a time of truce was unfair, and ordered it handed back to the French.

The following summer, 1352, many knights of the new order joined an expedition in Brittany led by followers of the imprisoned Charles de Blois. After capturing the town of Rennes, the French marched towards the English-held fortress of Ploërmel, but en route at Mauron they encountered a small Anglo-Breton force led by Sir Walter Bentley and Tanguy du Chastel. After a bloody fight, with the English longbows wreaking their usual execution, the French were routed. Forty-five members of the Order of the Star were killed in the fighting, including Alain de Tinténiac, one of the heroes of the Combat of the Thirty.[16] Thereafter, despite Jean's attempts to revive it, the Order slid quietly into obscurity. Later kings would rescue the order and refound it.

Jean also suffered from poor health. The exact nature of his ailment is not certain, but it is notable that he rarely engaged in outdoor pursuits such as hunting and jousting.[17] This too probably did not endear him to his nobility, at a time when physical virility was one of the most prized attributes a leader could possess. His greatest weakness, however, was his impulsiveness. The chronicler Jean Froissart, not a fan of the king, observed that he took decisions too quickly and then was reluctant to reverse course even when it became clear that the original decision was wrong.[18]

The king's men

You shall know a great leader, it is said, by the quality of those around him; and conversely, a weak leader tends to surround himself with mediocrities. Very few of the men who were close to King Jean inspire much confidence. There was the ambitious, greedy Carlos de la Cerda, the avaricious chamberlain, Robert Lorris, and the powerful lawyer, Simon Bucy, both of whom saw proximity to the king as a chance to line their own pockets. But there were some clever men too. Pierre de la Forêt, another lawyer and churchman, served as Jean's chancellor for many years before becoming Archbishop of Rouen, and succeeded in ramming through a few reforms to the French royal administration. Renaud Chauvel, the future Bishop of Chartres, took over the main royal finances in the Chambre des Comptes and did what he could to stem the tide of debt that constantly washed around the king.

It is somewhat surprising to find that one of the men King Jean relied on the most was the veteran knight and captain Geoffroi de Charny. To his contemporaries, Charny was the symbol of chivalry, the exemplar of everything a chivalrous knight should be. Since the death of King Jean of Bohemia at the battle of Crécy, Charny was regarded as the foremost knight in Europe.

Born around 1300, Charny was now in his mid-fifties. He came from a noble family; he was descended on his mother's side from Jean de Joinville, friend and comrade of the sainted king, Louis IX, while in his father's family another Geoffroi de Charny, or Charney – possibly an uncle – had been a member of the Knights Templar and was burned at the stake along with the last Grand Master of Templars, Jacques de Molay, in 1314. Like Molay, Charny had originally confessed to heresy under torture, but then recanted; his courage was remarked upon with reluctant admiration at the time.

The younger Charny had fought in most of the major actions of the war so far, and had been taken prisoner at Morlaix in 1342. His captors had been so impressed by him that they allowed him to go freely back to France to raise his own ransom, without any kind of surety or pledge. Charny duly raised the money, probably in the form of a grant or loan from the crown, and was back in service the following year. He had survived the disaster of Crécy and played an important role in the siege of Calais, going on to command the French forces in the north who blockaded the port by land; as we saw in Chapter 1, he came very close to seizing the city back for the French. He was a subtle and intelligent captain as well as a brave one.

Charny had, quite literally, written the book on chivalry. The *Livre de Chevalerie*, or *Book of Chivalry*, was written in the early 1350s, quite possibly to accompany the foundation of the Order of the Star (Charny was one of its founder members, and probably advised the king on setting up the order).[19] As well as being a handbook on chivalry itself, Charny also uses the book as a manifesto for reform. The noble classes have forgotten what chivalry really means, he says; they have become idle and devote themselves too much to personal pleasure. The true ideal of chivalry is service, to the crown and to the people. He rebukes monarchs, too, for failing in their own duty of service. The powerful in society have a moral duty to set an example for the lower orders, and to the next generation of their own order. They should live modestly, be pious in their behaviour, courteous towards women and caring for the poor and the weak.

The knight's life is one of danger and suffering, Charny says, and he compares the hardships a knight should undergo to the penance done by monks and priests. Through suffering comes redemption. A knight never fears death, for he knows that in death will be found eternal life in heaven. A true knight is glad to die in battle. It is hard to read this book today without a shiver, for Charny was all too accurately forecasting his own end.

Charny was the sort of councillor that every king should have – wise, experienced, courageous and selfless – and he compares favourably to the men around King Edward and the Prince of Wales. Jean usually listened to him on military matters, to his profit. He had a few other good men around him too. The Constable of France, Jacques de Bourbon, Count of Ponthieu and a younger son of the Duc de Bourbon, was an able soldier and administrator who had formerly been captain-general of Languedoc, the post now held by Jean d'Armagnac. During the summer of 1355 Bourbon faced the formidable task of holding the fractious, unpaid French army together while simultaneously conducting secret negotiations with Charles of Navarre. He succeeded in the second task, and probably did all that was humanly possible with the first; the subsequent failures in Normandy should not be laid at his door.

But the post of Constable was both a powerful and a lucrative one, and many men coveted it. Bourbon found himself the target of political infighting and attacks. One of his principal opponents was Gauthier de Brienne, one of the more colourful and divisive figures at the French court.[20] His family came originally from Champagne, and were only distantly related to the Norman Briennes (of which family the executed former Constable, Raoul de Brienne, had been a member). One of his ancestors, Jean de Brienne, was an adventurer who had at various times been both King of Jerusalem and Emperor of the Latin empire of Constantinople. Jean's descendants had then carved out chunks from the wreckage of the Byzantine empire in Europe, and settled down to rule. Gauthier could claim a host of titles – Duke of Athens, Prince of Taranto, Count of Lecce and lord of Lefkada, to name just a few – but had actual possession of precious few of them. His father had been killed defending the Duchy of Athens against the mercenaries of the Catalan Grand Company, and Gauthier spent much of his early life and most of his remaining fortune trying to recover the duchy from the Catalans.

Moving on, he was briefly acclaimed despot of Florence, where he ruled the city with brutal efficiency until the Florentines grew tired of him and began to plot against him. In 1344 he returned to his ancestral homeland, France, and married the daughter of the Constable, Raoul de Brienne. He seems to have believed that this gave him a claim on the office of Constable itself and, even though his wife had died, began to campaign against Jacques de Bourbon.

Similarly, things were not well between the other two high military officers, the marshals. Jean de Clermont, lord of Chantilly and Beaumont, was a member of an old aristocratic family steeped in chivalric ideals. He had also been close to Raoul de Brienne and had served under his command on several occasions. He could be an effective military commander when given the resources, and was cautious and level-headed. His opposite number, Arnoul d'Audrehem, came from a relatively obscure background in the north of France and served with no great distinction in France and Scotland; he was one of the defenders of Calais, and was taken prisoner when the city fell. Ransomed back to France, he then served as captain of the fortress of Angoulême before suddenly, in 1351, being appointed marshal of France. It can be hypothesised that Audrehem had become a favourite of King Jean. Rash and reckless, he was one of the men on whom Jean relied for advice.

The king's sons were just too young to be of much influence on their father. The Dauphin Charles was 17 in 1355, and though he was nominally the head of government in Normandy, it is likely that local officials and the Constable, Jacques de Bourbon, held the real power. He was, however, a level-headed young man who showed promise of intelligence and spirit, qualities he would need in full in the years to come. He was also capable of following his own path. Whether on the advice of his officials or through his own inclination, he began conciliating the Norman nobles with a view to patching up relations between them and France.

The middle children, Louis, later Duc d'Anjou, and Jean, Comte de Poitiers (later Duc de Berry), barely trouble the historian at this point in their careers. Both would go on to achieve prominence, Louis in the failed pursuit of a kingdom in Naples, Jean as a collector and patron, the man who commissioned one of the most remarkable artistic achievements of the Middle Ages, the illuminated manuscript known as the *Tres Riches Heures*. The younger son, Philippe, the future Duc de Bourgogne, was 13 in 1355 but clearly already a young man of some character.

The *furor franciscus*

Like its English counterpart, the French army was composed of two principal types of troops, men-at-arms and foot soldiers armed with missile weapons – in this case, crossbows rather than the English and Welsh longbows.

The summonses to military service, the *ban* and the *arrière ban*, in theory applied to all adult males who could bear arms.[21] In practice, the authorities tended to be more selective. Formerly French armies had gone to war accompanied by vast masses of untrained, unarmoured peasant foot soldiers, some of them armed with nothing more than pitchforks, scythes or pruning bills. They had no defence against arrows, and could not stand up to charges by armoured men-at-arms; their main function in the field was to consume food supplies and then, when the food ran out, die in droves from hunger or disease, or else desert and make their way home. Crécy was the last campaign where France called up ordinary foot soldiers in large numbers. Most probably never saw action.

Men-at-arms in France were much like men-at-arms in England in terms of weapons and equipment, except that there were more wealthy knights in France and hence a large number of men who were well equipped with plate armour. In fact, numbers are one of the distinguishing features of most French armies of the day when compared with their English counterparts. France had a population perhaps three times that of England, and below the level of the great magnates there were thousands of families of local nobles and knights able to contribute men-at-arms to the French army.

In most of the battles of the early part of the Hundred Years War, the English fought at a numerical disadvantage, sometimes being outnumbered three or four to one. At Crécy, Edward had perhaps 8,000 or 9,000 men left from his original expeditionary force; while even allowing for the exaggerations of the chroniclers, Philippe of France probably had 40,000 men at his disposal, even if many of these never reached the battlefield.[22] At Mauron in 1352, Bentley and Chastel had no more than 2,000 men; their French opponent, Guy de Nesle, had at least 5,000.

It was the numbers of men-at-arms as well as their weight of arms and armour that made the French mounted striking force so effective. Crécy, Morlaix, La Roche-Derrien and Mauron had blunted the French reputation for invincibility, but the historical record could not be denied. On battlefield after battlefield, in wars stretching from France, across Europe, to the mountains of Asia and the deserts of the Middle East, French cavalry had shown what it could do. The *furor franciscus*, the massed charge of armoured horsemen – hooves drumming like thunder, horses whinnying, men shouting, banners snapping and streaming in the wind, sunlight gleaming off armour and then the lances lowered for the kill as the great mass of men prepared to charge home – was a terrifying sight. Few other armies could stand up to it. Most did not even try. They either retired behind fortifications, or fell back out of the way and sniped at the French from the flank until they grew weary, as the Turkish and Mamluk horse archers had done during the Crusades. Only the English, with their formidable longbowmen, were willing to stand and face them.

The French men-at-arms were proud of their military record, and proud of their fighting ability. Their feats of arms were enshrined in myths, dating back to the heroic paladins of Charlemagne – men like Count Roland and his companion Olivier – moving on to the heroes of the crusades, like Godefroi de Bouillon and Raymond de Toulouse, and then the contemporary heroes like Jean of Bohemia (counted as an honorary Frenchman) and Geoffroi de Charny. And the old knightly and noble families had their own heroes too. The Briennes and the Joinvilles had provided captains and commanders during the crusades. The counts of Alençon and Dammartin had famous knights in their ancestry, and both were fighting men in their own right; Dammartin had been at Crécy, and young Charles d'Alençon's father had been killed there. Alençon would later give up the profession of arms, handing over his title to his brother in order to enter the church; in 1365, he became Archbishop of Lyons. Eustache de Ribemont, after Charny perhaps the most respected knight in France, could trace his family lineage back to the time of Charlemagne. An ancestor, André de Chauvigny, a knight from Poitou, had fought with distinction on the Third Crusade in the service of King Richard of England, and had later taken part in Prince Arthur's rebellion against Richard's successor King John; captured by John, he was imprisoned and starved to death.

To these men, chivalry was real. Courage and honour were what they lived for, what they breathed; and if their notions of honour were sometimes rather confused, permitting them to sack cities and slaughter defenceless civilians, we still have to recognise that by their standards, they were living according to their code.[23]

The maltreatment of civilians is something that happens in every war, and our age has no right to criticise medieval man for his callousness and brutality. What is different is the attitude to plunder. Pillage was one of the chief pastimes of the medieval soldier, and towns, villages, farms – and churches and abbeys too – were routinely looted of everything of value they might possess (and what could not be taken away, including the buildings themselves, was usually burned). This practice was often justified in military terms; by laying waste the countryside, one was denying valuable resources to the enemy and forcing him to commit money and time to relief work and rebuilding. That was true, but that thought was not uppermost in the minds of the soldiers. From the loftiest banneret to the humblest archer, their primary goal was enrichment. War offered them a chance to make a fortune, to pay off debts, to buy estates, to move up the social scale. And the thought that this enrichment came at a cost of destitution and misery to others, including women and children, seems not to have troubled their minds.

What is more, this attitude was positively encouraged by the commanders of armies, who saw plunder as a cheap way to reward their men, and by the code of the times. 'War without plunder is like sausages without mustard', ran a proverb of the day, and two centuries earlier the troubadour Bertran de Born, himself a professional soldier, had written about the delights of robbing merchant caravans. The line between warfare and organised banditry could be a thin one.

One of those who frequently crossed that line was Arnault de Cervolles.[24] A Gascon from a good family, he had inherited the fief of Vélines in the Dordogne valley, not far from the town of Ste-Foy. Vélines was an ecclesiastical fief – his overlord was the Archbishop of Bordeaux – and Cervolles was known as 'the Archpriest'. Seldom has a nickname been less apt. Taking advantage of the increasing chaos along the Gascon frontier, Cervolles set himself up as a mercenary soldier, specialising in taking towns and castles by escalade; that is, bold surprise attacks aiming to scale the walls and get inside before the defenders could react. When not employed by one side or the other, Cervolles and his men turned to banditry, plundering villages and robbing caravans. By the mid-1350s he had been chased out of Gascony and took service in the French army, probably in the retinue of the Count of Alençon.

Of course, the French army was not the only one to harbour bandits and robbers. English men-at-arms, and Scots, German and Italian ones, also fought for plunder. The English knight Sir Robert Knollys, who had distinguished himself at Mauron and was one of the leading English captains of Brittany, later set up in business for himself as master of a Free Company, pillaging the Loire valley and openly proclaiming that he fought neither for king nor God, but for himself alone. In 1358 he launched a raid through the Auvergne towards Avignon, boasting that he would pillage the pope himself; this did not come to pass, but the trail of destruction Knollys and his men left across the Auvergne scarred the valley. In village after village, nothing could be seen but the still standing gable ends of burned-out houses. With grim humour, Knollys's men called these 'Knollys mitres', thinking that the points of the gables reminded them of the headgear of a bishop. Knollys himself was pleased by the joke.[25]

Brave to a fault, violent, idealistic and ambitious, the French men-at-arms liked fighting. And they were very good at it. Given a level playing field, they were probably the best in Europe. Even full-time professional soldiers like the Teutonic Knights in Prussia admired them, and were always glad to see a contingent of French crusaders arrive ready to fulfil their vows of crusade by striking a blow at the heathen. Under good leaders, they could indeed be invincible. But in recent years, good leadership had all too often been lacking.

Mercenaries

As well as the men-at-arms, the other important element in any French army was the crossbowmen. Unlike the English longbowmen, who were recruited domestically, the crossbowmen were mercenaries. They are usually referred to in chronicles of the day as 'Genoese', but they came from all over northern Italy, Provence, and probably further afield as well. Like the Flemish crossbowmen of earlier centuries or the Swiss pikemen of the 15th and 16th centuries, they were professional soldiers who fought for pay wherever an employer could be found.

Their captains and employers did mostly come from Genoa, or were of Genoese descent, but they did so without official sanction from the government of Genoa, whose relations with France were not particularly good. One of the primary contractors was Carlo Grimaldi, lord of Monaco. Grimaldi had seized the rock of Monaco in 1331 and set himself up as an independent overlord, providing mercenary soldiers and ships to anyone who would pay; the kingdoms of France, Majorca and Naples were among his clients. Carlo was growing old now, but his son Rainier acted as his agent and military contractor in France.[26]

The Doria family had been thrown out of Genoa during a popular rebellion in 1338, and though they were now allowed back in the city, they were not in favour. Like the Grimaldis, they turned to mercenary service probably as a way to secure an income. One of the family, Ottone Doria, had recruited and led the crossbowmen at the battle of Crécy, where he had been seriously wounded.[27] His kinsman Baldo Doria could now usually be found at the French court, ready to offer services when needed. There was no love lost between the Dorias and Grimaldis, and the mercenaries they hired and led had to be kept apart when in the field; the usual French policy was to post the two contingents to different theatres of war.

Regardless of where they came from and who hired them, the crossbowmen were armed and equipped in much the same way. Unlike the English archers, who wore no armour at all, the crossbowmen wore light body armour, usually quilted gambesons rather than more expensive chainmail, and steel caps. Often a white surcoat was worn over top of the gambeson as a kind of uniform.

The crossbowmen also carried pavises, large and heavy wooden shields which could be mounted on the ground with a wooden brace to hold them up. In theory, the crossbowman could shelter behind the pavise while reloading, then shoot over or around it and duck back into cover again.

The crossbows themselves were heavy and complex weapons. A steel bow, or prod, was mounted horizontally on a wooden stock. The heavy bowstrings were made of woven animal sinew, one of the strongest materials then available. A hand-crank, sometimes known as a 'cranqequin', was required to draw the bow and set the string. The crossbow bolt was then fitted to the string. The bolts were short, made of iron with steel tips and sometimes fitted with vestigial fins to ensure greater accuracy. As with longbow arrows, different tips were employed for different targets; bodkin points were used against men wearing mail hauberks, while square-headed bolts also known as quarrels were for penetrating plate armour.[28]

These were very powerful weapons indeed, and at short range a crossbow bolt could punch through plate armour without much difficulty. But the crossbow suffered from two problems. First, the weight of the iron bolts meant that both kinetic energy and accuracy fell off sharply at longer ranges. Beyond about 150 yards, crossbows were probably not effective against armoured targets. Maximum range would have been about 250–300 yards, the same as the longbow's. The second problem was the slow rate of fire. It would have taken a skilled archer indeed to fire four aimed shots a minute; three was probably nearer the average. Additionally, winding the bows was tiring work; even with the hand-crank, the steel prods were difficult to draw. In any kind of prolonged encounter, fatigue would have come into play, reducing the rate of fire and accuracy still further.[29]

The lessons of Crécy

Crossbows were very effective weapons, particularly during siege warfare. On the battlefield, however, at least in French service, they never quite came into their own. Partly this was because the French commanders never entirely worked out an effective tactical doctrine for their use. Here again the situation is in sharp contrast to English tactics, where commanders such as Northampton, the Constable of England, and Warwick and Reginald Cobham had worked out the best way of using the longbow effectively and then deployed the same tactical formations over and over again.

Part of the problem was that, given the advantage of numbers the French nearly always enjoyed, in most battles the French were on the attack, while the

English stood in defensive positions waiting for them. The French never did work out how to use their crossbowmen in an attack formation. There was a vague idea that the crossbowmen should advance ahead of the men-at-arms to soften the enemy up, then move aside to let the men-at-arms deliver their devastating mounted charge. However, in practice, in any duel between long-bows and crossbows, the crossbowmen nearly always came off worse, thanks to their slower rate of fire. At Crécy in 1346, standing on a higher elevation and therefore with greater range, the English longbowmen had slaughtered the Genoese crossbowmen before the latter could make effective reply. The problem was then compounded when the Comte d'Alençon, commanding the vanguard of the French men-at-arms, accused the Genoese commanders of treason and ordered his cavalry to ride them down, completing the massacre begun by the English.[30]

Ten years on, and there was still no indication that the French had really worked out how to use their crossbowmen to best advantage. Charles of Blois's experiment at La Roche-Derrien seems to have gone unnoticed. But that is not to say that no lessons had been learned. The French were certainly thinking again about how to use their men-at-arms. Much of the carnage at Crécy had been caused by archers shooting at the horses of the charging French. A falling horse would not only bring down its rider, but possibly other horses and riders as well, or at least make them slow or veer away. One needs only to watch a modern steeplechase such as the Grand National to see the kind of havoc that a single falling horse can cause.

One solution was to armour the horses, but this was expensive and slowed the horses down, meaning the time they and their riders were exposed to the arrows was greater. Nevertheless, by 1355 a few of the more well-to-do French knights and nobles had adopted some horse armour, mostly plates to protect the head and chest of the animal. But not every horse could be armoured, and commanders were increasingly ordering their men to dismount and fight on foot. A knight without a horse was a far cry from the romantic image of Charlemagne and his paladins or the heroes of the Round Table, but fighting on foot by no means unknown; combats with the sword on foot were part of the entertainment at most tournaments and jousts, indicating that knights were certainly trained to fight in this way.

At the battle of Mauron in 1352, Guy de Nesle had ordered his men-at-arms to dismount and attack on foot. They took heavy losses from English arrows, and Nesle himself was killed, but unlike at Crécy the French men-at-arms did push through to reach the English front line. Here the superior armour of the French made itself felt, and the Anglo-Breton force also took heavy casualties.

One wing of Bentley's little army nearly collapsed, and it was saved only by the courage and level-headedness of Robert Knollys, who rallied the men for a counter-attack which finally threw the French back.

So, a few lessons had been learned; but problems remained in plenty. The state was disunited, finances were strained to the point of collapse, the French army was still fighting with a tactical doctrine rooted firmly in the past, and it was led by a king who, though intelligent and brave, was also impetuous and suspicious of just about everyone outside his close circle of friends. He inspired little loyalty in his countrymen, and little fear in his foes. The chronicler Geoffrey le Baker, always ready to repeat gossip, maintained that Jean had starved his first wife to death, that he had enjoyed a long affair with a nun, and that he was a coward who shirked battle.[31] None of these things were true – Bonne of Luxembourg, Jean's first wife, had died of the Black Death – but it is clear that many English held their most important foe in contempt.

Betrayal in Normandy

But, as we have said, Jean could be astute when needed, and he and his advisors had seen that negotiating with Charles of Navarre, reprehensible though he might be, was preferable to fighting him. France could not afford a civil war, not now when the English were clearly preparing to invade again. The French knew, too, that Charles was also having trouble holding his factious army together. There were incidents of looting around Evreux and Pont-Audemer, with Navarrese troops plundering the villages of their supposed allies, and two Navarrese captains, Martin Henriquez and Pedro Ramirez, became so disgusted by the idea of peace that they took their men and several ships and sailed away to England, offering their services to King Edward.[32]

Throughout the remainder of the summer, through his son the Dauphin and his officials in Rouen, Jean continued to negotiate. On 10 September, a treaty between Charles and Jean was signed at Valognes in Normandy.[33] Charles nominally handed over several towns he had captured to the French crown, but he was still allowed to garrison these towns with his own troops. His other possessions were restored and he even received compensation for damage done by royal troops. On 17 September, Charles and the Dauphin met at Vaudreuil on the banks of the river Seine. They spent several days in talks, and seem to have got along very well. The Dauphin then accompanied Charles to Paris, where the King of Navarre was received in formal audience by the King of France. Here Charles asked for pardon for his wrongs, which

Jean was graciously pleased to grant; though, given subsequent events, he may have been crossing his fingers as he did so. Charles, for his part, then made an unusual statement justifying himself, claiming that he had 'done nothing against the King but what a loyal vassal should and ought to do'.[34]

At a stroke, the English strategy was in ruins. King Edward, well served as he usually was by his intelligence service, knew about the negotiations even before the defection of Henriquez and Ramirez, but it may have been this latter event that convinced him Charles was about to renege on his promises. At the end of August, even before the treaty between Jean and Charles was signed, Edward issued orders cancelling Lancaster's expedition and diverting most of its men and ships to a new and hastily planned punitive attack on northern France, from Calais into Picardy. Lancaster's men, still battling the winds along the south coast of England, received new orders; the duke would carry on to Normandy with part of his force, to see whether any of the remaining Norman rebels like Harcourt could be persuaded to remain in the field, but the rest of the army was ordered to sail back to Sandwich. News arrived from the north that the Scottish regent had agreed to a further extension of the truce between England and Scotland, which meant Edward could also call on the troops stationed along the border. More men, led by Lord Percy and the Bishop of Durham, Thomas Hadfield, came south to join the army bound for France.

The purpose of this expedition was punitive. Edward was angry and frustrated, but he also needed some kind of military success to show that all the preparation and cost incurred so far had actually been worthwhile. But the assemblage of men and provisions took time, as it always did, and it was October before the English army finally completed the crossing of the Channel to Calais. Even before the king left England, word came that the Scots had broken the recently established truce, and Scots forces under William, Lord Douglas and Patrick, Earl of Dunbar and March, were attacking the border posts. Edward ignored them. The north of England must look after itself. He was intent on attacking France; everything else would have to wait.

But things did not go according to plan. Anticipating his move, Jean moved to Amiens on the Somme where, with the Constable, Jacques de Bourbon, and Marshal d'Audrehem, he summoned the remnants of the army he had gathered in the summer. A new *arrière ban* was proclaimed and some of the peasant foot soldiers of the feudal levy in Picardy were called up too, but as usual they arrived too late to have much influence on events.

On 2 November the English army marched out of Calais, about 5,000 strong. Jean, at Amiens, had a force of about the same size. Realising he had little chance of victory in the field, Jean turned instead to delaying tactics, sending small parties of men to skirmish with the advancing English and also to carry away or destroy food and other provisions. There were not enough supplies in Calais to provide for the whole English army, and Edward had intended that his men should live off the land. But by the time they reached Hesdin in central Picardy, they were running out of food. Supplies of beer and wine had already given out. Edward had no choice but to retreat. His little army returned to Calais on 11 November, followed at a safe distance by the French.

Whether Edward was contemplating a second expedition, we shall never know. Word came again from the north of England, telling of a dire emergency. On the night of 6 November a small force of Scots led by Patrick of March and Thomas Stewart, Earl of Angus, slipped silently over the walls of the town of Berwick-upon-Tweed, the strategic fortress that guarded England's northern border. The garrison commander, William Greystoke, and most of his men were with Edward's army in France. Despite heavy fighting in the streets, the town was quickly taken. The castle, on the northwest edge of the town, held out and was soon reinforced from other garrisons along the Tweed, but more Scottish troops arrived and began a full-scale siege of the castle.

This time the Scots could not be ignored. Edward hurried back to England, taking most of his men with him, and began to raise a new army against Scotland. His plans for taking the war to France had collapsed; he had failed on every front.

Or, not quite. In September, the Prince of Wales and his little army had sailed away to the south. By December, word of their achievements was arriving back in London. On one front, at least, English arms had dealt France a humiliating blow.

CHAPTER 4

'We had a Little Trouble with the Black Prince'

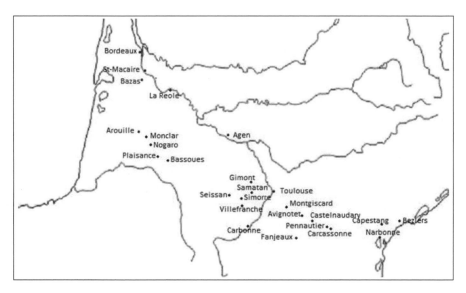

1355 campaign

The Prince of Wales and his men had reached Gascony on 20 September 1355 without incident. The situation on the frontier was stable; Jean d'Armagnac had retired to his base at Toulouse and appeared to have given up on campaigning for the year.

Prince Edward and his captains received a warm welcome. In one of those pieces of theatre that both the prince and his father delighted in staging, a ceremony was held at the cathedral of St-André, attended by Amanieu de la Mothe, the Archbishop of Bordeaux, and all his clergy in full robes, Present also were the worthies of the town in gowns and chains of office, led by Thomas

Roos, the mayor of Bordeaux, and local officials including John Chiverston the seneschal and his assistant John Stretelee (or Streatley) the Constable of Bordeaux. Most importantly, there were the representatives of the Gascon nobility. Here were the men whom the prince would rely on to defend Gascony and drive back the French: Jean de Grailly, the Captal de Buch; Bernard-Ezi d'Albret and his sons; Guilhem-Sans de Pommiers and his younger brother Élie; Augier de Montaut of Mussidan; Guilhem-Raimon de Madaillan from Rauzan; Aimeri de Biron from Montferrand and many others. They and their followers would play a prominent role in the events to come.

Before the high altar, a proclamation authorising the prince to act in the name of the king was read out. The prince swore to defend Gascony and to respect and preserve the ancient liberties and customs of its people. The nobles and people in turn reaffirmed their oath of allegiance to the English crown and promised to serve the prince in all his endeavours.[1]

The ceremonies over, a council of war was held the following day. The prince received reports of the activities of Jean d'Armagnac and the French armies, including detailed accounts of the fighting in the spring. According to the chronicler Geoffrey le Baker, the Gascon nobles complained that Armagnac was still trying to undermine the English and their allies and woo the Gascons away to an alliance with France. Although Baker goes on to say that 'the anger of the furious prince glowed white-hot' at this news, in fact the situation was already well known. Striking back against Armagnac was one of the reasons why the prince had come to Gascony in the first place.

The prince was still at Plymouth when news came of Charles of Navarre's imminent defection, and of the consequent change of plans and the new royal expedition into Picardy. It seems safe to assume that the prince himself received fresh orders at about the same time. Two priorities had asserted themselves. First, there was a need for military success, something to give good news to the populace at home, bolster royal prestige and justify the enormous expense of these expeditions. The king clearly hoped that his own venture into Picardy would achieve this end, but anything the prince could contribute would be helpful too.

Second, the strategic situation in the south needed to be rebalanced. The French needed to be driven back and some of the lands, castles and towns they had seized returned to English lordship. Along the valleys of the Dordogne, the Lot and the Garonne, the frontier had become a complex mess, with some towns and fortified places garrisoned by the French and others only a few miles away held by the English and their Gascon supporters. Delivering a decisive blow to the French in the field would weaken the French garrisons and make these towns easier to recover.

There is still some argument over the prince's actual aims when he arrived in Bordeaux that autumn, and it cannot be definitely proven that he set out to force a battle with Armagnac and the French. However, it seems likely that the possibility was at least discussed at the council of war. Defeating Armagnac would offer a number of advantages. As noted above, a military victory would increase English prestige, not just at home but in Gascony as well. A triumph on the battlefield might persuade those notables whose allegiance was doubtful, or who held themselves aloof from the conflict like Gaston Fébus, the powerful Comte de Foix, to climb down from the fence and join the English cause. Victory would also allow the prince to reward the men who already followed him, through allocations of plunder and ransoms, and bind them more closely to him. The objectives for the campaign to come, including Armagnac's own lands and then his base at Toulouse, seemed designed to force the count to come out and fight.

The lords of Gascony

Of all the issues he faced, the question of Gascon loyalties must have been the one that vexed Prince Edward and his councillors the most. Squeezed between the English and the French, the Gascons tended pragmatically to support the party that looked like it might come out on top; or else, the party that offered them the most personal reward. Changes of allegiance were frequent; even Jean de Grailly, the most loyal servant of the English crown in Gascony, kicked over the traces on one occasion and served the French for about a year before defecting back to the English.

The Gascons had a reputation for hot tempers and volatility, and some of that reputation may have been deserved. But in the 14th century they were fighting to preserve an independence, a culture and a way of life that were slowly being eroded away. In times past, Gascony had been an independent state in its own right. The Duchy of Vasconia, founded as part of the Frankish kingdom in the 7th century, had always been different from the rest of France; its language and culture were Basque, not French, and its territory ran from Bordeaux down across the Pyrenees to Pamplona. The southern regions eventually broke away to form the Kingdom of Navarre, and by the 9th century the rest of Gascony had declared itself independent of the Frankish empire.

Around the same time, the Basque tongue was displaced as the principal language of the region by Provençal, or the Langue d'Oc, a very different language from both Basque and French (Catalan, still widely spoken today, is a modern descendant of the Langue d'Oc). Gascon culture reached its zenith. Gascony was the birthplace of the troubadours, the famous singers and composers, men and women, who epitomised secular culture in the High Middle Ages; it was, arguably, the cradle of concepts such as chivalry and courtly love, which the troubadours enshrined in their music. When Duke Sancho VI died childless in 1032, Gascony was absorbed by the Duchy of Aquitaine (Occitan) to the north, but in cultural terms it was Gascony that colonised Aquitaine, not the other way around. Indeed, the name Aquitaine eventually disappeared, and the whole region became known as Gascony.

But with the union with Aquitaine came loss of independence. Aquitaine was a fief of the Kingdom of France, and its dukes, like those of Brittany and Normandy, owed fealty to the French crown. When Aquitaine became an English possession through the marriage of Duchess Alienor to Henry II of England, France became alarmed. A vast and wealthy tract of land had passed into the hands of the enemy. Almost immediately, French kings had begun scheming to recover Gascony. The English crown was equally determined to hold on to this rich and prosperous territory. Caught between the two sides, the Gascon lords had to make difficult choices.

For some, like Jean de Grailly, the choice was easy. Apart from that one aberrant year, he served the English and was their loyal friend throughout his life. The Grailly family held lands in the Médoc and also around Castillon, around 35 miles east of Bordeaux on the Dordogne.[2] His exact date of birth is unknown, but he is likely to have been born around 1320. The title Captal de Buch was hereditary in the family; 'captal' means something like 'great chieftain', while 'Buch' is the name of one of the family's castles.[3] He was prominent in English service by the early 1340s, and was named one of the founder knights of the Order of the Garter, one of the few non-Englishmen to be so honoured. He went on to fight in English service from Spain to Brittany; he also crusaded in Prussia alongside his friend and cousin Gaston Fébus, Comte de Foix.

Like Geoffroi de Charny and John Chandos – the latter was also a close friend – the Captal was held up as an exemplar of the chivalrous knight. There is some suggestion that he may have been the model for Chaucer's knight in *The Canterbury Tales*, though it is more likely that Chaucer's creation is an amalgam of several different historical figures.[4] He served the English out of honour and friendship, and though he was richly rewarded for his services, there was also something selfless about his loyalty. When the French captured the Captal in 1372, he was offered his freedom if he would swear an oath never to fight against France again. He refused to do so, and died in prison several years later.

Much more pragmatic, and more typical of the Gascon lords, were the Albret family. The patriarch was Bernard-Ezi IV, lord of Albret, probably in his fifties by this point but still hale and hearty and ready to lead his clan in war. He had married Marthe, sister of Jean d'Armagnac, so these two enemies were also brothers-in-law. When we consider that Jean's mother was Bernard-Ezi's sister, that one of Bernard-Ezi's daughters was married to the Captal de Buch, and the Captal's mother was the aunt of the Comte de Foix – and that is just a few of the strands in the tangled web of marriages and relationships that connected the Gascon nobility – the war in the southwest begins to look almost like a family quarrel.

Bernard-Ezi and Marthe had numerous children, several daughters and at least three sons – Arnaud-Amanieu, Bernard and another Arnaud – as well as an illegitimate son, Bertucat. Bernard had briefly been considered as a husband for the Prince of Wales's sister Isabella, but the lady had put her foot down firmly and declined. All four young men accompanied their father to war.

The Albrets were staunch loyalists to the English cause, and continued to be so as long as Bernard-Ezi was alive. But in the 1360s, when English fortunes were at their height, Arnaud-Amanieu and most of the rest of the clan changed sides and joined the French, leading a dangerous revolt against the English in Gascony. They had seen something in the wind that told them English sovereignty in Gascony could not last; and, of course, they were right. Arnaud-Amanieu was laden with honours by the French king; his son Charles went on to become Constable of France, and was partly responsible for another disastrous French defeat at the hands of the English, this time at Agincourt in 1415.

The Albrets were rich and powerful, but most of the Gascon lords who supported the English were relatively small landholders. Some had ambitions to expand their estates, preferably at the expense of their pro-French neighbours. One of the most hungry and restless was Augier de Montaut, lord of Mussidan in the valley of the river Isle, northwest of Bergerac. Mussidan was on the dangerous frontier facing east towards the French-held fortresses of Périgord; much of the Dordogne valley to the south was also French-held. Mussidan thus constituted an excellent advance base from which to operate against the French, and the English seneschal in Bordeaux provided the lord of Mussidan with money and supplies and encouraged him to attack his neighbour and rival, Roger-Bernard de Talleyrand, Comte de Périgord. A guerrilla war between Mussidan and Périgord, in reality a proxy war between France and England, had been going on for years.

Mussidan's support for the English was largely contingent on self-interest; so long as the English would help him to advance his own interests, he would support them. Much the same was true of most of the other Gascon barons, men like Guilhem-Sans de Pommiers and the ambitious Guilhem-Raimon de Madaillan who had recently expanded his own landholdings to include the town and fortress of Rauzan. All these men were allied to the English only so long as it suited them. At the cathedral of St-André they swore allegiance to the English crown, but the prince and his advisors were realistic enough to know that many of these men wore that allegiance lightly, and would throw it off at will.

To keep the loyalty of these proud, violent men, so full of chivalry and so taken up with their rivalries with each other, the prince needed to impose himself as a successful war leader. Victory in battle, and the riches of the spoils that came with it, was something that all of them would respect. The same was true when it came to impressing the neutrals. Of these, by far the most important was Gaston Fébus, Comte de Foix and Vicomte de Béarn.

Born in 1331, Gaston was now in his mid-twenties, a year younger than the Prince of Wales.[5] He was tall with golden blonde hair, which may have been responsible for his nickname, Fébus, or Phoebus, a name also applied to the sun god Apollo. Like the Prince of Wales, Gaston never missed an opportunity for publicity, and it is entirely possible that he coined the nickname himself. Brave, cultured, classically handsome, Gaston wrote poetry in Occitan and a famous book on hunting, the *Livre de chasse*, in French. He was passionate about hunting, and rode out from his castle at Pau to hunt in the foothills of the Pyrenees whenever he could. He was another role model of the chivalric knight and nobleman, and he cultivated this image assiduously.

Gaston's county, Foix, was one of the richest and most powerful of the semi-independent states-within-a-state that comprised Gascony. In theory, he held Foix as a vassal of the French crown, and he had done homage to Philippe VI. But Gaston was also viscount of the neighbouring state of Béarn, which he insisted was completely independent of any overlord. He refused to do homage for Bearn, and resisted all pressure from Paris to do so.

But when Gaston took over his lands, he also inherited a feud with his neighbour, the Comte d'Armagnac. Gaston's father had taken advantage of the chaos of war to expand his possessions northward, and in 1339 he seized the town of Miramont-Sensacq in the Landes. Jean d'Armagnac also coveted this town, and later in the year he attacked it, triggering a war between Armagnac and Foix. The French crown stepped in, enforced peace and took the town into royal hands, but the bad blood between Armagnac and Foix lingered. Upon his accession, Gaston Fébus kept the peace, but he remained aloof from the war, refusing to respond to calls from either king, Philippe VI or Jean, to support the French cause. In Bordeaux, there was a strong sense that Gaston was watching from the sidelines, waiting to see which way the war went; he would choose whichever side offered him most, and where he could gain the greatest advantage.

It was clear too that whoever could command the loyalty of Gaston, with his powerful private army, would have a clear advantage in Gascony. The English had their plans to win Gaston over, and it is likely that those plans had been laid even before the prince's expedition left England.

Twenty years older than Gaston, his bitter rival Jean, Comte d'Armagnac, was another whose loyalty was pliable. From his mother he had inherited the county of Rodez, in the high country northeast of Toulouse, and he also had lands in Quercy, further to the west; these, with his own country of Armagnac, meant he was a wealthy and powerful man. But he too was ambitious. His father had served the French crown on several occasions, and the Armagnacs, like their neighbours the counts of Comminges and Astarac, were loyal probably as a matter of policy; the French kings could exert more pressure than the English seneschals in Bordeaux. But Jean d'Armagnac seems to have been testing the waters, and even though he served under King Philippe VI in the 1340 campaign against England in the north, he was already considering whether the English might offer him a better deal.

In September 1346, shortly after the defeat at Crécy, Armagnac accepted an appointment as king's lieutenant in Gascony. Quite probably Philippe was aware that Armagnac's loyalty was wavering, and giving him more power and authority was meant to bind him more closely to the French crown. His second wife, Beatrice, was either a sister or a cousin of Jean de Clermont, the cousin of the French marshal. Initially, at least, Armagnac threw himself into his duties. As we have already seen, in the early years of King Jean's reign, Armagnac had been making life difficult for the English in Gascony, and had won the reputation of being an energetic and enterprising commander. But even so, his loyalty could not be taken for granted. By 1360, a few years after the events of this book, Armagnac was effectively operating as a free agent before going over to the English side – and then changing sides again and leading a rebellion against English rule. Even in 1355–56, while he continued to hold the French king's commission in Gascony, we are entitled to wonder whose side he was really on.

Armagnac's feud with Gaston Fébus dominated his political and military career, and was far more important to him than any question of fidelity to an overlord. The same is true of the other important pro-French Gascon nobleman of the day, Roger-Bernard de Talleyrand, Comte de Périgord. He too was an older man, in his mid-fifties by the time of the events described here. A second son, he had taken holy orders, but left the church when his older brother died childless and he inherited the county of Périgord. His lands too were rich, and included the fortified city of Périgeux, which dominated the upper valley of the river Isle, but he was at daggers drawn with the powerful lords of Mussidan further down the valley. Périgord's loyalty to France was one of strategic necessity; England supported Mussidan, so Périgord had perforce to turn to France for help.

Périgord's younger brother, Hélie de Talleyrand, also plays a part in the events of this book. Patronage and influence had secured him a place in the church while he was still a child – he became a canon at the age of six – and after a period studying law, in 1324 he was ordained Bishop of Limoges when he was still only 23.[6] In 1328 he moved to the bishopric of Auxerre, and in 1331 he was appointed a cardinal by Pope John XXII. His appointment had been the result of sustained pressure by King Philippe of France, who was determined to pack the college of cardinals with as many Frenchmen as possible, and Talleyrand repaid the favour by leading resistance to all attempts to relocate the papacy from Avignon back to Rome, and to ensure the election of French or pro-French popes. A shameless collector of benefices, Talleyrand also held several ecclesiastical posts in England, and was at various times Archdeacon of Richmond, Archdeacon of London and Dean of York cathedral. Before the war he had been a familiar figure in London and was well known, if not entirely trusted, at court.

Talleyrand, like most Gascon noblemen, believed in looking after his own. His sister Agnes married Jean, Duke of Durazzo, one of that family of adventurers descended from Charles of Anjou, younger brother of the saint-king Louis IX. Agnes's troublesome younger son, Robert of Durazzo, had what might be called a chequered career: captured and imprisoned during an audacious attempt to take over the Kingdom of Hungary, imprisoned again in Italy on a charge of murder which he may or may not have committed, and then excommunicated for a plundering raid during which he seized the castle of Les Baux in Provence. His uncle the cardinal managed to get him out of all these scrapes and, probably to keep an eye on him, took the young man into his own household. Durazzo became one of the cardinal's men-at-arms, serving in his bodyguard.

These were the friends, the neutrals and the foes with whom the prince had to deal in Gascony. They were proud, cultured, violent men who would break an oath of loyalty without thinking twice. Their own feuds and quarrels meant far more to them than the dynastic and political struggle between England

and France, and it is almost impossible to overestimate the strength of their self-interest. To get them on side and keep them there, the prince needed to do two things. First, he needed to ensure they got the rewards of land and money that they wanted to keep them sweet. Second, he had to impress them with his power and resolve, and prove himself a worthy leader in their eyes. This he now proceeded to do.

'To ravage the county of Armagnac'

The first step was to carry the war to Armagnac and concentrate on him. As we noted earlier, the prince may have intended to force Armagnac to come out and fight. If he refused to do so, then the next best thing would be to cause as much destruction as possible in his own county of Armagnac, thus damaging the count personally and hopefully impressing his rival, Gaston Fébus, with the prince's power. If time permitted, other pro-French nobles like Pere-Raimon, Comte de Comminges, and Centule, Comte d'Astarac, would also receive similar treatment. And so, as the chronicler Geoffrey le Baker says, 'with the agreement of the council of his lords, he [the prince] dispatched his troops to ravage the county of Armagnac'. This, he goes on to say, 'gave great comfort to the loyal lords of Gascony'.[7]

The decision made, the prince's staff moved with remarkable speed. The Gascon lords brought in their men; including, significantly, a contingent from Béarn, part of the holdings of Gaston Fébus, though that worthy himself still continued to sit on the sidelines. The Béarnais served under Élie de Pommiers, brother of the lord of Pommiers. Stores including food, wine and fodder for the horses were sent up the Garonne by boat to the port of St-Macaire, the designated jumping-off point for the campaign. Horses were sent to pasture in an attempt to regain the weight and fitness they would have inevitably lost during the sea voyage. The accounts of the Prince of Wales's household show purchases of food and firewood, as well as, inevitably, a few luxuries: the prince ordered a dozen boxes of confectionery, presumably as a gift, and also received a present of two falcons.[8]

On Monday 5 October, just over two weeks after he arrived in Bordeaux, the prince led his army out of St-Macaire and south towards the frontier. Haste was the order of the day. It was late in the year to launch a major campaign. In October, the weather in southwest France is still often quite fair, but later would come the winter rains, softening the ground and turning unpaved roads into quagmires. The prince and his advisors knew they had only a small window of opportunity in which to strike their blow at Armagnac.

The first day's march, through friendly territory, was a short one; the second day, Tuesday, was a brutal march of 23 miles through the desolate country of the Landes, mostly covered in pine forests with few towns or villages. The sandy soil of the Landes is also arid, and at that season of the year even the few streams and ponds that do exist are largely dry. The army ploughed on through the heat, the horses in particular suffering terribly, and Baker noted that many animals died.[9] The troops camped that night outside the town of Castets-en-Dourthe. During the night some of the Welsh archers, probably under the influence of drink, broke into the town and did a fair amount of damage before they could be restrained. The prince was later forced to pay compensation to the townspeople.

Passing through Bazas and Castelnau, on Sunday the army embarked on another very long march which killed yet more horses. By evening they had reached the town of Arouille, on the frontier of the County of Armagnac, 81 miles from Bordeaux. Arouille, like several towns nearby, was a bastide, one of the many towns planted in Gascony under English rule, and it had continued to be an English possession until fairly recently. Quite who owned it now was uncertain; Baker thought the garrison captain, 'William de Reymon', was English, but it is more likely that his real name was Guilhem Raimon and he was a Gascon.[10] He may have been a local nobleman who set himself up as protector of Arouille and its neighbours. At all events, he seems to have been happy to surrender the towns to the English once again, and Arouille was handed over peacefully.

In the field outside Arouille, Prince Edward began to prepare for war. The battle standards were ceremoniously unfurled and displayed, and several esquires in the army including a man named Janekin, or John, de Berefort were knighted; this was customary when opening a campaign. The prince then re-organised the army into three divisions. More Gascon troops had been arriving during the march, and Prince Edward now had somewhere between 8,000 and 9,000 men at his disposal, about a third of them English and Welsh and the remainder Gascons.

The vanguard division was placed under the command of those two distinguished veterans, Thomas Beauchamp, the Earl of Warwick, and Reginald Cobham.[11] This division was something of a family affair; Warwick's brother, John Beauchamp, and his son-in-law the young Roger, Lord Clifford were also with this division. A knight from Hampshire, Sir Thomas Hampton, was the standard bearer.

The main body, the largest division, was commanded by the prince personally with the Earl of Oxford to assist him. There too were the knights and esquires of his household, including Bartholomew Burghersh and John Chandos. Other knights with this division included John Willoughby de Eresby, Roger de la Warre who had been knighted by the prince at Quettehou in 1346 and fought alongside him at Crécy, Maurice de Berkeley, Thomas Roos the mayor of Bordeaux – the Middle Ages was a time of multi-tasking, when civic officials could also be fighting men – and John Bourchier, a distant ancestor of the 16th-century translator of the chronicles of Jean Froissart. Many of the principal Gascon lords were here too, including the Captal de Buch and Aimeri de Biron, the lord of Montferrand. The rearguard was commanded by the earls of Suffolk and Salisbury, along with Guilhem-Sans de Pommiers and another contingent of Gascons.

This division into three was standard for most armies of the day; the French used it as well as the English. It allowed for a good deal of operational and tactical flexibility. On the march, the three divisions might stick closely together, especially if the enemy were nearby, or they might spread out across the country and use different roads, which reduced congestion at key points such as bridges and allowed more opportunities for foraging and plundering. On the battlefield, the three units could fight independently or work together to support each other. At Crécy and several other engagements, the English commanders had put the two smaller divisions together in the front line – which meant, paradoxically, that the rearguard fought alongside the vanguard – while the main body was held in reserve, but other permutations were also possible.

Chevauchée

After this reorganisation, which took most of Monday, 12 October, on the 13th the Anglo-Gascon army marched forward into Armagnac. The first stage of the advance led them uphill out of the forested plain of the Landes and into an open, populous, agricultural countryside rich with fields. pastures and vines. The advance was slow and deliberate, often no more than 8 or 10 miles a day. This was now a *chevauchée*, a seemingly innocuous term meaning literally 'riding' or 'promenade', but which in the 14th century came to have much darker connotations. A *chevauchée* was a campaign of organised destruction, and as the Hundred Years War developed, these *chevauchées* were becoming more and more frequent.

The purposes of a *chevauchée* were simple: to weaken the enemy; to destroy resources such as food which might be of strategic benefit to him; to reduce the tax base by destroying wealth; and to force the enemy to commit money to relief work and reconstruction which might otherwise have been spent on

The rolling countryside of Sauveterre

war. In cases such as the *chevauchée* through Armagnac, there might also be secondary purposes: to punish the enemy and exact retribution, or to force him to come out and fight, to defend his lands and vassals. In every purpose but the last, the *chevauchée* in Armagnac must be considered a success.

Yet we need to look behind that military success and see what it really meant. It is easy to talk of raids like this in a cold-blooded fashion, noting the movements of troops and evaluating the damage done, but we need to be clear about what actually happened. The instructions given by the commanders to their troops were clear. Every farm, every village, every town the army passed was stripped bare. Every form of movable wealth was carried away, and all that could not be taken was destroyed. That meant families robbed of their money, their jewellery if they had any, and their clothes and household possessions. There are stories from the Hundred Years War of raiders carrying off even basic things such as kitchen utensils and mattresses, anything that might be sold elsewhere for a profit. All livestock, pigs, sheep, goats, cattle, were rounded up and driven away, most likely to be slaughtered and eaten by the troops at a later date, and food and fodder were also carried off. Any animals that could not be taken were killed on the spot. Once the work of plunder was done, houses and outbuildings were set on fire (though if the army needed buildings for shelter, the burning might not take place until they were ready to depart). In extreme cases, orchards and vineyards might be cut down, and any crops still in the field destroyed.

The victims of the *chevauchée* were left destitute, robbed of everything they possessed and without a roof over their heads or any food to eat – if they were lucky. The more humane commanders gave orders that civilians should not be physically harmed, but those orders were not always respected. Medieval armies, like most armies, contained their fair share of criminal elements. Sometimes, convicted criminals were allowed to enlist in exchange for a pardon. Rape and murder happened during these raids, and it would be naïve in the extreme to pretend they did not. Similarly, church property was supposed to be respected and left untouched, but again, the commanders were not always able – or willing – to enforce their orders. The lust for plunder and for burning was simply too strong.

The *chevauchée* of 1355 was by no means the worst of its kind; for the full horror, one needs to read accounts of the Free Company raids in the 1360s, when lawless men like Robert Knollys and Arnault de Cervolles, the Archpriest, raided, burned and slaughtered their way across southern France. The Prince of Wales was, mostly, able to keep his men under control – there were exceptions, such as the assaults on Montgiscard and Castelnaudary, below – but it was not easy. As we saw, even before they left friendly territory, some of the archers had gone on the rampage at Castets-en-Dourthe. And as for the protection offered to church property, this was more honoured in the breach than in the observance. Keeping men hungry for plunder away from rich churches and abbeys was never a realistic proposition.

By the evening of Tuesday the 13th the army had reached the town of Monclar, another bastide, located in the valley of the river Douze. The town's castle had a small garrison, which promptly surrendered. The town itself seems to have been deserted, which is unsurprising. Most people, on hearing that the English and Gascons had arrived and were scorching their way across the countryside, would have packed whatever they could carry and fled to safety. Prince Edward and his household made themselves at home in the empty town, but during the night the arsonists set to work, and flames suddenly leaped up. The prince was forced to flee the burning town in a rather ignominious fashion, and passed the rest of the night in a hastily pitched tent in a field outside Monclar. Throughout the rest of the campaign, he never again spent the night in a town, preferring the safety of the open fields where, in Baker's glib words, 'he might always be ready for the enemy'.[12]

And so for the next 10 days the army plundered and burned its way south across Armagnac, leaving a trail of smoking ruins behind it. Each day the tale is the same – of towns taken, looted and burned, villages reduced to ashes, castles stormed. The Anglo-Gascons did not have things all their own way. Here and there, pockets of resistance flared up, isolated and uncoordinated, small garrisons fighting against enormous odds but determined to hold out. The first blood was shed. A few miles south of Monclar the castle of Estang put up fierce resistance. The veteran knight John de Lisle, leading the assault on the battlements, was wounded by a crossbow bolt. The wound was mortal, and Lisle died the following day, to the sorrow of the prince and the other captains. Lisle was the first of the founder members of the Order of the Garter to be killed in battle.[13]

By Friday the 16th the army had reached the heavily fortified town of Nogaro. Here again the garrison was determined to resist, and threw back the assaults of the English and Gascons.[14] The prince and his commanders did not press the issue; other, easier targets were waiting for them further south. Thirteen miles south lay Plaisance, another fortified bastide. The town was abandoned and deserted, but a small garrison under the Comte de Montluzon held out in the castle. Montluzon does not seem to have put up much of a fight, and he and his men soon surrendered to the Captal de Buch. Another castle, at Galiax to the west of Plaisance, was captured the following day. Plaisance itself was burned to the ground as soon as the army was ready to depart.

From Plaisance the army changed course a little, veering to the southeast. The ground was rising now, the peaks of the Pyrenees visible on the horizon. Numerous small rivers ran down from the mountains towards the plains to the north, cutting deep valleys into the hilly country. The going became harder. Climbing and descending hills was tiring for men and horses, but it was the presence of the wagons loaded with provisions and plunder that really impeded the army now. Taking wagons down a steep hill is nearly as fatiguing and time-consuming as dragging them up; the wagons cannot be allowed to go too quickly, or they will overrun their draught teams and injure the horses. For a time the army followed the road towards Auch, the ancient city which had once been capital of all Gascony and now was the seat of the counts of Armagnac, but it is likely that the prince's intelligence gatherers already knew that Armagnac himself was not there. On hearing of the prince's advance, he had retreated east towards Toulouse.

On Monday, 19 October, after a difficult march through hilly country, the army reached Bassoues. The town was owned by the Archbishop of Auch and the prince gave firm orders that none of his men were to enter the town. On this occasion his orders were respected. Bassoues provided food for the army, but otherwise escaped undamaged.[15] Next along the road was Mirande, a big

The Pyrenees in autumn from near Carcassonne

bastide town on the banks of the river Baise. An assault was considered, but after assessing the strength of the walls and the garrison, the prince and his captains decided to bypass the town instead. The prince spent the night at the Benedictine abbey of Berdoues a few miles upriver.

Prince Edward had achieved his first objective. He had torn a smoking strip across the County of Armagnac, destroying several towns and castles and causing an immense amount of damage to his enemy. The question now was, what next? There had been virtually no resistance. The French seemed to have been taken completely by surprise. The Comte d'Armagnac, still gathering his forces in Toulouse, did not have enough men to stop the Anglo-Gascon advance. Clermont, the marshal, was still far away to the north, beyond the Dordogne. There was nothing to stop the prince from advancing still further, even as far as Toulouse itself.

The advance on Toulouse

The losses taken at Estang, including the death of a veteran captain, had made Prince Edward cautious. Apart from the half-hearted assault on Nogaro, he had

The donjon at Bassoues-en-Armagnac

attempted no more attacks on strong fortified positions, bypassing Mirande rather than attempting to storm it. Such attacks, even if successful, were bound to be costly in terms of lives, and he wanted to keep his little army intact in case Jean d'Armagnac should sally out to give battle.

But Armagnac showed no signs of doing so. In the absence of any correspondence or other documents, we can only guess as to why, but two possibilities present themselves. First, Armagnac had been stymied earlier in the year, starved of men and money with most of the French crown's scanty resources diverted to the crisis in Normandy. Second, despite – or perhaps because of – the devastation caused in his own lands, he may have been contemplating a change of allegiance. If French power was so weak that English armies could plunder his lands with impunity, Jean may have reasoned, then he was entitled to ask whether he was actually on the right side. It seems highly likely too, given the complex familial relationships of the Gascon nobles, that he was aware of English overtures to his rival the Comte de Foix. What we do know is that, for whatever reason, Armagnac did not stir from his citadel in Toulouse until French royal officers, Clermont the marshal and Bourbon the Constable, arrived and he had to make some show of doing his duty.

Prince Edward, for his part, perhaps unaware of Armagnac's weakness or vacillation, now chose to advance directly on Toulouse with the aim of facing his enemy down. Ahead lay the little County of Astarac, and the army proceeded to burn its way across the land with the same thoroughness as before. On Friday, 23 October, the town of Seissan was taken and burned, apparently against the prince's orders.[16] (Why he should wish to save the town is not clear; perhaps it too was ecclesiastical property.) Pushing on through the hills and steep valleys, the peaks of the Pyrenees marching always to their right, on Saturday the main body of the army reached Villefranche on the river Gimone; the rearguard occupied a deserted Benedictine abbey near Simorre and the vanguard occupied the town of Tournans. All three towns were empty, their inhabitants having fled to safety in Toulouse.

On Sunday they marched again, fording the Gimone and moving on into the County of Comminges. Bypassing the heavily fortified town of Lombez they reached Samatan, which was undefended and deserted. It too was plundered and burned, and a Franciscan friary in the town, despite being church property, was not spared the flames. The ground over which the army marched was growing flatter and more open now, the mountains further away and the land rich with agricultural wealth, but as Geoffrey le Baker says, 'all was laid waste by fire and the sword'.[17] The night of Monday the 26th brought them to the town of St-Lys, less than 15 miles from Toulouse.

On the 27th the army rested. It had still seen no serious fighting. The prince and his commanders now faced a difficult choice. Ancient, rich and powerful, a centre of trade and commerce on the banks of the broad river Garonne, Toulouse was a large city. Its population before the Black Death may have been as high as 45,000; if we take the standard measure of a population decline of one-third during the plague, then the city could still have been as large as 30,000 people.[18] It was also heavily fortified. The city walls were 7–8 feet thick and more than 15 feet high and studded with towers, nearly 30 in all.[19] During the Albigensian Crusade, the military campaigns aimed at stamping out the Cathar heresy in the 13th century, Toulouse had withstood three lengthy sieges by French royal armies much larger than the force the Prince of Wales had at his disposal.[20] Although, as we have mentioned, Armagnac was short of fighting men, he could call out the town militia of Toulouse to defend the city, and this would give him a considerable advantage in numbers.[21]

Storming these massive walls in the face of a well-organised defence would be a bloody affair, and there was no guarantee of success. A siege was equally undesirable. The prince lacked artillery. Unlike his father's campaign in 1346,

Simorre church

there were no cannon with the army, nor were there siege towers, catapults or trebuchets. Siege engines could be built, but this would take time, and as already noted, the season was far advanced. And if Prince Edward had hoped that Armagnac would sally out and meet him on the field, he was badly disappointed. Armagnac held discretion to be the better part of valour, and stayed behind Toulouse's fortifications.

Returning to Bordeaux and putting his army into winter quarters would have been disappointing, to say the least. The damage done in Armagnac, Astarac and Comminges had been considerable, but it would hardly dent France's fighting power, or advance English war aims. There would be no battle, no ransoms, and so far there had been only a modest amount of plunder. Prince Edward needed results, and he needed them quickly. Holding a council of war on the 27th, he committed his army to a breathtaking gamble. He would bypass Toulouse altogether, leaving it behind him, and continue the *chevauchée* eastward, advancing into the heart of Languedoc.

The move was risky for two reasons. First, by advancing, the prince would leave Armagnac and his little army standing across his line of communications, barring his retreat to Bordeaux. If Armagnac were to be reinforced – for example, by Clermont and his troops further north – he might be able to cut the Anglo-Gascon army off and leave it stranded in enemy territory. Second, to bypass Toulouse, the English needed to ford two formidable rivers, the Garonne and the Ariège, and no one even knew for certain if this could be done. Fording the rivers would leave the army very vulnerable; if Armagnac should suddenly sortie out of Toulouse and attack them while in mid-river, the result would be disastrous.

But Prince Edward had seen river crossings under fire before. Nine years earlier, in 1346, the English had fought their way across the river Somme at the ford of the Blanchetaque. The prince had been in the vanguard at that battle, and that memory was almost certainly in his mind on the morning of 28 October as he led his army out of St-Lys, bypassing Toulouse and heading towards the valley of the Garonne south of the city.

'War's fury had never entered their land'

A march of about 13 miles brought the army to the banks of the Garonne near Pinsaguel. A ford had been found, possibly on the advice of one of the Gascon men-at-arms, Amanieu de Fossat. He had formerly held lands near Toulouse, including the town of Montgiscard, but in 1338 he had been declared a rebel and his lands seized by the French seneschal of Agen. Fossat had taken refuge with the English, and as Peter Hoskins suggests, was likely acting as a guide to the prince's army as it traversed around Toulouse.[22]

The ford would probably have been impassable at most times of the year, but in late October before the arrival of the winter rains it was possible for men, horses and wagons to cross the river. Even so, says the chronicler Geoffrey le Baker, the river was 'difficult, rock-strewn and completely terrifying'.[23] Baker goes on to say that no one had ever crossed this ford before on horseback; this may be hyperbole, but there is no doubt that the crossing was difficult and some of the English and Gascons were swept away and drowned in the rushing waters. All the time, too, the army would have been braced for an attack; Toulouse was just a few miles away over the horizon.

But no attack came. Pressing on, the army came to another river, the Ariège, smaller but faster and, says Baker, even more dangerous. We should spare a thought here for the teamsters and their horses, struggling to drag heavily laden wagons and carts across the stony bed of the river against the strong current. The exhausted army camped at Lacroix-Falgarde on the far bank of the Ariège. They had bypassed Toulouse with minimal losses. The way into Languedoc was wide open.

Jean d'Armagnac, for his part, was caught flat-footed. He had not expected, or believed it would be possible, that the English could bypass Toulouse so easily and quickly. He seems to have fallen into a classic trap of military thinking, assuming that the enemy will do what one wants him to do. Military logic had suggested that the prince, stymied before Toulouse, would recognise that winter was drawing in and retreat west. Shocked when the prince did the exact opposite, he sat in Toulouse for the moment and did nothing. He would have known by now that reinforcements were on their way from the north, led by Jacques de Bourbon the Constable of France; as the Anglo-Gascon army was fording the Garonne, Bourbon was at Montauban, about 35 miles north of Toulouse. Bourbon quickly learned of Prince Edward's flanking movement and was furious, rebuking Armagnac sharply for his inaction. Yet Bourbon himself was curiously passive in the days that followed.

The prince's army marched swiftly on. On the 29th they reached the prosperous town of Montgiscard and summoned it to surrender. The townspeople, believing themselves secure behind the protection of Toulouse, had not fled, and now they decided to fight. But Montgiscard's fortifications were rudimentary, and the town militia were reduced to hurling stones at their attackers. Despite taking some casualties, the prince's army stormed the walls and entered the town. Here for the first time we hear of the killing of civilians, including women and children.[24] It is hard to tell whether they were killed deliberately or were caught up in the fighting, but we are entitled to wonder what Amanieu de Fossat thought as he watched his former subjects being butchered by his allies.

Once the fighting died down, Montgiscard was looted from top to bottom and then burned. Its church did not escape the flames, nor did 12 windmills used for grinding flour in the fields outside the town. 'After this,' says Geoffrey le Baker, 'there was scarcely one day's riding on which our men did not take by storm towns, forts and castles, all of which they despoiled and consigned to the flames.' The inhabitants, he writes, were helpless and did not know what do to: 'war's fury had never entered their lands before then.'[25] More than a century had passed since the crusaders had swept through Languedoc, exterminating the Cathar heretics, and the country had known peace ever since. It would not know peace again for a long time to come.

On the 30th the English burned the town of Baziège and then swept on southeast to Avignonet, following an old Roman road, the Via Aquitania, the main route connecting the Atlantic with the Mediterranean. Most of Avignonet had been abandoned, its people fleeing after hearing of the disaster

Carcassonne on the horizon from 10 miles to the west

at Montgiscard, but a few of the town's notables had taken shelter in the castle. To no avail; the castle was quickly stormed and the notables dragged out and held to ransom, while the town and its church were consigned to the flames. Another 20 windmills were burned. All respect for church property seems to have been disregarded. A large Augustinian abbey at Mas Saintes Puelles was burned the following day, after which the army marched on to Castelnaudary. Its fortifications were rudimentary; Hoskins, following local historians, suggests they were a mixture of stones, wooden beams and piled earth.[26] Just as at Montgiscard, the townspeople chose to fight, and once again they failed; the English archers swept the ramparts with storms of arrows, driving the defenders back, and the men-at-arms stormed the walls. The army rampaged through the town, pillaging at will, capturing and holding to ransom those who had wealth, beating up those who did not.

After a day of rest at Castelnaudary the army moved on, burning the town and castle along with several churches and convents. By Tuesday, 3 November, they were standing outside the walls of the city of Carcassonne, a little under 60 miles southeast of Toulouse.

Carcassonne was an even more formidable proposition than Toulouse had been. The city was divided into two parts; the old town, known as the Cité, southeast of the river Aude, and a newer district, the Bourg, across the river on the northwest side, the two linked by a single bridge, the Pont Vieux. The Cité, situated on a hill more than a hundred feet high, was protected by massive fortifications, nearly 40 towers and bastions and gatehouses along a circumvallation of stone ramparts. (The walls still stand, though they were heavily restored by the French engineer Eugène Viollet-le-Duc in the 19th century.) The Bourg, on the other hand, had no fortifications. It had been founded by King Louis IX in the aftermath of the Albigensian Crusade at a time when the Languedoc was at peace; no fortifications were deemed necessary.[27]

Warned by the refugees fleeing down the Via Aquitania from the northwest, the people of Carcassonne were well prepared. Most of their movable wealth had been taken into the Cité for safety, and most of the population of the Bourg evacuated there too. A few brave volunteers remained behind, stretching chains across the street to impede the passage of horsemen and preparing to fight on foot with sword and shield. Their efforts were in vain. The English and Gascons jumped their horses over the chains, and archers coming up behind shot down the militia swordsmen before they could put up much resistance. The survivors fled across the Pont Vieux into the safety of the Cité.

Prince Edward billeted his troops in the Cité, where there was an abundance of food and wine waiting to be plundered and consumed. On Wednesday he rested his men, and knighted several who had distinguished themselves, including the sons of Bernard-Ezi d'Albret, and one of the prince's own household, Roland Daneys, who went on to become Constable of Cardigan Castle and a wealthy landowner in Rutland and Leicestershire. Ralph Basset of Drayton, already a knight, was appointed to the rank of banneret, making him one of the senior captains in the army.

Shortly after these ceremonies were concluded, a delegation came out of the Cité under a flag of truce. The townspeople begged the prince to spare the Bourg from further destruction, and they were supported by the religious communities of the city, the cathedral canons and the Dominican, Franciscan, Augustinian and Carmelite convents, who wrote a joint letter begging the prince to listen to the pleas of the people. As a sweetener, according to Geoffrey le Baker, the town was willing to pay a ransom of 250,000 gold crowns if the prince would march away.[28]

We suspect the real figure might not have been quite so high, and that Baker was indulging in the medieval proclivity for exaggeration. At all events, it was not enough to impress the Prince of Wales. He may have been tempted; he kept his army for another day in the Bourg of Carcassonne, resting while the commanders deliberated, but that evening the orders were given. The following morning, Friday, 6 November, the army set fire to the Bourg, burning every building – civil and ecclesiastical alike – and then marching away southeast towards their next destination, Narbonne.

From Carcassonne to Narbonne is about 40 miles. The army covered the distance in three days, marching past the lake of Marseillette – now vanished, drained by the construction of the Canal du Midi – and burning every town they passed, with the exception of Sérame, which was the property of Lady Yseult of Brittany, a personal friend of the Prince of Wales. Out of respect for her, the town was spared. Leaving the valley of the Aude, they crossed some rough and broken country, the army splitting into two separate columns and then both converging on Narbonne, which they reached at the end of 8 November.

Unlike Toulouse and Carcassonne, Narbonne was no longer flourishing. It had formerly been a major seaport on the Mediterranean, but in the early 14th century its harbour had silted up and the coastline had receded, leaving the city stranded several miles inland. The imposing cathedral, begun in the 13th century, was still unfinished, and even before the Black Death its population had been in decline. Even so, the population in the 1350s may have been as much as 30,000, as large as that of Toulouse. Like Carcassonne, Narbonne too was divided into two districts, a heavily fortified Cité, the old quarter, and the newer mercantile district, the Bourg, across the river.[29]

The defence of the city was in the capable hands of the local vicomte, Aimeri of Narbonne. He had a garrison of 500 men-at-arms at his disposal, as well as a sizeable local militia, and the walls of the Cité were plentifully equipped with stone-throwing catapults. He had plenty of advance warning of the enemy's advance, and had already moved all women and children into the Cité. Unlike at Carcassonne, no attempt was made to defend the Bourg, and the prince's army marched in without opposition. Several citizens of Narbonne who failed to get away in time were captured and held to ransom.

Scarcely had the English and Gascons settled in and begun to loot the houses, however, than Vicomte Aimeri's artillery opened fire. All through the night and the next day his catapults launched showers of stones in the direction of any of the enemy who showed their face in the Bourg. A number of English were wounded, and some killed. The prince ordered his archers forward to try to suppress the fire of the catapults, and the French defenders took casualties too, but the catapults continued to throw stones and the English casualty list grew longer. By the end of the 9th, it was clear that not only was there no chance of storming the Cité, but even the Bourg could not be held for much longer.

On the morning of the 10th, the army spread out through the Bourg and set fire to every building, then marched through the burning streets and out of the city. Some of Aimeri's men-at-arms sallied out and attacked the rearguard as they withdrew, even capturing a couple of the prince's baggage wagons – small recompense for the damage done to Narbonne, but a victory nonetheless. At least one French commander was capable of acting with skill and daring in the field.

From Narbonne, Prince Edward's army marched due north into the valley of the Aude, halting at the town of Cuxac. His intentions at this point are not entirely clear; he may have been contemplating advancing to threaten the town of Béziers. Cuxac was too strongly fortified to be attacked. The army camped in the fields outside the town, and the prisoners taken in Narbonne were summoned. Those who could afford to pay a ransom were released. Those who could not were executed on the spot. It is hard to see what purpose this barbaric act served. The laws of war allowed for the execution of prisoners if supplies are short and they cannot be fed, or if upon their release they would immediately take up arms again, but neither case was true here. The release of the poor prisoners would have been an act of mercy, and quite why Prince Edward did not choose this course is unclear. The executions were one of the darker shadows in this bleak campaign.

The march west

The end was now in sight. The army had encircled the town of Capestang and was once again negotiating with the townspeople, offering them a chance to pay a ransom to make the troops go away, when news came in. Bourbon and Armagnac had finally stirred from their base at Toulouse and were advancing towards them, and more French detachments were closing in from the north and east. The prince's council were unanimous. It was nearly the middle of November, and they were almost 250 miles from their base in Bordeaux. It was time to go home.

The going was hard. The army had perforce to follow a different track than it had taken on the march east; that route had already been stripped bare of food, and fresh sources of plunder were needed if the army was to sustain itself. The route now was through hilly country, and many of the rivers and streams were still dry. On at least two occasions there was no water for men or horses. As an experiment, the horses were given wine to drink; paradoxically, there was no shortage of wine, and a large quantity of muscat had been looted during the day's march. But the experiment had the predictable result; many of the horses became ill, and some died. And the enemy were now very close. Reaching the town of Homps on 12 November, the vanguard discovered that Jean d'Armagnac had spent the previous night there before withdrawing west. The prince was convinced that a battle was imminent, and that evening he held a ceremony to create more new knights, including one of his chamberlains, a Hainault man named Theodoric van Dale.[30]

But the battle did not come. As the prince advanced, passing north of Carcassonne, the French retired before them, clearly unwilling to give battle.

Once again, we can only speculate as to why. Bourbon may have felt that even with his own troops and those led by Clermont, the marshal, the army was not yet strong enough to face down the English and Gascons, and as a veteran soldier he would have had a healthy respect for the English longbowmen. Bourbon was not ready to fight – not yet.

And as it became clear that the French were retreating, the English resumed their work of destruction. By 14 November they were back in the vicinity of Carcassonne, one division actually lodging in the town of Pennautier, just a few miles from the city. The next day, crossing the old line of march, the army swung further south. One division veered off to the left to attack and burn the prosperous town of Limoux. The towns of Fanjeaux, Villar-St-Anselme and Lasserre-de-Prouille also went up in flames.

Twenty windmills were burned outside Fanjeaux, and as the columns of smoke rode into the sky, the prince and his suite called in at the Dominican friary of Ste-Marie-de-Prouille, only about a mile away. There followed one of those bizarre scenes that so often occur in medieval warfare. The friars – Baker says there were about a hundred of them, as well as 140 sisters of the Dominican order living in their own house nearby – made the prince welcome and entertained him. In a move that sounds like it had been planned long in advance, another Dominican friar in the prince's entourage, Richard of Leominster, presented the brothers and sisters of Ste-Marie-de-Prouille with a very substantial gift of cash, £32.[31] In exchange, Prince Edward and 'many others' of his following were admitted as *confraters* of the Dominican Order, a kind of lay membership that granted them some privileges without having to take holy orders – rather like the organisations of 'friends' that support art galleries and philharmonic orchestras today. All this gentle ceremony took place under a cloud of smoke, with the orange lights of fires raging on the horizon.

On Monday the Prince of Wales's own division drove a French garrison out of the town of Belpech, but spared both the town and its castle as they were the property of the Comte de Foix, whom the prince was anxious to placate. (The French, we can surmise, had seized the town without the permission of Gaston Fébus, for the purpose of delaying the English advance.) During the morning of Tuesday the 17th the army advanced into the valley of the river Hers, still on the boundary with the County of Foix, and that afternoon at the abbey of Boulbonne, Gaston Fébus himself awaited them. Again, this must have been planned in advance; the idea that Gaston just happened to be waiting astride the prince's line of march is too much of a coincidence. Prince and count spent several hours together in talks, and one can imagine the tenor of the conversation from the prince's side. See how my army has humiliated France; join us and you can share in the wealth and glory, but if you choose to join the French, we will treat your lands like we treated those of Armagnac and Comminges.

The two men seem to have parted on amicable terms. The prince rejoined his army, which moved on down the valley of the Hers and then turned west before reaching Toulouse. The Ariège was crossed once more, and the town Miremont seized without opposition and burned. On the 18th the army reached the upper Garonne again, to find the river swollen with water; the weather had changed and it was now raining heavily. The English had hoped to seize some ferry boats at Montaut, but the boats had been removed, probably on the orders of either Bourbon or Armagnac, thinking perhaps to trap the English behind an impassable river. But once again the prince's scouts found a ford and his army filed across to the west bank, where they seized and burned another town, Noé, and then pushed their way upriver. Along the way, a daring band from the prince's division crossed the swollen river *again* to burn another town, Marquefaue, rejoining the main army in time for a short, violent fight with the local garrison at Carbonne.

Confrontation

This rapid move across and then up the Garonne took the French by surprise. Bourbon, Clermont and Armagnac had sortied with their combined forces from Toulouse, and it seems clear they had hoped to trap the English against the supposedly impassable Garonne. The prince rested his tired army on the 19th while the French moved cautiously closer, camping within a few miles of the English rearguard. Preparing to march again on the 20th, the prince sent out a strong reconnaissance party of men-at-arms led by Bartholomew Burghersh, John Chandos, James Audley and Baldwin Botetourt, to determine exactly where the enemy was.

Around mid-morning, Burghersh's men collided with a smaller French party on a similar mission, led by Pere-Raimon, the Comte de Comminges. The French came off considerably the worse, sustaining casualties and losing Comminges and around 30 others as prisoners. Further on, Burghersh's men swooped down on part of the French baggage train, killing the teamsters and destroying wagons and provisions. Surprised and disoriented by the sudden attack, one French detachment fled west with the English in pursuit. Later in the afternoon, four French knights were discovered in the church at Mauvezin, where they claimed sanctuary. They were left unmolested, but their horses and arms outside the church were seized and taken away.

Another body of French also moved west, crossing the river Save, one of the many fast-flowing streams that runs down from the Pyrenees to join the Garonne. It was still raining heavily, the rivers in full spate, and the French had broken down the bridges over the Save. The English moved downriver, tired men and horses and heavy wagons ploughing through the muddy tracks, the French in clear view on the far side of the river, barring the route back to Bordeaux. The rest of the French army was gathering, and it was clear that a confrontation was coming. The battle Prince Edward had sought might be about to happen after all.

On Sunday, 22 November, the English found a passable ford on the Save and crossed the river, advancing towards the town of Gimont. They found the French army standing on a hill outside Gimont in full battle array with standards unfurled, barring the English path. Prince Edward halted his men, sending one party north to take the little town of Aurimont, probably with a view to holding it as a bastion and taking up a defensive position. The army passed a tense night in the rain, and in the dull morning light began to assemble and take up battle formation. They were in the midst of doing so when a reconnaissance party brought astonishing news. The French were gone. During the night they had withdrawn from Gimont, and were still falling back. The way forward to Bordeaux was wide open.

Once again the question comes: why? Quite simply, it seems that Bourbon, Clermont, Armagnac and their captains were not prepared to risk a battle. Perhaps the violence of Burghersh's little raid had shaken their confidence, or that of their men; perhaps they still did not have enough men. At all events, they had conceded the field. The Prince of Wales was free to bring his campaign to a triumphant conclusion.

'Accomplished much that was excellent'

Of the rest of the campaign there is little to tell – a succession of dreary, uncomfortable marches through cold rain and mud with little sniping skirmishes between outlying detachments. The French had not yet given up entirely, and continued to harass the prince's withdrawal, though to no real effect or purpose. The hardships were caused mostly by the weather, and there were again problems with lack of water; Baker reports that on 24 November the shortage was so acute that the horses were once again given wine to drink, 'but were still too drunk next day to be able to walk straight, and many of them died'.[32]

The church at Mauvezin

By 28 November the army was at Mézin on the edge of the Landes, back in friendly territory. The men of Béarn were given leave to depart for their homes, and other contingents of Gascons peeled off as the army moved on north. The remainder reached La Réole on 2 December and began moving into winter quarters, while the prince and his entourage continued on to Bordeaux.

What had been achieved during the past two months? There had first of all been a decisive humiliation of French arms. Apart from a few isolated garrisons, especially the aggressive defence of Narbonne, the Anglo-Gascon army had encountered no resistance. Twice the French had advanced to fight, and twice they had refused the challenge. That failure was noted on both sides. The Gascon nobles, the Captal de Buch and the Albret family and others, who had seen the campaign brought to a successful conclusion, had been greatly heartened. Losses had been minimal; Sir John de Lisle was the only notable English captain to be killed, and losses among the other ranks may have amounted to a few hundred; losses due to illness and accident, including drowning while fording swollen rivers, almost certainly outnumbered battle casualties.

An immense amount of destruction had been caused along the 500-mile trail from the Atlantic to the Mediterranean and back again. The French historian Georges Minois reckons that more than 500 villages had been burned.[33] Thousands had been reduced to poverty, and with food stocks burned or plundered, many would have been near starvation.

By the end of the year, some reconstruction work was already underway; royal funds had been sent to Carcassonne, Castelnaudary and other places to begin the rebuilding.[34] But while the bigger towns received help, many of the smaller places and villages did not, and the scars of the raid remained for many years. 'We had a little trouble with the Black Prince' was how the mayor of commune of Mauvezin near Toulouse put it rather dryly as we followed the line of march; in fact, the entire place had been burned, with only the church surviving. Some of the towns described by Baker as rich and prosperous in 1355 are nothing but tiny hamlets today, and their decline into obscurity may have begun with this devastating raid. Well might Minois dub Prince Edward the 'cavalier d'Apocalypse'.

Reconstruction work and aid to refugees did indeed divert money that might have been spent on arms the following year. And yet, apart from the psychological humiliation, the French army had suffered few losses. France could still wage war, and there was no reason to suggest that, come the following year, an even stronger French army would take to the field. The English would be glad that they had bolstered the loyalty of their Gascon allies, for they would need them. The thing Prince Edward desired most, a decisive victory in battle, was yet to come.

CHAPTER 5

'I Shall Kill Them with this Sword!'

After two months of arduous marching, it was time to rest. By early December, most of the Gascons had returned to their homes; only a few hundred remained under the command of the Captal de Buch, Augier de Montaut of Mussidan and young Élie de Pommiers. In Bordeaux, John Wingfield, the governor of the prince's household, and the clerks of the civil administration found there was much to do. Payments were made for service to men-at-arms and archers alike, compensation was paid for lost horses, plunder was sold and the proceeds distributed, ransoms paid and prisoners released once the money had arrived.

If you choose to believe the prince's chatty but unreliable biographer, Chandos Herald – his real name is unknown, but he appears to have been a herald in the service of Sir John Chandos – the prince and his household passed the rest of the winter in leisure and pleasure: 'the prince turned back towards Bordeaux and abode there until the whole winter was passed. He and his noble knights were there in great joy and solace. There was gaiety, noblesse, courtesy, goodness and largesse; and he quartered his men, as I think, in his castles round about, and there they took up their abode.'[1]

The reality was somewhat different. The prince passed Christmas 1355 in Bordeaux, lodged in the palace of the archbishop, but not in his usual high style. The household accounts record a few payments for gifts and luxuries; there is a record of a purchase of a quantity of sugar, a very expensive luxury, and also the purchase of a pair of hand-drums for a minstrel named Hankin. Prince Edward knew that he needed to give his men – and horses – a few weeks off, to rest from the rigours of campaign. But he also knew one of the first rules of war: when you have your foot on your enemy's throat, keep pressing down.

Once again, the French had expected Edward to behave in the conventional fashion: pay off most of his troops, put the rest into winter quarters in various scattered garrisons, and sit the winter out. That was exactly what they themselves had done. Bourbon the Constable and Clermont the marshal had both returned to Paris, with most of their troops paid off. Armagnac was involved in some personal business of his own with the king of Aragon; very possibly, an intrigue against Gaston Fébus of Foix, whose lands abutted Aragon – the counts of Foix and the Aragonese bishops of Urgell were joint sovereigns of the little principality of Andorra – and who was also on friendly terms with Aragon's fractious neighbour, Charles of Navarre. The few French garrisons remaining were commanded by relatively junior captains such as Jean le Maingre, nearly always known by the name 'Boucicaut', and his colleague Philippe de Chambly, known for equally obscure reasons as 'Gris Mouton', the Grey Sheep.[2] Gris Mouton seems to have been a family nickname, as his elder brother Pierre was also called the same thing, and so were several generations of Chamblys before them.[3] Boucicaut and Gris Mouton were the John Chandos and James Audley of the French army: energetic, vigorous, skilful and usually to be found where the fighting was hardest, but they had just 600 men under their command, and the garrisons in French frontier towns and castles amounted to only a few hundred more.[4]

Prince Edward's own force was not large. The historian Jonathan Sumption estimates that he had available about 2,200 English and Welsh troops, along with the Gascons mentioned above, perhaps 3,000 in all. But he had the advantage of speed and, above all, tactical surprise. When he launched his attacks in early January, the French were caught off guard. Once again, Edward had done the opposite of what everyone expected him to do.

Even before Christmas, on 20 September, Edward had given his orders. His striking forces were in position. The marshal, the Earl of Warwick, held an advanced base at La Réole on the Garonne, and he was supported by a second detachment including Reginald Cobham, John Chandos, James Audley and Baldwin Botetourt. A third force, the largest of the three, around 1,000 men led by the earls of Oxford, Suffolk and Salisbury, had its headquarters at St-Emilion on its hill overlooking the Dordogne about 30 miles from Bordeaux, with a forward detachment under the Earl of Salisbury at Ste-Foy, another 15 miles upriver. Further north, seemingly unremarked by the French, the Captal de Buch, the lord of Mussidan and Élie de Pommiers had gathered their forces around the town of Cognac, reinforced by 240 English men-at-arms and Welsh archers under Bartholomew Burghersh.[5]

In early January 1356, as provisions were gathered and shipped up the great rivers, Prince Edward moved his field headquarters to Libourne, also on the Dordogne a few miles west of St-Emilion. From this position he could watch the progress of all his forces and move to their assistance if required. A few days later the final orders went out, and the English advanced.

Warwick struck first, moving up the valley of the Garonne and bypassing the town of Marmande, a bastide originally founded by Richard Coeur-de-Lion but which had been in French hands for several years. Further upriver he took another French town, Tonneins, cutting Marmande's line of communications and supply. Turning east, his little force moved up the valley of the Lot, mopping up more French posts and further isolating Marmande.

Hard behind him came the second detachment under Cobham and Chandos, who moved up the Garonne to take Port-Sainte-Marie, midway between Marmande and Agen. Despite having a garrison of 300 men, the captain of this river port surrendered without a fight.[6] Cobham put a garrison into the port, further strengthening the English grip on the Garonne. Pressing on, the English reached Agen, 40 miles from Marmande and about 85 miles from Bordeaux. The town was too strongly fortified for Cobham to take by assault, and the French garrison inside the walls was too weak to come out and fight.[7] Stalemate ensued; the English burned several mills and captured an outlying castle, then moved on east, where they overwhelmed the small French garrisons at the town of Castelsagrat and the castle of Brassac. Cobham then learned that Boucicaut and Gris Mouton were a few miles away at Moissac with their gallant 600, but both sides played it cautiously; Cobham established another garrison at Castelsagrat and then withdrew.

In the valley of the Dordogne, the force under Oxford, Suffolk and Salisbury opened its account by seizing the castle of Montravel, midway between Castillon and Ste-Foy. This forward French base had long been a thorn in the English side, interrupting communications along the river. The army then pushed on upriver, advancing more than a hundred miles from Bordeaux and meeting little opposition. In the high country of the upper Dordogne valley they established two more garrisons, at Souillac, not far from the hill town of Rocamadour, and the fortified abbey of Beaulieu-sur-Dordogne. These garrisons embarked on a series of raids into the highlands of Quercy.

The most audacious raid was carried out by the Captal de Buch. Leaving Cognac, his little Anglo-Gascon force mopped up the French garrisons of several nearby castles and then made a sudden dart towards Poitiers. There was much alarm in Poitiers, but this was a feint. Turning south, the Captal launched a surprise attack on the city of Périgeux.

Périgeux had originally been two settlements, the old Roman town of Civitas Petrocorium, known in medieval times as the Cité, and the later Frankish town of Puy-St-Front, organised around the abbey and later cathedral of St-Front.

The two were formally united in 1251, but each retained its own walls and fortifications. Approaching by night, the Captal's men stormed the walls of the Cité before the garrison could react, seizing the western half of Périgeux.

Another stalemate then ensued. The walls of Puy-St-Front were stronger than those of the Cité, and its garrison was now on full alert; there would be no chance of a surprise attack. The prince, learning of the situation, ordered the Cité handed over to the lord of Mussidan, who garrisoned it with his own Gascon troops. The city was now divided between the two warring camps, which must have been a hellish situation for the citizens trying to go about their daily lives.

Roger-Bernard, the Comte de Périgord, could not muster enough men of his own to dislodge Mussidan's garrison – at least, not without destroying half the city in the process. He decided instead to negotiate, and asked his younger brother Hélie, Cardinal Talleyrand, to act as intermediary. The cardinal met with the Prince of Wales – whether the meeting took place at the latter's headquarters in Libourne or in Périgeux is not clear – and offered an undisclosed sum of money to buy off Mussidan and restore the city to the count's control. The prince refused indignantly. His purpose, he said, was to restore English authority in Gascony and to compel, by force if necessary, all King Edward's subjects to recognise him as their rightful overlord, and he would not rest until that had been done.[8]

By March the fighting had died down. The garrisons established upcountry continued to harass the French; in April, Warwick led another raid into Quercy, and more French posts along the Garonne were retaken, notably Mas d'Agenais in the early spring. These expeditions, carried out by small, highly mobile forces, had arguably been more successful than the *chevauchée* of the previous autumn. The frontier had been pushed back and a number of towns regained. The French citadel of Marmande, once on the frontier, was now stranded behind enemy lines. And the Gascon nobility had been impressed too. A number of fence-sitters – Bertrand de Durfort and his brother Gaillard, the lord of Grignols and Duras, and the lords of Caumont and Limeul – quietly made their way to Bordeaux and pledged allegiance to the English cause.

The home front

During the autumn messages had been sent back to London by sea, informing the government of the prince's progress, but probably the first detailed account of the autumn *chevauchée* only reached London in January. Sir Richard Stafford, one of Prince Edward's trusted councillors, carried a letter from the prince to the Bishop of Winchester, acting as regent while the king was away on campaign. This letter was fairly matter-of-fact; other correspondents such as Sir John Wingfield gave more detailed accounts.[9] These letters were also intended for public consumption; copies of the prince's letter, at least, would have been made and sent around the kingdom, and the letter would have been read aloud in public places in London and other cities. Thus the establishment and the general public both would have kept apprised of events.

Stafford was also instructed to ask for fresh orders from the king. To launch another expedition in the spring, the prince would need more men and more money, but he also needed to know how best to coordinate his actions with other English forces that might be operating further north.

But when Stafford arrived, the king was still in the north, dealing with the Scots. It will be recalled that the town of Berwick-upon-Tweed had been captured by the Scots in a surprise attack, but the castle was still holding out. At the end of Chapter 3, we left King Edward hurrying back to England to deal with the situation. Arriving at Newcastle-upon-Tyne just before Christmas, he quickly began to muster ships and men-at-arms and archers from all across the north of England. On 6 January the army began to move north. A detachment led by another famous fighting man, the Hainault knight Sir Walter Manny, rushed ahead and relieved the siege of the castle, and then began undermining the walls of the town, preparing for an assault to recapture.

For their part, the Scottish force in Berwick took one look at the size of the army and fleet Edward was bringing against them, and did the sensible thing: they offered to surrender the town in exchange for being allowed to withdraw unmolested. The king accepted the offer and the Scottish army marched out of Berwick, no doubt thinking that the matter was over. Far from it; Edward was determined to punish Scotland and force the country to bend to his will. In late January he struck north from Roxburgh, burning and scorching his way across the lands of of the Earl of Dunbar and March, one of the leaders of the assault on Berwick.

The other major landowner in the lowlands, William, Lord Douglas, had arranged a temporary truce with the English, allowing him time to evacuate his tenants and carry away all livestock and provisions. Other landowners did the same. As the English advanced towards Edinburgh, they found the winter landscape empty and desolate. They reached Edinburgh to find that the city also had been evacuated. Short of food and fodder, Edward burned part of Edinburgh and then retreated back towards the border. On the way, he was ambushed in the forest near Melrose by Lord Douglas and his men, and his own bodyguard was very roughly handled, losing a number of men and only just managing to get the king to safety.[10] The English army also suffered losses to hunger and cold.

By the end of February the king was in Carlisle, back on English soil, and the army was paid off while he himself returned to London. For his part, Douglas launched a vigorous attack on the garrisons the English had planted in Scotland, retaking several castles and then punishing several Scottish notables who had supported King Edward (who claimed the throne of Scotland as well as that of France), attacking their livestock and houses. A truce was finally arranged on the borders, to the fury of Douglas, who was clearly using the chaos as a chance to enlarge his own lands and power at the expense of his Scottish neighbours.

Douglas was a restless and violent man, who a few years earlier had murdered his godfather, the vicious Sir William Douglas of Liddesdale, and effectively bullied the Scottish regents into allowing him to steal Liddesdale's lands. Ambitious and energetic, he was not interested in peace. Gathering a group of about 300 like-minded followers, including his cousin Archibald 'the Grim' Douglas and William Ramsay of Colluthie, Douglas departed for France, and in March this company presented itself at the French court and offered its services to the crown. Jean of France, desperate as always for men, accepted gratefully.

With Berwick recovered and a tenuous peace re-established on the Scottish border, King Edward was free to turn his attention towards France once again. His strategic position was still quite strong. He could, if he wished, re-open the war on three fronts. Calais gave him a base for further incursions into Picardy and the rest of northern France. The pot of rebellion in Normandy was still bubbling; Charles of Navarre's reconciliation with King Jean had not lasted, and the Harcourts and others were supporting him. And in Gascony, the winter campaigns had given the Prince of Wales some very useful forward bases from which to launch further incursions into France. However, as usual, money was tight and troops were in short supply. The question was how to make best use of the clear strategic opportunities, in a way that also made best use of resources. The king listened to accounts of events in France, and pondered.

'Rendered obedient to the king'

Over in France, for a little while that winter, things had gone reasonably well for King Jean. As we saw in Chapter 3, by the end of the summer of 1355 Jean was effectively bankrupt and had to suspend payment on his debts until the following Easter. Unable to squeeze out more money by debasing the coinage still further, he took the desperate step of calling on the Estates-General, the representatives of the three estates: the nobility, the clergy and the commons. The estates, dominated by the powerful Provost of the Merchants of Paris, Étienne Marcel, were surprisingly ready to help. Their representatives voted to pay for an army of 30,000 men, the funds to come from new taxes including the infamous *gabelle*, or salt tax.[11] In exchange, the Estates-General wanted to control the administration of the tax themselves, raising the money and handing it over to the treasury, rather than trusting corrupt royal officials. The Estates-General also demanded a say in war policy, stipulating in particular that Jean must not agree a truce with the enemy without the consent of the representatives.

Jean had little choice but to agree. The new tax was not popular; in March 1356 there was a bloody revolt in the northern town of Arras, with several representatives of the Estates-General killed by rioters, quite possibly while trying to collect the new taxes. On the Wednesday after Easter a small force of royal troops under the marshal, Arnoul d'Audrehem, arrived in Arras and arrested a hundred of the ringleaders of the revolt. Twenty of them were publicly beheaded, the rest thrown into prison at the king's pleasure. 'By this means,' wrote the chronicler Froissart, 'the town was rendered obedient to the king.'[12]

Other threats to Jean's authority were more serious. Charles of Navarre had not long made his peace with Jean before he began to plot against him once more. He, the Comte d'Harcourt and several other Norman nobles and disaffected members of the court – including, apparently, Jean's chamberlain, Robert de Lorris – planned to seize the Dauphin, the king's eldest son and heir. Once he was safely a prisoner, revolts would be raised in Normandy and Paris, with the aim of forcing Jean from his throne and perhaps even killing him. The Dauphin himself, who had become friendly with Charles of Navarre, may have been a party to the plot, or at least known of its existence.[13]

Somehow, Jean got wind of what was about to happen. He acted with uncharacteristic restraint – at first. The Dauphin was quietly arrested and brought before the king. Father and son talked for some time and reached a settlement. Jean would give Normandy to the Dauphin as his personal fief, along with the title of Duc de Normandie, and would pay off some of his debts. The Dauphin would abandon the cause of Charles of Navarre and pledge allegiance to his father. As for Charles himself, the king made light of the affair and appeared not to take it seriously.[14]

Rumours of the plot soon broke the surface, and gossip in both Paris and Normandy spoke of new plots on both sides. Charles of Navarre's agents spread the word that the reconciliation of the king and his son was spurious, and Jean intended to arrest his son and perhaps even kill him, as he had killed the Comte de Brienne. For his part, Navarre devised a new plot to kidnap and murder the king. This plot too was discovered in March just before the attempt was due to be made, but Navarre was not deterred. Jean's patience, always a somewhat frangible thing, finally snapped.

The day 5 April 1346 found the Dauphin in Rouen, where he had called a council of the leading notables of Normandy, including Navarre and the Comte de Harcourt, to plan the defence of the duchy in advance of a renewal of hostilities with England. The mayor and provost of Rouen were also present. After discussions, the group dined together in the great hall of Rouen castle. They were in the midst of dinner when the doors burst open and King Jean strode in, wearing full armour and accompanied by Marshal d'Audrehem and a hundred men-at-arms from the royal household.[15]

As the company sat stunned, Audrehem drew his sword and shouted theatrically, 'If anyone moves, I shall kill them with this sword!'[16] Jean then dragged Charles of Navarre out of his chair and arrested him. One of Charles's esquires drew his dagger to defend his master, and he too was disarmed and arrested. The rest of the company, the Dauphin excepted, were then taken away under guard. The Dauphin protested furiously; the king ignored him.

There was not even a pretence of a trial. That afternoon the Comte d'Harcourt and two other Norman nobles, along with the esquire who had drawn his dagger, were taken to the execution ground outside Rouen's walls and beheaded. Charles of Navarre – who we should remember was King Jean's son-in-law – was spared execution, but he was dragged away to prison in Paris. Two of his retainers were taken away with him and one, a Norman named Friquet de Fricamps, was tortured to make him reveal details of whatever plots Charles might be planning. Friquet eventually escaped and made his way to England, but Charles would spend the next 18 months in a prison cell.

If Jean thought this was an end to the problem, he was wrong. Charles's younger brother Philippe, Comte de Longueville, usually known as Philippe of Navarre, rallied the Navarrese and rebel Normans, the latter led now by the dead count's uncle Godefroi d'Harcourt. Évreux, Charles's seat in eastern Normandy only 60 miles from Paris, was garrisoned and made ready to withstand a siege, as was Pont-Audemer, further to the west. Philippe withdrew his remaining forces into the Cotentin peninsula, where the most disaffected rebels were based, and called for help. The captain Martin Henriquez was sent back to Navarre to raise men there, while two other envoys, the Norman knight Guillaume de Carbonnel and a Picard rebel named Jean de Morbeke, a relative of the Denys de Morbeke who was currently in the Prince of Wales's army, went to England. King Edward, still mulling over his strategy for the coming summer, was doubtless delighted to see them. Philippe offered to do homage for his and his brother's lands and to recognise Edward as King of France, in exchange for military assistance.

Chaos in France

Such assistance the king was only too happy to provide. Another expedition, led by the Duke of Lancaster, was preparing to go to Brittany, but hearing of an opportunity to cause trouble in Normandy, in early May 1356 Edward changed his mind. Lancaster would go to Normandy to support the rebels. Orders went out for the mustering of troops and ships and the gathering of supplies. Judging by the effort and money expended to equip it, this expedition had top strategic priority. All the supplies gathered by royal purveyors, all the men raised by the captains of companies, were earmarked for Normandy.[17]

And what of Gascony? From his actions, it would seem that all of King Edward's attention was focused on Normandy and the strategic possibilities there. It is not clear whether he issued any specific orders for Gascony at all. Sir Richard Stafford, trying to raise reinforcements for the Prince of Wales, was told to make do with 300 – later increased to 600 – archers from Cheshire.[18] The same was true of supplies. One of the prince's agents in Cheshire, Robert Pipot, tasked with purchasing 2,000 sheaves of arrows, 1,000 bows and 400 gross of bowstrings, reported that none could be found 'because the king has taken all to his use'.[19] Pipot was forced to offer financial inducements to the fletchers of Cheshire to work extra hours in order to produce all the arrows he needed, and ships once again had to be impressed from the prince's own ports in Devon and Cornwall. Only in the prince's own domains was he able to recruit or gather supplies and money at all. Eventually Stafford was able to squeeze out a few more men, but only after a series of irritating delays. He had planned to sail for Gascony in April, but it was June before he was finally able to set out.

If Edward was fixated on Normandy, so too was Jean. The *arrière-ban*, the summons to military service, was issued on 14 May, and men-at-arms and crossbowmen began gathering at Chartres. The response to the summons was so poor that it had to be repeated several times.[20] Meanwhile the Estates-General, who had so blithely taken upon themselves the task of gathering revenue, had begun to learn that collecting a tax is rather more difficult than proclaiming one. Money came into the treasury in a thin trickle. By early summer the mints were running out of silver, and there was no coin with which to pay the troops.

Jean, aware that Philippe of Navarre was treating with England and that English troops might arrive to reinforce the Norman rebels, did what he could. A small force, all that could be mustered, was sent under Marshal d'Audrehem to capture Évreux. An assault on the walls succeeded in capturing part of the town, but attacks on the castle failed bloodily. Another scratch force under experienced captain, Robert de Houdetot, was sent to attack Pont-Audemer, and enjoyed a similar lack of success.

In the midst of this financial and administrative chaos, the king had to be reminded that he had also promised to send an army to the south, to defend the frontier and make certain there was no repeat of the damaging *chevauchée* of 1355. Rather grudgingly, he gave orders for a second army to muster at Bourges, south of the Loire. Its commander was an uninspiring figure, one of the king's younger sons, the 15-year-old Jean, Comte de Poitiers, but at least he had two relatively level-headed commanders to advise him, Clermont the marshal and the veteran captain Boucicaut. But this army too was short of money and men, and the muster proceeded only slowly.

Meanwhile, all hell was breaking loose in the south. The English and Gascons were advancing, not in organised expeditions now but in short, fast strikes all along the frontier from Saintonge to Quercy. Little bands of men slipped into the interior, often by night, capturing castles or abbeys or fortified houses in which they set up bases. Some were English, some were Gascons, some were freelances who owed only nominal loyalty to the English cause. These garrisons lived by plunder, terrorising the locals and nibbling away at the French-held towns like so many predatory mice. As the climate of fear and violence rose, the rule of law began to break down. It became increasingly difficult to tell the difference between soldiers and bandits.

By mid-summer the more venturesome of these bands were raiding and robbing as far north as Poitiers. Jean ignored them. To him, nothing mattered now but the recovery of Normandy. On 28 May at Cherbourg, Philippe of Navarre had issued a defiant proclamation, in effect a declaration of war against France. It was a challenge Jean could not ignore.[21]

Lancaster's expedition

The vanguard of Lancaster's expedition sailed from Southampton on 1 June and reached the now traditional invasion landing place at St-Vaast on the Cotentin peninsula the next day. It took some time to ferry all the men across, and it was not until 18 June that all of Lancaster's men had been assembled around the town of Montebourg. His force was small, only 1,300 men, but it was augmented by another 800 from Brittany led by Robert Knollys and 300 Navarrese and Normans led by Philippe of Navarre.[22]

Lancaster's force rode out of Montebourg on 22 June. All the men were mounted, and they moved fast. Their first task was to rescue the beleaguered garrisons at Pont-Audemer and Évreux. They were successful in the first instance; Houdetot, hearing on 29 June that Lancaster was already across the river Dives and coming straight towards him, abandoned the siege of Pont-Audemer and withdrew east. The beleaguered garrison welcomed Lancaster with delight. He spent three days at Pont-Audemer, repairing the damage done by the besiegers to the walls, filling the storerooms and replacing the garrison with a contingent of English troops.

Lancaster's arrival and rapid movement across Normandy caused alarm in Paris. Fearing a repeat of the attack in 1346, when the English had burned the suburbs of Paris before turning north into Picardy, Jean mustered as many men as he could and moved north from Chartres to block the passage of the river Seine. He ordered the Comte de Poitiers to postpone his march south, and most of the troops gathering at Bourges, including Clermont and Boucicaut, were sent north to join the king. By the end of June, the king had around 8,000 men-at-arms under his command, plus an indeterminate number of Genoese crossbowmen. But he had mistaken Lancaster's intention. The duke was still aiming to relieve the siege of Évreux, and only after he had left Pont-Audemer and started his march towards that place did he learn that the garrison of Évreux, fearing the castle was about to fall, had done a deal with the besiegers to let them march away safely.

Lancaster and Philippe of Navarre were now stymied, facing a very much larger French force which was beginning to move towards them, if somewhat ponderously. They had a dart at the French-garrisoned castle at Conches-en-Oude, and drove off a French detachment laying siege to the Navarrese castle of Breteuil, before moving south to the town of Verneuil. This too was in French hands. The townspeople had fled into the shelter of the castle, taking their valuables with them. Learning of this, Lancaster ordered his men to assault the castle. After three days of bloody fighting, in which the English and Navarrese sustained heavy losses, the garrison finally surrendered. Verneuil was pillaged from top to bottom.[23]

The expedition to raise rebellion in Normandy was rapidly fizzling out into just another plundering *chevauchée*. But Lancaster could not remain in the field for much longer. By 8 July the French royal army, led by King Jean in person, was only a few miles away. Lancaster departed swiftly, the French giving chase, and there followed a rapid pursuit across central Normandy. At L'Aigle, with the French vanguard once again only 3 miles from the English army, King Jean sent heralds to challenge Lancaster to stand and fight. Smoothly, Lancaster declined; his business in Normandy was done, he said, and it was time to move on elsewhere. The following day he led his men through dense forests west of L'Aigle, and by 13 July he was back at his starting point, Montebourg in the Cotentin.[24]

Another stalemate ensued. The northern Cotentin, a bastion of the Harcourt family, was solidly for the Navarrese cause; to attack it and reduce all the rebel strongholds might take King Jean the rest of the summer. Similarly, Lancaster could not venture far from his base, or the French would use their superior numbers to cut him off. Both sides began to chip away at each other's positions. Jean captured a few more Navarrese castles and towns in central Normandy, including Thilliers, but then became bogged down in another siege of Breteuil. Sancho Lopez, the captain of Breteuil, had already seen off one besieging force, and was not about to be intimidated by another; he had strong walls and plenty of supplies.[25] With that obsessive streak which was so much a part of his nature, Jean sank his teeth into Breteuil and refused to budge, not even when word of encroaching danger from the south began to reach his ears. It was another month before Breteuil finally agreed to capitulate.[26] For his part, Lancaster pushed the boundaries of rebel-held territory a little further south, taking the town of St-Lô and installing a garrison there.

In and of itself, Lancaster's raid had not achieved very much. Pont-Audemer had been saved, a few towns taken, but Lancaster had swiftly been forced back to his base by overwhelming numbers. But there was one unintended consequence of the expedition. The army destined for the south had effectively been disbanded to support the advance into Normandy, and the young Comte de Poitiers had still advanced no further than Bourges. There was a yawning strategic gap in the south, and into the gap the Prince of Wales was now ready to step.

The gathering storm

In the absence of a French royal army, the defence of the south against the English rested once again on the unreliable shoulders of Jean d'Armagnac. Once again, he had too few men and too little money to stem the tide. Even the little force commanded by Boucicaut and Gris Mouton had been withdrawn north to join the army gathering at Bourges. Armagnac had only whatever men he could raise locally; and after the chaos of the previous autumn and the defections of the spring, that was not as many as it might have been.

Anglo-Gascon raids had reduced parts of Saintonge, Poitou and the Limousin to anarchy, and in June another damaging raid by the energetic Augier of Mussidan into Quercy had added to the chaos there. Armagnac, who for all his faults was an astute commander, recognised that the Prince of Wales would not rest idly during the summer. He braced himself for another campaign, but once again he made the error of assuming that the prince would do what everyone expected him to do, namely, launch another *chevauchée* into the Languedoc.

For many years, historians tended to not credit medieval war leaders with much strategic sense. Their campaigns were seen largely as plundering raids that happened by accident, without clear goals or desired strategic outcomes. For example, it was argued that Edward III's expedition in 1346 had originally intended to go to Gascony, but somehow got lost and landed in Normandy instead, and that Edward had no clear idea of strategy but simply wandered at random across France until he encountered Philippe's army at Crécy. That view has now been comprehensively rebutted,[27] but when we come to examine the strategic thinking behind the Prince of Wales's campaign in 1356 we find a similar prejudice among historians old and new. It is argued, by French and English historians both, that the campaigns of 1355 and 1356 were simple plundering raids, *chevauchées*, undertaken for no other purpose than the collection of booty and ransoms.[28]

But let us pause for a moment to consider what Prince Edward knew, and when. It seems quite clear that the prince was aware of events in Normandy, and knew of the outcome of Lancaster's expedition. The prince's own letters to the government in London confirm as much. According to the chronicler Geoffrey le Baker, the prince also knew that his father, King Edward, was planning to raise a third army and lead it to France, probably through Calais. The orders for assembling this army did not go out until 20 July; however, the plans for the royal expedition would have been laid long before, and it is likely that Richard Stafford knew of the king's intentions before he departed for Bordeaux in June.[29]

It has also been suggested that Prince Edward, hearing of Lancaster's plan, marched north with the idea of effecting a junction between their two forces; the combined army might then force the French to give battle.[30] It seems more likely, however, that by the time he set out from Bergerac in early August – or shortly thereafter – the prince already knew that Lancaster was retreating towards the Cotentin, and that Jean and the French royal army were pursuing him; the prince may even have known about the bogged-down siege of Breteuil. The possibility that he and Lancaster were in contact by land should not be discounted; the distance from Breteuil to the northernmost English outposts in Poitou was only about 200 miles, and mounted couriers could have covered the distance in a week or so.

It seems certain too that Prince Edward knew that the remnants of the French army destined for the south under the Comte de Poitou were still at Bourges. Looking at the map and the prince's movements, it seems quite clear to us that Bourges was his intended destination from the beginning of the campaign. His own statement in letters home at the end of the summer confirm as much.[31]

Think what we may of him as a person, there is no doubting that Prince Edward was a highly gifted military commander. He had a number of talents, one of which was the ability to spot a strategic weakness. With the main French army pulled away to the north, that little French army at Bourges was vulnerable. If he could defeat it, perhaps even take the Comte de Poitier prisoner, he would have the victory on the battlefield that he wanted. He would have also cleared out the entire French army south of the Loire, and have a free hand to reduce towns and cities and post garrisons where he wished. Control of the Limousin and Poitou would be his; and if he could also seize a crossing point on the Loire, he could join hands with the Anglo-Breton garrisons in Brittany.

How much Prince Edward knew about the terrain into which he was about to advance is debatable. The previous autumn he had relied on Gascon lords such as Amanieu de Fossat. Some of the men in his army had been with Derby (now Lancaster) during his attack on Poitiers 10 years earlier, and more recent English raiders had penetrated equally far north. But the country beyond Poitiers was likely to have been more mysterious. No English army had travelled through this country for a couple of centuries.

It is 250 miles from Bordeaux to Bourges. To advance so far from his base into unknown country against an enemy who was close to his own base and benefitted from interior lines of supply and communication was audacious in the extreme. But, as the events of the previous autumn had shown, the Prince of Wales was nothing if not audacious.

The arrival of Richard Stafford with reinforcements and supplies from England was the beginning of a period of intense preparation. On 6 July, the prince joined his army already beginning to muster at La Réole on the Garonne. At first sight it looks like the prince was moving in the wrong direction, but this was almost certainly a feint to deceive the Comte d'Armagnac and force him onto the defensive. Weapons, supplies and wagons were gathered, and the Gascon lords rode in with their men to swell the ranks of the little army. Prince Edward had probably about the same number of men available as in the previous year. The historian Georges Minois estimates that his force included 3,500–4,000 men-at-arms, 3,000 archers and around 2,000 Welsh, Irish and Gascon foot soldiers, for a total of around 9,000 men.[32] Stafford's recruits probably just about made up for the losses suffered during the autumn and winter campaigns but did not increase the total. As before, at least half the army – if not more – would have comprised locally recruited Gascons.

However, the prince and his advisors realised that Bordeaux could not be left entirely undefended. As well as the frontier garrisons, a local defence force of around 2,000 men was left behind under the command of John Chiverston the seneschal of Bordeaux, Thomas Roos the mayor of the city and Bernard d'Albret, younger son of the old patriarch Bernard-Ezi d'Albret.[33] This was an insurance policy, in the unlikely event that Armagnac should decide to move onto the offensive. That left around 7,000 fighting men available for the incursion into France.[34] Non-combatants – grooms, drivers, priests, clerks, blacksmiths, fletchers, servants and so on – probably swelled the total to about 10,000.

The captains were the same men we have seen in action already: the earls of Warwick, Suffolk, Oxford and Salisbury, Reginald Cobham, John Chandos, James Audley, Bartholomew Burghersh, Baldwin Botetourt and the other competent, trusted men whom the prince had gathered around him over the past decade. In another time and another milieu, Admiral Nelson sometimes referred to his captains as a 'band of brothers'. Looking at the men around the prince, one gets the same feeling of comradeship, of a sense of men embarked on a great venture together, who will fight for each other and die for each other. The second thing that made Prince Edward a great commander was his ability to bind men like those to him, and inspire their loyalty and devotion. For men like Chandos, Audley and Burghersh, service to the prince was something that went beyond feudal loyalty, beyond any question of reward and largesse, important though these things undoubtedly were. Their service was based on a personal bond, and for most of the men around the prince, that bond was broken only by death.

The Gascons too were the same captains as before: the Captal de Buch, the younger members of the Albret family led by Arnaud-Amanieu, the aggressive Augier de Montaut from Mussidan and quite probably his son Raimon as well, the brothers Pommiers, the lords of Montferrand and Rauzan, and newcomers to the cause like the Durforts. There was also a smattering of foreigners. We have referred already to Denys de Morbeke, the Picard exile. Others like Eustache d'Abrichecourt were from Hainault, Queen Philippa's birthplace, and had come to England in her suite – or in Abrichecourt's case, followed earlier relatives who had done so.

Once the troops had assembled, on 22 July the prince abruptly moved his main striking force from La Réole to Bergerac, 40 miles away on the Dordogne.[35] This was to be his real jumping-off point for the campaign. News of this movement reached the French court at almost exactly the same time as word of King Edward's proposed new expedition was transmitted by French spies in London. On 26 July King Jean called his councillors together in the siege lines around Breteuil and issued his orders. The Estates-General had failed to deliver the promised taxes, and the king was desperate for money. The coinage was to be devalued again, and more troops were to be raised as a matter of urgency: men-at-arms called up under the feudal levy, more crossbowmen to be hired from Doria and Grimaldi. But Jean was, as usual, running behind the times. Even while his new army was beginning to assemble, the Prince of Wales marched from Bergerac, heading north.

CHAPTER 6

'We are Determined to Defend Ourselves'

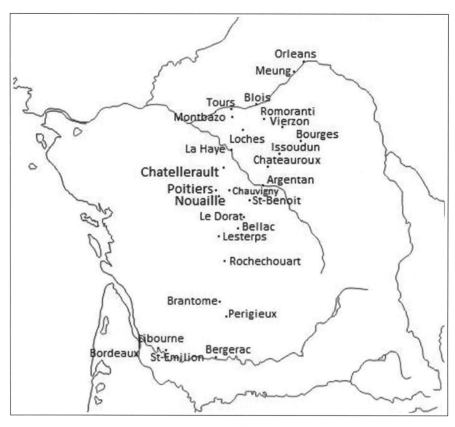

Campaign of 1356

Thursday, 4 August to Sunday, 7 August

The first stage of the march saw the army advance 30 miles north from Bergerac to Périgeux. During these first couple of days, at least, the troops marched through ostensibly friendly country and were not in battle array. Leaving the valley of the Dordogne with its vineyards, they climbed into a country of rolling hills and dense forests of scrub oak, with villages and castles few and far between. There was only one direct road from Bergerac to Périgeux, through St-Martin-les-Combes and Vergt, and it is likely that most of the army followed this, strung out in a single long column with the baggage wagons near the rear. Progress was slow; the descents into the river valleys are steep, the climbs back out of them equally so. As we saw in the campaign the previous autumn, these hills would have caused problems for the baggage train in particular. The vanguard of the army reached Périgeux on Saturday the 6th, but the last of the army did not straggle in until sometime on the 7th.

Périgeux, it will be recalled, was now a divided city. The old district of the Cité was in the hands of a garrison installed by the lord of Mussidan, while the newer district of Puy-St-Front was still controlled by townspeople loyal to the pro-French Comte de Périgord. The townspeople, seeing the prince's army coming out of the hills and winding down the road into the valley of the river Isle, were terrified, thinking their last hour at come. Nevertheless they stood to arms, preparing to defend their homes. The prince and his captains, eyeing the strength of the walls and remembering that Puy St-Front had already defied the Captal de Buch earlier in the year, decided to leave well enough alone. The inevitable pillagers set to work in the faubourgs outside the wall, looting and burning the abandoned buildings. Watching them from the safety of the cathedral of St-Front, Pierre Pin, the Bishop of Périgeux, issued a decree threatening the looters with excommunication.[1] It is highly doubtful that this had any effect whatever. The army camped in the fields outside Périgeux for the night.

Monday, 8 August to Thursday, 11 August

To the relief of the people of Périgeux, the Anglo-Gascon army departed the following morning, marching up out of the valley of the Isle and following the road through rolling scrub forests towards Brantôme. After a march of about 13 miles the main body halted at the castle of Ramefort, overlooking the

The old bridge at Brantôme

valley of the river Dronne. Reconnaissance parties rode on as far as Brantôme itself, 3 miles away.

Why the army did not advance all the way to Brantôme, which had a fine Benedictine abbey and a large and powerful castle guarding the bridge over the Dronne, is something of a mystery, as indeed are the army's movements for the next few days. The historian Peter Hoskins offers an entirely plausible explanation: on approaching Brantôme, the English scouts discovered that the castle, and possibly even the town itself, were in the hands of the French.[2] The countryside north of Périgeux was a no-man's land, with French and English outposts scattered across the landscape, so it is quite conceivable that Brantôme was still under French control. And even a small French force holding Brantôme castle could block the bridge and the road north.

On the following day, the 9th, the army advanced the short distance to Brantôme, and if Hoskins is right, tested the defences and concluded that there was no safe way across the river. The banks of the Dronne are steep, often with sheer cliffs protruding out of the heavily wooded slopes, the ground impassible for horses and wagons. The army waited outside Brantôme while an alternative route was sought, and then on the 10th the main force moved along the valley to Quinsac. This town was undefended, and the English and Gascons were able to cross the Dronne and, on the 11th, march north up and over the hills to Nontron. Several lakes outside Nontron provided a source of fresh fish, a welcome change from the staple diet of salt meat and pease porridge on which most of the troops lived.

Rochechouart chateau east tower

Friday, 12 August

This day saw a long march of more than 25 miles from Nontron northeast past Augignac, Piégut and Vayres. By the end of the day the ground was beginning to level out, the forests of pine and scrub oak giving way to more pastures and cultivated fields. Eighty miles from Bergerac, the army was now entering the Limousin, a high plateau rich with agriculture and, then as now, a place where fine cattle were bred. There were no more friendly garrisons in the castles and towns now. The debatable lands of Périgord lay behind them. Ahead lay enemy country.

At the end of the march was the town of Rochechouart, its high castle on a cliff thrust out into the river Graine. We can be sure that Rochechouart was garrisoned by pro-French forces, because its lord, the Vicomte Jean de Rochechouart, was already with the French army in the north. Rochechouart was a powerful landowner, and thanks to privileges granted to the town by his grandfather, he had a good relationship with the town; the townspeople were willing to stand fast against the English in accordance with his wishes. Rochechouart himself was a loyal servant of the house of Valois. Ten years earlier, he had charged uphill into the arrow storm with the rest of the French army at Crécy, and survived. Now, he was serving with the king's army in Normandy.[3]

Even had Prince Edward wished to storm the town, there is no question of his army being ready to do so after such a long march. The army settled down to make camp on the south bank of the Graine, across from the town, and passed a watchful night.

Saturday, 13 August

The Graine was a tributary of a much larger river, the Vienne, which would have to be crossed before the advance could continue. The English could bypass Rochechouart to the east, ford the Graine and continue north to the Vienne, and perhaps try to seize the bridge at St-Junien. But St-Junien too was strongly fortified and defended, and moving east would also bring the English within reach of the garrison of the powerful French city of Limoges, only about 20 miles from Rochechouart. It was no part of Prince Edward's design to get involved in assaults that would slow his march and cost casualties, not at this point in the campaign. His eye was fixed firmly on the end game.

Instead, on Saturday morning the army turned northwest, following the line of the Graine up to its junction with the Vienne at Chabanais and then carrying on to the Benedictine abbey of La Péruse, a march of about 12 miles. Here most of the army rested for the remainder of the day while foraging parties went out to gather food and fodder. Prince Edward could count himself well satisfied; the preliminary march into enemy country had gone without a hitch. Now the real campaign was about to begin.

Sunday, 14 August

In the morning the army struck camp and marched down to the banks of the Vienne, and forded the river. As he waited for the troops to cross the ford, the prince unfurled his standards, signalling that the campaign had now begun. Fresh orders were issued. From now on, every man was to go armed and armoured as if they were in the presence of the enemy. No one should wander away from the main body of the army without permission;

only organised scouting and foraging parties were permitted to do so. Every man was to receive the sacraments and the eucharist: 'In this way they would be ready for fight with rebels against the king's peace,' says Geoffrey le Baker, 'and whether they lived to win honour on earth or died to win honour in heaven, they would in both places be rewarded.'[4]

It is likely that the dividing of the army into the traditional three divisions took place here also, once the Vienne had been crossed. The officers of each division were probably the same as before – the veteran Warwick leading the vanguard, the prince himself in command of the middle division, and Suffolk and Salisbury, wise older head and impulsive young one, in command of the rearguard. Most if not all of the baggage train would have accompanied the prince's division.

From now on the three units of the army marched down separate, parallel roads, sometimes covering a front as broad as 15 miles. The prince also gave orders for scouts to be deployed to cover the line of march and guard against surprise attack, 'so that our men might not be taken off their guard as the enemy suddenly sprang at them from ambushes in the woods'.[5] Two of his most trusted captains, John Chandos and James Audley, were put in charge of reconnaissance. Baker also gives us an insight into the prince's leadership style:

> At the same time the prince himself saw to the planning of the marches and the daily moving of the camp. Just as though the enemy were at hand, he had the camp guarded at night. He set careful groups of watchmen, and would himself go round them accompanied by his nobles. On these rounds of inspection he would sometimes visit the vanguard, at other times the rearguard, and sometimes the middle-guard, for he did not want any part of his forces to be exposed to danger through lack of order.

The picture that emerges – which is likely to be authentic; Baker had access to men who had served on the campaign – is of a meticulous commander who takes proper precautions at all times, is attentive to detail, and cares about his men. The little visits to each division in turn were in part tours of inspection, to reassure the prince himself that all was well, but he was also making sure that he was visible to his men. They were left in no doubt that he was there and in command, and they also knew that he was interested in their welfare. His presence reassured his troops and gave them confidence. It sounds simple, and it is: show yourself to the men, and they will respect you. But far too often military leaders have neglected this principle, and have paid for it dearly.

We know the course taken by the army for the remainder of the campaign with some certainty thanks to an itinerary copied into a contemporary chronicle known as the *Anonimalle*; this too was probably based on an official document from the campaign.[6] After crossing the Vienne the army advanced 10 miles to the town of Lesterps. The first skirmish of the campaign was fought here, as a small garrison attempted to defend the walled Augustinian abbey adjacent to the town. After an initial resistance, the French soon surrendered. The town and abbey were protected as ecclesiastical property, but in the countryside, the pillaging and arson had begun. The smoke of burning farmsteads would have been clearly visible in nearby towns such as Confolens, and probably even in Limoges. Couriers raced away down the roads towards Paris, spreading the word. The English were coming.

Monday, 15 August

During the course of that Monday the army remained encamped around Lesterps. It might seem strange that the prince would not continue his advance; Bourges was still a long way away, and haste was surely in order. But 15 August is the day of the Assumption of the Blessed Virgin Mary, one of the holiest feast days in the later medieval calendar, and it was important that the occasion be marked. Once again, the prince was a shrewd enough leader to know that his men would fight better if they were assured of the salvation of their souls.

We don't know the details of the celebration at Lesterps, but we can be sure that there was one. Ten years earlier, with the English army on the outskirts of Paris poised to begin its race north towards the sea and its date with destiny at Crécy-en-Ponthieu, Prince Edward had been present at a spectacular feast hosted by his father the king, at the abbey of Poissy on the banks of the Seine. Edward had appeared dressed in a red robe trimmed with ermine, and the lavish meal had featured geese, hens, doves, mutton, beef and fresh fish.[7] Now, the prince would have had his own ceremonial robes packed away in his baggage, in case visiting dignitaries needed to be entertained. And, thanks to the plundering of the last two days, there was plenty of food, for nobles and commoners alike.

The priests travelling with the army, including the Dominican friar Richard of Leominster, blessed the army and called upon God's aid, while the smoke of yesterday's burning hung in the air around them. Once the feast was over, the scouts went out and the rest of the army prepared to march. The advance would resume in the morning.

Tuesday, 16 August

On Tuesday the army struck northeast from Lesterps, skirting the higher hills known as the Monts de Blond that lay to the east. The highlands of the

Massif Central rose blue on the horizon. The countryside was populous, or had been; the attack on Lesterps would have alerted the locals, and already the refugees were streaming away to the shelter of fortified places such as Limoges or Poitiers. There was plenty to burn and plunder, including castles at Le Fraisse and Mortemart, both of which were taken without a fight. Mortemart belonged to another of the Rochechouart family, Aimery the lord of Mortemart, probably a cousin of Jean the viscount. He too was away serving with the royal army in the north, and probably did not learn of the destruction of his home for some time.[8]

Again, it might seem that the burning and destruction were unnecessary, and would slow the army down when it should be making all haste towards Bourges. In fact most of the pillage and burning was carried out by small mobile groups operating away from the main army, and it is unlikely that any of this activity impeded the pace of the march. As ever, it was the need to keep in touch with the supply train that slowed things down. The army could plunder much of the food it needed, but other vital stores – including the vital sheaves of arrows – had to be carried in wagons.

And, as well as rewarding his men with plunder, the prince was again proving a point. He could advance where he liked, burn and destroy what he wished, and the enemy could not stop him. His stock with his own men and his Gascon allies increased still further; so did the demoralisation of the enemy.

Keeping to the west of the Monts de Blond, the army marched across a gently undulating plain. Ahead, cutting across the line of march, were a number of rivers – the Vincou, the Gartempe, the Creuze, the Indre – which over time have cut deep, steep-sided valleys into the plain. In many places the valleys are lined with sheer cliffs; elsewhere, the slopes down to the river are usually forested and steep. Crossing points were few, and most were heavily guarded with very strong castles. On the evening of the 16th after a march of nearly 20 miles, the army came to the first of these crossing points; the town of Bellac, guarded by a castle on the clifftop high above the bridges over the Vincou.

As with Rochechouart, the position would have been difficult and costly to take by force, but luck was on Prince Edward's side. Bellac was owned by Marie de Châtillon, a member of the illustrious French noble house of St-Pol; but Marie was also the second – and much younger – wife of Aymer de Valence, the English Earl of Pembroke. The town had been part of her dowry, and reverted to her after the death of her husband in 1324. Although she had only been married for three years, the widowed Countess Marie chose to remain in

England and lived there for the rest of her life, becoming a popular figure at court. A few years earlier she had founded a house of scholars in Cambridge that later evolved into Pembroke College.[9] Her high rank and connections were such that both sides respected her. In England, she had been specifically exempted from the orders to arrest all French subjects, issued at the outbreak of the war; in France, the crown had issued an ordinance protecting her property from seizure, even though she was now a subject of the King of England.

This quirk of ownership saved Bellac. Out of respect for the countess, the prince gave orders that no harm was to be done to the town or its inhabitants; and presumably, backed these orders up with sufficient threat of force that the pillagers and arsonists in the ranks were moved to obey. Presumably, in return, Bellac's crossbowmen were willing to hold fire and let the prince's army cross the river. The army camped near Bellac that night, sending out scouts as far as the river Gartempe a couple of miles to the north.

Wednesday, 17 August

The march this day was a comparatively short one, only about 8 miles. In part this was because it took some time to get the army and its transport across the two rivers, the Vincou and the Gartempe, but French resistance also held up the advance for some time.

The resistance came at Le Dorat, a strategic crossroads town which could not be easily bypassed. Le Dorat also belonged to Pierre de Bourbon, the brother of the Constable of France, and as it happened the Constable's wife, Jeanne de Châtillon – probably either a cousin or a niece of Marie of Pembroke – was in residence in the town.[10] Both these things made the town an attractive target. But the vanguard, moving in to occupy the town, met with resistance from garrisons in both a small castle and a fortified church. There seems not to have been an all-out assault; instead, the English sat down around the two positions, the archers no doubt taking the occasional potshot at any target that showed itself on the walls, and waited for the defenders' nerve to crack.

That took the rest of the day. We don't know whether Jeanne herself played an active role in organising the resistance – women sometimes did command castles when their husbands were away at war – but whoever was in command, they had a strong will. Not until evening did the defenders finally agree to surrender. Their fate is not known, but it seems that Jeanne and her entourage, at least, were allowed to go free. The town, as usual, was pillaged and burned, and the army camped in the fields nearby.

Le Dorat

Thursday, 18 August

A hundred and forty miles from Bergerac the army halted for the day around Le Dorat. The two river crossings would have produced a certain amount of disorder, and parts of the army may still have been catching up. More importantly, there was the need to scout ahead. Prince Edward's caution may have been the result of the fact that he was now deep in enemy territory and lacked knowledge of the ground ahead, especially the key river crossing points. This day allowed him a chance to conduct reconnaissance and plan the next step of his advance.

While the army waited, detachments were sent out to scour the countryside. Several more small castles were captured and burned.

To the north, the French were beginning at last to stir. Word of the Prince of Wales's advance had reached Paris, and was passed on to King Jean at Breteuil. Realising the danger to the force still waiting at Bourges, on the 18th Jean sent orders to his son, the young Comte de Poitiers. He was to withdraw his army immediately behind the line of the river Loire, and wait for reinforcements. It is possible that, as a precaution, some bridges over the Loire were also broken down, though as we shall see, others remained standing. Jean himself remained at Breteuil. The importance of Breteuil as a strategic objective had never been high; now, with danger looming in the south, the town no longer held any importance at all. Yet, stubborn as a dog with a bone, Jean persevered with the siege.

Friday, 19 August

Once more the army advanced over open country, this time meeting no resistance. Lussac-les-Églises, now a small village but then a prosperous market town, was the next stop. The prince's men occupied the deserted town without resistance, and plundered it in the usual way before camping around the town that night. Among the provisions seized was a large quantity of fresh fish, which again provided a welcome relief from the usual campaign diet. Scouts were already probing forward towards the valley of the Creuse, looking for signs of the enemy. They found none. The way to the north was clear, and Bourges was less than a hundred miles away.

Saturday, 20 August

The town of Argenton had been selected as the crossing point over the next river, the Creuse. The army marched towards this, keeping the central highlands

The abbey church at St-Benoit-du-Sault

to their right and the Brenne, a difficult country of lakes and forests with few roads, to their left. The castle of Brosse, perched on a spur of high ground overlooking the line of march, was taken and burned. A few miles further on the main body of the army reached St-Benoit-du-Sault, a fortified town on high ground overlooking the river Portefeuille. Again there was no resistance; much if not all of the town was probably deserted, its inhabitants having fled to join the growing numbers of refugees streaming away from the line of the army's advance. The troops occupied and pillaged the town and its ancient Benedictine abbey, where they found a surprise; the strongboxes of the abbey, forced open, yielded a small fortune in gold coins with an estimated value of around £2,000.[11] Recall that the pay of the average foot soldier was three pence per day.

After a march of some 16 miles, the army camped around St-Benoit to count its loot and prepare for the onward march to Argenton. Meanwhile, 200 miles away outside Breteuil, King Jean's advisors had finally prevailed upon him to see sense. Jean's pride would not permit him to march away and abandon the siege. Instead, money was scraped together from somewhere to bribe Sancho Lopez, the garrison captain, to give the place up. Lopez and his men were allowed to march out freely and go where they wished, and Breteuil was restored to French control. Honour satisfied, Jean hurried back to Paris.

At Chartres, 50 miles southwest of Paris, the new army was gathering. Men were trickling in slowly. The chronicler Froissart speaks of men-at-arms from Auvergne, Berry, Burgundy, Lorraine, Hainault, Vermandois, Picardy, Brittany and Normandy assembling at Chartres under the direction of the two marshals, Clermont and Audrehem.[12] William Douglas and his band of Scottish adventurers had arrived as well. Douglas called on the king in Paris, and seems to have impressed him; later, Jean applied to Douglas for advice on how to fight the English. Several contingents of German men-at-arms were on the way, provided by allied princes such as the counts of Saarbrücken and Nassau-Weilberg; another ally, Count Amadeus of Savoy, also provided a party of men-at-arms, and there was a Swiss contingent under Graf Rudolf of Neuenburg-Nidau. The Genoese crossbowmen had begun arriving too. There were even a few Spaniards in the service of Enrique de Trastámara, illegitimate son of King Alfonso of Castille; he and his followers had fled to France after plotting against his half-brother King Pedro. The Comte de Poitiers, who had withdrawn east from Bourges to the town of Decize on the Loire, was summoned to move his troops downriver to Tours to effect a junction with the main army.

Slowly, the French royal army was beginning to come together, but money remained in desperately short supply and it was not clear how long Jean could hold this force together. He too needed something decisive, a victory that would satisfy his men and restore his battered prestige.

Unsure of Prince Edward's exact direction or strategic aims, Jean issued orders that all towns in the provinces along the Loire, Anjou, Maine and Touraine, as well as further south in Poitou, should be garrisoned and their fortifications put into good repair. All victuals and fodder should be taken into fortified places and held in store, so that the prince's army could not live off the land. This last measure, a kind of scorched earth policy, was in theory a good idea; in practice, given how far north the prince already was, the order came rather too late. Finally, the French commanders also dispatched two reconnaissance parties, each of about 200 men-at-arms. One was led by Philippe de Chambly, 'Gris Mouton', the other by Jean le Maingre, 'Boucicaut', with Amaury de Craon as his lieutenant. Their task was to cross the Loire and move south, searching for the enemy. Once they had found Prince Edward's army they were to report its movements, guiding the French army to intercept the prince.

Who was overseeing military dispositions at this point is not entirely clear. Clermont was supposedly tasked with organising the defence of Tours and other towns along the Loire; of Audrehem, we hear very little after the operations in Normandy concluded. There was also a new Constable of France. Jacques de Bourbon, weary of the political infighting and smarting from the criticism he had received for his handling of affairs in Languedoc the previous autumn, had resigned the post in May. His replacement was Gauthier de Brienne,

Duke of Athens, who had long coveted the post. But of Brienne too we hear almost nothing during the build-up to war. He does not seem to have been a particularly effective constable; fortunately, perhaps, he did not last long.

In the midst of all these preparations a peasant from Champagne arrived at court, begging to see the king. Given an audience, the man said he had been sent a sign from heaven. A divine voice had told him that the king should avoid a confrontation with the English this summer. 'Go and tell King Jean who his real enemies are,' the voice had commanded. King Jean treated the man kindly, rewarded him and sent him away, but took no heed of what he had said. Before the summer's end, he must have wished he had taken the peasant's advice.[13]

Sunday, 21 August

On Sunday the English army continued its rapid march north, covering the 14 miles over the rolling plain to Argenton. The town, unfortified, lay in a valley around the south end of the bridge over the Creuze, the whole protected by another large and strong castle on a promontory overlooking river and town. The castle's garrison was commanded by André de Chauvigny, son of the lord of Chauvigny.

The first troops on the scene surrounded the castle and summoned Chauvigny to surrender. Chauvigny refused; he had been charged by his father to keep the castle safe, and he would defend it to the death. A bloody fight broke out, during which the English used a makeshift battering ram, an ox-cart filled with earth, to try to smash down the gate. Braving the arrows of the English longbows, the defenders leaned over the parapets and threw down heavy stones and beams, driving the assailants back. Two knights are said to have been killed, though it is not clear if they were English or Gascons.[14] Arriving on the scene, the prince called off the assault. There was no need to take the castle, which could be isolated and bypassed, and he was unwilling to risk further loss of life. Once again, he needed to keep his army intact and ready for battle.

Monday, 22 August

The army remained camped around Argenton, watched by André de Chauvigny and his men still trapped inside their beleaguered castle. Once again Prince

Edward was looking for intelligence of the terrain ahead, and the enemy. Despite the speed of his movements over the last couple of days, he remained cautious. He was too experienced a soldier not to know that, by now, Paris would know his army was approaching. It was to be expected that the French would be mustering an army against him. All through that day, small highly armed parties rode out from the main body, sometimes venturing many miles to the north and east. They burned and laid waste to the farms and villages they came across, but mostly they looked for the enemy.

Once again they saw nothing. Gris Mouton and Boucicaut and their French reconnaissance parties were still approaching from the north, probably only just now crossing the Loire. Apart from isolated garrisons like the one at Argenton, the land was empty. Yet all the same, tension was rising. The fighting at Argenton had been a foretaste; a larger clash could come at any moment.

At Bourges, the people had not waited for instructions from the king to put the city into a state of defence. When the Comte de Poitiers marched away he left behind a garrison, commanded by Guy Dalmas, lord of Cousans, and the Picard knight Hutin de Vermeille. These now began preparing for an attack. The walls were strengthened and people and livestock brought in from the surrounding area for safety. All along the valleys of the Cher and the Loire, at Issoudun, Vierzon and Romorantin, townspeople and garrisons made the same preparations. Everyone waited for the storm to break.

Tuesday, 23 August and Wednesday, 24 August

Satisfied that the road ahead was clear, Prince Edward advanced again. After setting fire to Argenton the army marched onward, covering 20 miles across the plains towards Chateauroux. The three divisions were marching more or less parallel to each other, the rearguard to the east and the vanguard to the west of the main body.

Chateauroux was an unfortified market town on the banks of the river Indre. It too belonged to the Chauvigny family, whose property was beginning to take quite a beating. The main body occupied the town and secured the crossing, while the other two divisions camped at Déols and St-Maur, northeast and west of the town respectively, and both also on the river.

Here once again, Prince Edward paused for a day to send out his scouts. There is something almost catlike about his stalking of the French during this part of the campaign: rapid pace, then pause, rapid pace, then pause again. The 24th was the feast day of St Bartholomew, and with ample provisions in hand from the storerooms of Chateauroux, the English and Gascons were well fed. It was the last day of leisure for some time.

Thursday, 25 August

The English army marched again, this time directly towards Bourges. At some point during the day, Prince Edward split his force into two groups. He himself with the main body continued straight towards Issoudun, while another force led by Warwick swung out to the right, circling around the city to the east.[15] We can assume from their speed of movement that most, if not all, of this second force was mounted, men-at-arms and archers on horseback. From their movements, it seems clear that the plan was to seal off Bourges and trap the French force believed to be gathered there. The prince did not yet realise that the Comte de Poitiers had been ordered to withdraw.

By evening the main body had reached Issoudun, a fine town on the banks of a small river, the Théols. Issoudun was divided into two parts, the heavily fortified old quarter around a strong castle called La Tour Blanche, built originally by Philippe Augustus in the early 13th century, and a more modern *bourg*. This too was fortified, but not as strongly as the castle district. The garrison and townspeople were armed and prepared to resist.

Details at this point are very sketchy, and it is not clear when the assault on Issoudun took place. A first attack on the castle district may have been attempted that evening, but after a march of 20 miles it seems more likely that Prince Edward would have settled his men and ordered rest and food before attempting to reduce Issoudun the following morning. Meanwhile, Warwick's detached force had moved on, pushing northeast and drawing close to Bourges.

In Bourges itself, Cousans and Vermeille could almost certainly see the smoke of burning as the English army scorched its way towards Issoudun 25 miles away. The same smoke may have attacted the attention of Gris Mouton and his reconnaissance party, moving down from the north. Cautiously, they rode on towards Bourges. The second party under Boucicaut was operating further to the west, beyond Vierzon.

Friday, 26 August

We do not know the name of the garrison commander at Issoudun, but he – or she – was a captain of some resolve and courage.[16] The English attack on the keep was beaten off, with what casualties we do not know. The town resisted at first, but the English set fire to the houses inside the gate – probably using fire arrows – and the flames forced the defenders back. The English and Gascons then stormed the town, looting it from top to bottom. As they plundered, the flames began spreading from house to house. Fire consumed the entire town, burning every structure to the ground including a fine church. Completing their work, the English also burned the suburb of St-Paterne on the south side of the river.

The rest of the day was spent in mopping up at Issoudun. There seem to have been several more attacks on the castle, all unsuccessful; the prince, once again conscious of the need to not waste manpower, may not have pressed the assaults fully home. Away to the northeast, Warwick's men were prowling around the walls of Bourges, setting fire to the suburbs. Warwick would have seen very soon, however, that there was no sign of any French army; there were no royal banners on the walls and towers of Bourges. The quarry was no longer there.

On his own initiative, Warwick sent out scouts across the area, including a strong reconnaissance party of several hundred men led by John Chandos and James Audley. This group struck north, and late in the day came to the pretty market town of Aubigny-sur-Nère, 30 miles from Bourges. The town was undefended, and Chandos and Aubigny let their men pillage it before burning it down. The English were now only about 20 miles from the Loire.

We can surmise – and again, owing to the lack of information in the chronicles, all of which are rather fuzzy at this particular point, surmise is all we can do – that by the end of Friday the prince knew that the French army had retreated from Bourges. It is also highly likely that by now, his scouts had encountered outriders from Gris Mouton's little force and he knew that there were at least some French troops in the area (and, similarly, Gris Mouton was aware of the English presence and was shadowing the army's movements). He ordered a two-pronged advance. Warwick was to complete his sweep around Bourges, circling north of the city and burning the countryside as he went before turning back to the west. The prince would wait a day for him to get into position, and then both forces would advance northwest in concert, heading down the valley of the Cher towards Tours on the river Loire.

What was Prince Edward's intention at this point? The theory that he was setting out to meet the Duke of Lancaster has, we think, already been disproved (see Chapter 5). It is possible that he was hoping to seize a crossing point over the Loire and, as the chronicler Geoffrey le Baker suggests, march north to meet his father.[17] If so, he would have been doomed to disappointment; a fleet of galleys hired by France from the Kingdom of Aragon was cruising in the English Channel, terrorising shipping, and King Edward had already deemed it too risky to cross to Calais and had cancelled the expedition. The Prince of Wales would not yet have known this. But it is hard to imagine a commander of Prince Edward's calibre thinking that he could fight his way north through the heart of France to Calais with a force of just 7,000 or 8,000 men. Other equally effective options lay before him.

Although he made his fair share of mistakes, Edward usually had a decent idea of what his enemy was doing. He must have guessed – and very shortly, he would know for certain – that a new French royal army was mustering to confront him. The end of hostilities in Normandy would release the troops originally earmarked for the army in Bourges. (How strong this army would be or how great a threat it would present, he did not guess until it was almost too late; but that is another matter.)

We think Edward turned his army towards the Loire in order to trail his coat. If he could advance down the Loire valley, blazing a trail of destruction as he went, he would strike another blow at the French economy and French pride; and unlike the previous autumn, this time he might tempt the French to cross the river and fight him. He knew he could easily match any French army of a similar size to his own. And if the French did not fight, then, well, there was the tempting possibility of seizing a crossing point further downriver and linking up with the English garrisons in Brittany. Having advanced this far into French territory without significant opposition, there were still plenty of opportunities to wreak havoc.

Saturday, 27 August

The Prince of Wales remained at Issoudun, receiving reports from his scouts while the embers continued to flicker among the ruined buildings of the town. The troops had managed to salvage provisions and a large quantity of wine before the town burned down, and so once again were well provided for.[18] The siege of the castle, La Tour Blanche, continued, and finally the English succeeded in forcing the gates, at what cost we do not know. Froissart says merely that 'they slew the greater part whom they found in it'. Massacring the garrisons of castles that resisted was an unfortunate commonplace of medieval warfare, designed to encourage others to lay down their arms rather than fighting back.[19]

Warwick completed his passage around Bourges to the north and reached the valley of the river Cher, a day's march southeast of Vierzon. In the absence of Chandos and Audley, he sent out an advance party under the Captal de

Buch to burn the countryside and also to act as scouts. Chandos and Audley, returning from their raid on Aubigny, set a course to rejoin Warwick.

They had almost rejoined Warwick's division when they stumbled across a party of French – Gris Mouton and his 200 men-at-arms, skulking around the flank of Warwick's advance. Sensing an advantage, Chandos and Audley launched their men into the attack. There was a fierce little fight in the broken country north of the Cher – mounted men-at-arms hacking at each other, archers dismounting and shooting into the bodies of their enemies at close range – and then Gris Mouton's men broke and fled, leaving their dead on the ground. Gris Mouton himself was among those who escaped. Eighteen French men-at-arms, cut off from their fellows, laid down their arms.[20]

In the Middle Ages, there was no tradition of prisoners sticking to giving their name, rank and identity number to their captors. Indeed, prisoners seem to have gossiped quite happily about their own armies and their movements. The prisoners taken by Chandos and Audley divulged that the French royal army was mustering at Chartres, with the intention of marching south and confronting the Prince of Wales as soon as the muster was complete. As we said above, this news probably came as no great surprise. What the prince did not yet know – because Gris Mouton's force had set out before the muster at Chartres was complete – was how strong a force Jean was preparing to bring against him.

A more cautious or more prudent commander might have decided to withdraw at this point, turning back south towards Bordeaux and safety. But Edward was a gambler. He was confident – perhaps overconfident – and determined not to come away from this campaign without some more tangible reward. The advance towards Tours and the Loire would continue as planned. If Jean wanted a battle, he was welcome to one.

Sunday, 28 August

On Sunday morning the Prince of Wales's division marched away from the ruins of Issoudun, passing on down the valley of the Théols through La Ferté and Lury towards Vierzon 20 miles away. They were joined en route by Warwick's men, moving down the valley of the Cher, and both forces converged on the town.

They found Vierzon a smoking ruin. The Captal de Buch's raiders had already passed through the town the previous day, and in a fierce attack stormed both town and castle and put everything to the torch. The town's ancient Benedictine abbey was among the buildings burned. Respect for ecclesiastical property, enforced at the start of the campaign, had once again become a dead letter.

Further on, the Captal's men encountered French scouts near Villefranche-sur-Cher. In the ensuing skirmishes one of the Gascon captains, Nompar de Caumont, took a few more prisoners. They confirmed that all the crossing points over the Loire were fortified and strongly held by the French. Any chance of crossing the river would seem to have gone – if, indeed, Prince Edward had ever intended to do so.

It was at this point, says Froissart, that the prince held a council of war and decided to return towards Bordeaux.[21] He did eventually make this decision, but not yet. For the moment, he was still content to trail his coat. Indeed, it seems that he had abandoned his earlier active strategy and was now waiting for the enemy to make his move. His reaction would depend on what that move was.

The prisoners taken by Caumont came from the second reconnaissance force under the command of Boucicaut and Amaury de Craon. From now on, French scouts dogged the movement of the English army, passing information back to Chartres. For the time being, at least, the French had better intelligence than the English. They proceeded to put it to good use.

So far the campaign had moved rather slowly, the prince striking north without meeting significant resistance, the French fumbling and hesitant in their response. All that was about to change. The clash, long looked for and long sought by both sides, was coming.

For, on 28 August, King Jean arrived in Chartres and joined the royal army gathering in the fields around the town. His marshals and officials had worked miracles to pull together this unruly, underpaid army and put it into the field. Quite how many men he had available is a matter of pure conjecture. Estimates range from 15,000 to 30,000; the higher figure might be correct if we include the usual non-combatants. Roughly 10,000 of these were men-at-arms, including the German and Swiss allies, and there were perhaps 5,000 crossbowmen, though some of these might have been detached for garrison duty along the Loire.[22] The remainder of the fighting men were probably lightly armed foot soldiers raised through the feudal levy, though as discussed in Chapter 3 the French had begun to reduce the numbers of these. At all events, it was potentially a formidable force, if it could be held together long enough to take the field. The men-at-arms alone outnumbered the Prince of Wales's entire force.

Monday, 29 August

On Monday the army continued its advance down the valley of the Cher, heading towards the town of Romorantin. As usual, scouting and foraging parties went out in advance of the main army. One of these, led by Ralph Basset and John Willoughby, rode forward rather incautiously and walked straight into a French ambush. Outnumbered and surrounded, Basset and Willoughby could do nothing but surrender.

But Boucicaut, who had led the ambush, was not allowed long to enjoy his victory. More English and Gascon men-at-arms were pushing forward towards Romorantin, and another, much more powerful detachment of around 200 men-at-arms – led by Bartholomew Burghersh and Augier of Mussidan and including such veteran fighters as Walter Paveley, Nele Loring, Hugh Despenser and Eustache d'Abricourt, and the young Gascon Petiton de Curton – was coming down the road. Reacting quickly to their presence, Boucicaut drew his men off the road, out of sight. Then, once the English had passed, he moved swiftly out to attack them from behind.[23]

But Burghersh was a wily old soldier, and he was not to be ambushed that easily. Hearing the French coming, he split his men-at-arms into two parties, ordering some to peel off the road to the right and the others to the left. Half a dozen English and Gascons who did not move swiftly enough were ridden down and knocked off their horses, but otherwise the French charge met only with empty air. Then, once the French had passed and before they could regroup and turn, Burghersh turned the tables and launched his own attack.

This was medieval combat in the classic style, armoured and mounted men-at-arms charging at each other with lances trying to unhorse their opponents, and then when the lances broke, drawing swords and closing in to continue battering at each other. Men were thrown from their saddles onto the ground, but some managed to collect themselves and rejoin the fighting on foot. The fighting was very heavy, with casualties on both sides, but neither the French nor the English seemed inclined to break off. 'No one could tell,' said Froissart, 'so valiantly was it disputed, to which side victory would incline.'[24]

Eventually the rest of the English vanguard, led by Warwick and Cobham, hove into view. Boucicaut, realising the numbers were very much against him now, called his men off. The French raced west, down the road towards Romorantin, chased hard by the English and Gascons. Along the way, the latter rescued Basset, Willoughby and their fellow prisoners, who picked up their swords and joined in the fray. More French who fell behind were killed or captured, but Boucicaut, Amaury de Craon and about a hundred of their men managed to reach Romorantin just in time, rushing into the town and slamming the gates in the faces of their pursuers.

At this point Boucicaut made a brave decision. He could have carried on retreating towards Tours, 60 miles away, held by a strong French force under the Comte de Poitiers, and so saved himself. Instead, he chose to stay put, and hold Romorantin as long as possible. Boucicaut judged, rightly, that the Prince of Wales would not want to leave this fortified place with its strong garrison in his rear as he advanced. If he could hold the English up for a while, this would give the French royal army time to complete its assembly and advance across the Loire to challenge Prince Edward's little army.

Romorantin was walled, but Boucicaut did not have enough men to hold the perimeter. He abandoned the town and shut his men up inside the castle. This was a very strong place, with a flooded moat and walled enclosure around a powerful central tower, the keep. Food, water and wine were brought into the castle from the town. As the rest of the English army came pouring down the valley, the French prepared to resist.

The main body of the English army halted at Villefranche-sur-Cher, 5 miles short of Romorantin. They had marched 20 miles, and the prince doubtless judged it was best to rest his men and move on to the town in the morning. Elements of the vanguard, following Burghersh and his men, occupied Romorantin itself, surrounding the castle and waiting for the rest of the army to come up.

Tuesday, 30 August

The next morning the remainder of the Anglo-Gascon army marched up to Romorantin, finding billets in the town or making camp in the fields outside. Arriving on the scene, Prince Edward studied the castle. As noted, it was a very strong position, clearly well garrisoned and under a determined commander; the English already knew Boucicaut and his reputation. They decided to try negotiating, and John Chandos went forward under a flag of truce to inquire whether the French might be willing to surrender.

There followed one of those polite exchanges which in medieval warfare nearly always presage an act of organised mayhem. Chandos, approaching the castle gate, was stopped by a French sentry who asked his name. Chandos gave it, and Boucicaut himself came courteously down to the gate to greet him. Chandos invited the Frenchman to surrender, promising that he and his men could go free if they did so. Boucicaut refused: 'We have no sort of inclination to accept any such terms, nor to commit such an act of folly without necessity; for we are determined to defend ourselves.'[25]

Chandos returned to the prince and reported. The prince consulted his captains, and they were agreed. Romorantin would have to be reduced as quickly as possible so the march could continue. But taking Romorantin would not be easy. The attack would have to be methodical and well organised.[26] The rest of the day was spent in preparation, and the assault scheduled to begin in the morning. Men went through the town gathering hurdles and taking wooden doors off their hinges to use for crossing the moat. Others gathered firewood, oil and incendiaries, while the captains and companies told off as part of the storming party prepared their weapons.

Wednesday, 31 August

Early the next day, the assault on Romorantin castle began. Detachments of archers went forward first, surrounding the castle and shooting a hail of arrows at any defender who dared show his face on the ramparts. Under this covering fire, more men came forward carrying pick-axes and mattocks. Launching their makeshift rafts, they paddled across the moat and set to work on the foundations of the walls, trying to undermine them. Others approached the castle gate, piling firewood against the heavy wooden doors and then dousing it with oil.

Braving the arrows, the defenders bombarded the storming party with heavy stones and pots of hot lime, a rather unpleasant form of chemical weapon which burned and blinded the enemy. The resistance went on for some time, and the English and Gascons took casualties; a Gascon esquire in the Captal de Buch's retinue, whom Froissart calls Remond de Gederlach, was among those killed. But the wood heaped against the gate was set ablaze, and the fire consumed the gate itself. Once the flames had subsided more English and Gascons splashed across the moat and stormed through the burning embers, while others raised ladders against the walls and began to scale the ramparts, covered all the time by the relentless arrows of the archers. The French retreated from the walls and there was bloody fighting in the courtyard as they tried to reach the safety of the keep. Boucicaut, Craon and many others succeeded in getting inside the keep and barring the door. Those who did not make it inside were cut down and killed.

The outer ward of the castle had been taken but the keep continued to resist, and its high walls could not be scaled. Prince Edward ordered his men to regroup and rest. Tomorrow, they would try again.

Meanwhile, detached parties were riding out as usual, to forage and pillage and watch for the enemy. All of Boucicaut's surviving men were trapped inside Romorantin; Gris Mouton was nowhere to be seen. The countryside seemed empty. Finding no trace of the enemy, the prince ordered his scouts to push on as far as Tours.

Thursday, 1 September

At sunrise the trumpets sounded, mustering the army, and fresh assault parties went forward, running into the courtyard of the castle and attacking the keep, covered as ever by the archers. The defenders, at the windows of the tower and on the ramparts of the roof, were well protected by thick stone walls. The tactic of the archers in such cases was to maintain a steady rapid fire, shooting dozens of arrows at the windows and crennelations. Not all the arrows would hit their targets, and many would rebound from the stone walls, but some would get through; and any defender who tried to look out of the window or over the rampart ran the risk of getting an arrow in the face.

But that did not deter Boucicaut and his men. They continued to drop stones and other missiles on the heads of the English and Gascons who tried to batter down the door or undermine the foundations of the tower, and assault after assault was driven back. After several failures the Prince of Wales came to the castle with his esquires to see the situation for himself. With the prince was young Bertucat d'Albret, bastard son of Bernard-Ezi. Seeing the attack wavering, the prince rushed forward, encouraging his men and exhorting them to fight on. He was greeted with a volley of heavy stones, one of which struck Bertucat d'Albret on the head, crushing his helmet and killing him. Furious, the prince vowed never to leave Romorantin until he had taken the keep and winkled out the French resistance.[27] But his anger was to no avail. Sunset came, and still the French in the keep held out, defiant.

Meanwhile, the scouts were reporting back and some startling intelligence had come in; the French army had been spotted, only about 30 miles away. Shocked by this, the prince consulted his captains; should they abandon the siege and retreat, or should they continue? In the end they decided to stand fast. It was not clear how strong the French force actually was. Also, the prince was still more than willing to give battle, provided the odds against him not be too great.[28] The decision was made to carry on the siege, and wait for further news of the enemy.

In fact, the scouts were mistaken. The force they had seen was probably nothing more than the remnants of Gris Mouton's reconnaissance party, still in the field and carrying out its brief of watching the enemy. The French were still holding the line of the Loire; the Comte de Poitiers was in Tours, while elements of the vanguard marching down from Chartres were only just now reaching the river line at Blois and points further east. By now, the French knew the prince was besieging Romorantin, and they would have been hoping Boucicaut would hold the English up as long as possible so they could get their army across the river. They too were anxious for a battle.

Back at Romorantin, it was clear that new tactics would have to be employed. Prince Edward ordered three catapults to be constructed, one by the Earl of Suffolk's retinue, the second by Bartholomew Burghersh's men, and the third by a Gascon captain who is not named; the Captal de Buch or Bernard-Ezi d'Albret are the logical choices.[29] While some men worked on the catapults, others collected more incendiary material. Froissart says the English used Greek fire, but true Greek fire is complicated to prepare and handle, and it is unlikely that the English carried stocks of it with them on campaign. More likely, they gathered oil, pitch and other inflammables and made them into missiles for the catapults. If the French could not be prised out of the castle, they would be burned out.

Friday, 2 September

At Romorantin, the assault resumed. The catapults were dragged forward and brought into position. The defenders in the keep could only watch helplessly as the catapult arms were winched back and the baskets loaded with their burning missiles. At a word of command, the catapults were released; the arms snapped forward against the crossbar and streaks of fire hurtled through the air to splash against the stone walls of the keep.

The fire, of course, would not damage the walls. But there was plenty of wood in the keep too; the roof was made of wood, and so were the floors inside. If a fire could be started, the defenders would soon be smoked out. All that day the catapults kept up their slow, steady bombardment, the air growing thick with smoke while the archers continued to prowl and snipe at anyone who lifted their head. Boucicaut had no crossbowmen to counter them.

Under cover of the archers and the catapults, the men with picks and mattocks came forward again. Other men accompanied them, holding heavy wooden shields known as 'tortoises' over the heads of the workmen to protect them. Slowly and methodically they began undermining the foundations of the tower in an attempt to collapse the structure. The defenders tried to drop more stones and lime on their heads, but the tortoises deflected most of the missiles. Both sides took casualties, and the siege went on.

Outside the town, another enemy company had been spotted. This one was made up largely of Welsh exiles who rejected English authority and had taken service in France; their captain was a man named Gryffyd Micco. Quite what their purpose was is not clear; the historian Georges Minois thinks they were trying to relieve the siege, but their strength was quite unequal to such a task. More likely they had been sent from Tours as scouts, perhaps to bolster Gris Mouton's depleted party. Whatever their intention, they never reached their goal. They were caught in the open by the English and Gascons, and annihilated.[30]

Saturday, 3 September

At Romorantin the inevitable end finally came. Burning missiles from the catapult set the roof of the keep on fire. Boucicaut and his men held out for as long as they could, but finally, burned and choking with smoke, they could stay in the burning building no longer. Receiving a promise of fair treatment, the smoke-blackened men stumbled out of the keep and laid down their arms. Not long after they came out, the tower, weakened by fire and undermining, collapsed.

This was the second time Boucicaut had become an English prisoner; he had only been released after his previous capture in February 1355. Amaury de Craon surrendered too; unlike Boucicaut, who was released before the end of the year, Craon spent another four years in captivity.

The prince had his victory, but it had been bloodily won and had cost him four valuable days. The French had made good use of the time Boucicaut so gallantly purchased for them. More intelligence was reaching the prince, and he knew now that the French were marching hard south from Chartres. He had learned also of the presence of the Comte de Poitiers and his little force in Tours.

While the army rested and recovered from the rigours of the siege, the prince and his captains deliberated again. Tours was on the south bank of the Loire, and could be easily attacked. It had the reputation of being a strongly fortified city, but even so, some chance might present itself. If this detachment could be defeated, the French army would be weakened; if young Poitiers himself could be captured, even better. Bold as ever, Prince Edward made up his mind. He would continue the advance to Tours, into the teeth of the enemy, and see what opportunities presented themselves.

CHAPTER 7

'Choose a Place for Battle'

Sunday, 4 September

The Prince of Wales's army remained at Romorantin, resting and regrouping after the violence of the siege. It was a month to the day since they had left Bergerac and begun the long march north. The prince kept his word to the prisoners; the important ones such as Boucicaut and Craon were kept for ransom, but the poorer men-at-arms who could pay no ransom were set free. It was not uncommon for prisoners who could not be ransomed to be killed out of hand; we saw an instance of this the previous autumn in the Languedoc. On this occasion, it is pleasant to record that the defenders of Romorantin did not suffer for their bravery.

The French, for their part, were now on the move. King Jean probably left Chartres on this day, arriving on the Loire four days later. Other contingents were already marching south, using different roads to avoid congestion, on a front from Tours all the way upriver to Blois and Meung. Clermont, the marshal, arrived in Tours with another advance party, bolstering the garrison. At some point too, orders were sent to Normandy instructing the Dauphin to gather as many men as he could and march to join the royal army on the Loire. The Dauphin duly obliged, stripping his garrisons and collecting around 1,000 men-at-arms, and then riding south to join his father.

Tours itself was a wealthy city of about 12,000 people.[1] It was walled, but the ramparts were in a poor condition. Plans for repairing them had been drawn up with the encouragement of the king, but the city had balked at the cost of the work and then dragged its heels, and the work had not yet been completed. Like the Languedoc, this part of France had not seen war in more than a century, and people had forgotten the need for defence. Clermont did what he could to repair the defences, even demolishing a couple of churches in order to procure a supply of stone for the walls. He evacuated the unwalled suburbs and brought their people into the shelter of the city, where many took refuge in the churches or the great abbey of St-Martin.[2] For the moment, this was about all Clermont could do.

Also in Tours was the Cardinal de Talleyrand, younger brother of the Count of Périgord. Earlier in the summer he and his colleague Cardinal Nicola Capocci, the papal legate in France, had been sent to mediate between King Jean and his enemies, specifically the imprisoned Charles of Navarre and King Edward of England. They had met with Jean several times in the siege lines outside of Breteuil, but Jean had stubbornly refused to consider making peaceful overtures to either of his foes. Giving up on peace-making, Talleyrand withdrew to Tours, perhaps with the idea of going to Périgord and seeing if a peaceful resolution to the military deadlock in the city could be found. But the Prince of Wales's incursion northwards made it too dangerous to travel. As a churchman, the cardinal should have been sacrosanct; threatening or committing violence against his person was an offence punishable by excommunication, but all armies were full of lawless men who did not fear God. To ensure his safety, the cardinal travelled with a small bodyguard of men-at-arms, commanded by his scapegrace nephew Robert of Durazzo.

Most of the men were French, but included in their number was a Spanish Knight of St John, an intriguing figure named Juan Fernández de Heredia.[3] He had joined the Knights – one of the famous military-religious orders of crusading knights, similar to the now defunct Templars – in 1328, and had spent most of his career gathering power and wealth for himself and his family (despite taking a vow of celibacy upon becoming a Knight of St John, Heredia had several illegitimate children). He was now Grand Prior of Castile and Aragon, with ambitions to rise higher still. What he was doing in Talleyrand's train is not known for certain, but it is likely that he was trying to acquire Talleyrand's interest and favour.

Monday, 5 September

On Monday morning the English set fire to Romorantin and departed, leaving the burning town and wrecked castle behind them. The weather, which had been fine for the past several weeks, continued to hold and the army was able to make 20 miles, passing Selles-sur-Cher and halting for the night at St-Aignan, a handsome town on the banks of the Cher. Some of this area had already been burned by scouting and raiding parties over the past several days, and now the army completed the work of destruction, burning everything else left standing. The smoke of burning could almost certainly be seen by the French garrisons stationed along the Loire.

Once again, the English advanced without meeting resistance. Clermont, a cautious if capable commander, believed rightly that the safety of Tours was his most important objective and kept his men inside the city. Let the Prince of Wales advance and scorch what he wished; Clermont knew what the prince did not, namely that in a few days' time the French royal army would be ready to cross the river. The prince would then surely be compelled to retreat.

Tuesday, 6 September

The English continued to advance towards Tours, now just 40 miles away. By midday the army had reached the town of Montrichard, which had a heavily fortified castle commanding the road along the north bank of the Cher. Realising the prince's intention to march on Tours, Clermont had thrown a garrison into Montrichard in hopes of barring the way. The English scouts reported that the castle was far too strong to be taken quickly; another significant operation on the scale of the siege of Romorantin would be required. Events were moving quickly now, and the prince may have begun to regret spending so long at Romorantin.

Rather than attacking Montrichard, the prince and his commanders decided to bypass the town. However, in order to do so they had to leave the main road and circle around through the forested high ground to the north of the town, posting flank guards in case the garrison should decide to launch a sortie. This manoeuvre took time to complete. Dragging the baggage train – which as well as carrying arrows and other supplies was now hauling a considerable amount of loot – through the forest was slow and difficult work. The army camped that night just beyond Montrichard, having covered 12 miles since morning.

Wednesday, 7 September

The English army marched down the valley of the Cher, following the north bank of the river. They encountered no opposition. At the end of the day, after a march of 18 miles, the English and Gascons came out onto the banks of another river, much larger and broader than the Cher. This was the mighty Loire, the river that drained a third of France.

Usually at this time of year the water levels in the Loire were low, with broad banks of sand and gravel forming islands amid the channel. The river was probably even fordable in places. But there had been heavy rains in the highlands to the south and east, and the Loire was swollen and turbulent; the only way across the river now was by bridge.[4] There was a bridge at Tours, but it was protected by the walled city on the south bank. Other nearby bridges appear to have been broken down, probably at the orders of Marshal Clermont.[5] This was a wise precaution. We have argued earlier that the Prince of Wales's aim up to this point had been to move down the Loire valley, rather than cross the river in force, but if the chance to send raiding parties across the river and wreak havoc on the north bank had presented itself, the prince would doubtless have taken it.

Ahead, the spires of Tours could be seen on the horizon. The army halted at Montlouis on the south bank of the Loire. The weather was turning; thunderstorms were moving up from the west and it had begun to rain. To the crack of thunder and amid flickering flares of lightning, the army made camp.

In Tours, Marshal Clermont and Cardinal Talleyrand watched the glow of enemy campfires through the rain. The threat to the city was very real. Tours lies on a long tongue of land between the Loire and the Cher, which run together just west of the city. Only from the east could the city be attacked by land, but it was from the east that the English were now coming. Clermont had to hope that his troops, augmented by seven hastily raised companies of volunteers from the town, and the patched-together walls, would be enough to hold them back.

Thursday, 8 September

The storms continued and heavy rain fell all day. The prince halted most of his army at Montlouis and sent out a strong force of about 1,200 men under Bartholomew Burghersh to approach Tours more closely.

These men had a miserable time of it. The roads and tracks had dissolved into mud and the rain soon soaked them through. Burghersh's column approached Tours without hindrance and advanced to the unwalled eastern suburbs of the town with the intention of burning them, probably by using fire arrows to set light to thatched roofs. But the rain was so heavy that the fires would not light. The garrison of Tours was standing to arms on the ramparts. Burghersh judged his little force was not sufficient to mount an assault, and pulled back. His troops spent a highly uncomfortable night in the open near the town;

some of the men found shelter in troglodyte houses, cave dwellings cut into the banks of the Loire.

Sixty miles upriver, King Jean of France and his household reached the town of Meung on the north bank of the Loire and rode through the rain into the castle, where they spent the night. Reports reaching Jean and his officers from Tours told of how the Prince of Wales was camped in front of Tours, threatening the city. The main body of Jean's army was arriving behind him, on a front from Orléans downriver as far as Amboise. Orders went out to the various contingents, detailing which crossing points they should use. Clermont was told to hold Tours against any assault, while the Comte de Poitiers was ordered to leave the city and join his father at Blois, midway between Tours and Meung.

We are entitled to ask why it had taken the French so long to arrive. King Jean had left Breteuil on 20 August, nearly three weeks earlier, and yet he was only now arriving on the Loire. Of course, Jean and his commanders and administrators faced a plethora of problems. We have referred several times already to the crippling shortage of money. But there was also a long wait for some of the contingents to arrive. The German, Swiss and Savoyard allies had a long distance to travel, and when they did arrive it was necessary to give the men, and especially the horses, time to rest before setting out on campaign. Among Jean's own subjects, personal dislike of the king himself may have meant that some lords and knights moved slowly and reluctantly in answer to the royal summons.

Then there was the question of supply. Jean was campaigning inside his own country; unlike the Prince of Wales's men, his troops could not pillage and live off the land (though doubtless some did, when they thought they could get away with it). The provisions to feed 20,000 men, even for a month, took time to assemble and required hundreds of wagons for transport. As well as the men, there were the horses. Given that many men-at-arms had more than one horse, and including remounts and draft animals, we can safely assume that there were at least 20,000 horses in the army, and possibly closer to 30,000. Fodder had to be provided for these. The horses also required grooms to look after them and farriers to re-shoe them when they threw a shoe; the farriers needed horseshoes, tools and forges, and these all required more wagons. Similarly, the men-at-arms needed armourers to keep their mail and plate armour in good repair, and the armourers also needed tools and forges. The Genoese crossbowmen required wagons to carry their ammunition and their heavy shields, the pavises, while they were marching. The wealthier knights and nobles took their own personal baggage on campaign with them, including brightly coloured pavilions and furniture. And so on it went.

The army had initially mustered at Chartres, around 50 miles north of Orléans. When the movement south began in early September, it took several days to transfer this mass of men and wagons down to the Loire. The roads south from Chartres would have been heavily congested, and towards the end the weather turned bad; the same rains that bogged down Burghersh's men as they marched towards Tours would have affected the marching French as well. And finally, there were only a limited number of crossing points over the Loire. Thanks to the rains that swelled the river, the French, like the English, were unable to ford the Loire and would have had to cross by bridge. If the entire mass of men, horses and wagons were to pass over a single bridge, the process would take days. It made sense to split the army into different columns and use as many bridges as possible, but this also took time.

All of this matters because the French army, while large and powerful, was also rather cumbersome. Although the mounted elements of Jean's army could move at speed, when doing so they tended to outrun their support troops, including the crossbowmen, and the supply train. Thus, when Jean did move rapidly to take advantage of the situation, he was often then forced to halt and regroup his disordered army. Each time he halted he lost whatever advantage he had gained.

Friday, 9 September

In the pouring rain, Burghersh's column continued to prowl outside the walls of Tours, perhaps hoping to tempt the enemy into a sortie. That would have suited Burghersh perfectly; cutting off a French detachment and perhaps even seizing a gate into the city in a *coup de main* would have given the English an excellent chance of prising open the defences of Tours. But Clermont, his garrison weakened by the withdrawal of troops to accompany the Comte de Poitiers upriver, recognised the danger. He kept his men within the walls.

Back at Montlouis, the rest of the English army camped in the rain while the prince and his captains waited for news from their scouts. They were aware of the presence of the French army assembling on the north bank, but were still uncertain of its exact strength or intentions. With the confidence of a born gambler, the Prince of Wales held his position and waited for the enemy to show his hand.

Further up the Loire, King Jean moved downriver from Meung to Blois, a distance of about 25 miles. He was now less than 30 miles from Prince Edward's position at Montlouis. Jean was, of course, fully aware of the prince's location and probably his numbers too. At Blois, Jean was reunited with his son, the Comte de Poitiers. Two of his other sons, Louis and Philippe, were already with him. The Dauphin was on his way, marching down from Normandy with further reinforcements. His strength gathered, Jean sent out more orders. Despite the bad weather, the army would begin crossing the river the following morning.

Saturday, 10 September

Still the storms and rain continued, and still Prince Edward remained at Montlouis. Historians have puzzled over this, wondering why he did not either bypass Tours and continue downriver, or turn back south.[6] The answer lies in the bad weather. Dragging heavy wagons down the muddy tracks that passed for most roads in the Middle Ages would not be easy, and it was worth waiting for the weather to improve; and, of course, the rain would slow up the French as well. Waiting a day for the weather to improve was a risk worth taking.

Another factor now enters the picture as well. While camped outside Tours the prince received word from his cousin the Duke of Lancaster. When Jean left Normandy, he took the Dauphin and most of the royal troops with him. This restored Lancaster's freedom of movement, and at some point in late August he left his base in the Cotentin and struck south. By early September an advance party under Robert Knollys was raiding near Angers, 70 miles downriver from Tours. The prince had to consider whether to continue with his own plan to move downriver and perhaps link up with Lancaster, or to be satisfied with what he had achieved so far and turn south for home. The idea of joining Lancaster was a tempting one, as his own letter home written later in the year makes clear.[7] As yet, of course, the prince still had no idea of the full strength of the French army.

He was about to find out. Jean of France crossed the Loire at Blois with his household and thousands of men-at-arms. After them came the rumbling wagons of the supply train. Other contingents crossed at Orléans and Meung, and one detachment crossed at Amboise, just 8 miles from Montlouis.[8] Even using multiple crossing points, it took all day for the French army and baggage train to cross the river in the rain and assemble on the far side. Those contingents that crossed further upriver began marching hard down towards the king's position.

Sunday, 11 September

News that some of the French had crossed the river at Amboise would have reached the English camp by the previous evening. The Prince of Wales suddenly realised he was in a dangerous position, boxed in between the Loire to the north and the Cher to the south. A strong French attack from the east would drive him west, pinning him against the walls of Tours. His first priority was to get out of this potential trap. There was no time to make any further attempt against Tours itself.

The rain had stopped, but the roads were still wet and muddy. Moving as swiftly as the conditions would allow, the Anglo-Gascon army crossed the Cher south of Montlouis and moved on to the next river, the Indre. A march of about 12 miles brought them to Montbazon, a fortified town with a bridge over the river. The English approached cautiously, but the town was undefended and deserted. Part of the army seized the town and passed over the bridge; others crossed the river at nearby fords, a difficult and dangerous operation given that the Cher too had been swollen by the recent rains.[9]

Had Jean moved swiftly after crossing the Loire at Blois, he might well have been able to trap the prince at Tours. The ground around Tours was flat, open and wet, and the English would not have been able to take advantage of favourable terrain. A confrontation there would have been interesting, to say the least. But, not for the first time, the size of Jean's army hampered him. He needed to concentrate his forces, and that took time. The day was spent waiting on the riverbank opposite Blois while the contingents that had crossed at Orléans and Meung came marching down to join him. The last of these probably only straggled in late in the day.

Monday, 12 September

French scouts riding out from Amboise noted the departure of the English and reported back to King Jean. The king himself marched to Amboise, a testing journey of 21 miles in still difficult conditions. At this point the two armies were about 16 or 17 miles apart as the crow flies.

Prince Edward remained at Montbazon for the day. Again, we are not quite certain why. It seems probable that he still had some idea of linking up with Lancaster's men, but doubts would have begun gnawing at his mind. Suppose he marched west, and it turned out that Lancaster had withdrawn north again, or no crossing of the Loire could be forced?

The other two options were to withdraw south, or to remain in the field and seek a position where he could force a battle. As the day went on and reports came in of the strength of the French army moving down towards Amboise, that third option began to fade. This was the largest army France had put in the field since the fall of Calais nine years earlier, a formidable force nearly three times the size of the little Anglo-Gascon army.

The chronicler Geoffrey le Baker insists that the prince continued to seek out the French so as to fight a battle.[10] But if the prince wanted to force a battle, that was easily done; all he had to do was stand and wait for the French to come to him. His actions over the next few days tell us otherwise. There can be no doubt that the prince and his captains, learning of how heavily they were outnumbered, chose the prudent option of withdrawing south.

As they deliberated at Montbazon, considering their next move, the English commanders were startled to see a party of men approaching under a flag of truce. The surprise rather quickly turned to displeasure. Leading the party were two papal envoys, the cardinals Talleyrand and Capocci, demanding an audience with Prince Edward.

Pope Innocent, it seemed, had decided to try his hand at peace-making once again. Capocci, who had returned to the papal court at Avignon after the failure of their attempt in the spring, had sought out Talleyrand at Tours and the two of them then followed the track of the English army to Montbazon. In the conference that followed, it appears that Talleyrand did most of the talking. Urbane and well spoken, he was a better diplomat than the blunt-spoken Capocci, a member of a Roman princely family whom the historian Georges Minois describes as 'a man of brutal manner, devoid of all diplomatic ability'.[11] Capocci and Talleyrand also disliked each other, which is hardly surprising given the difference in their characters.

Talleyrand opened the meeting by informing the Prince of Wales that the Dauphin had just reached Tours with his 1,000 Norman men-at-arms. King Jean, he said, was very close at hand, and intended to force a battle with the English as soon as possible, perhaps as early as Wednesday. But battle could be avoided, Talleyrand said, if the prince would agree to a truce. His intention was to act as go-between and broker an armistice between the prince and King Jean, a truce which could hopefully be the basis for a lasting peace.

The prince, however, was in no mood to talk peace. Talleyrand was viewed with suspicion at the English court, where he was strongly suspected of being a French stooge. Was he genuinely here to talk peace, or was he trying to delay the English, holding them up until the French could arrive? This was probably unfair; the indications were that Talleyrand genuinely desired to act as broker and bring about peace. He may have been doing so for selfish reasons – settling the dispute between England and France would add hugely to his own reputation, perhaps even make him a candidate for the papal throne one day – but in his wish to make peace, if nothing else, he was honest.

Edward, however, was not interested. As he himself later wrote home, 'We made answer to him, that we had no power to make peace without the command and wishes of the king, our dear lord and father.'[12] The prince's own instructions from his father when he set out for Bordeaux the previous year had specifically precluded him from making a separate peace with the enemy; only if he was surrounded by enemies with no chance of rescue was he allowed to conclude a truce. The prince also pointed out that King Jean was already advancing with an overwhelmingly superior force to attack him; therefore, there was little likelihood that the king would agree to a truce. Why would he want to do so?

Rebuffed, Talleyrand and Capocci rode away to find the French army and speak to King Jean. They fared little better with him. The ravaging of some of the richest provinces of central France was an insult the king could not ignore. A truce now would allow the Prince of Wales to get away scot-free, and that would not be acceptable to either the king or the nobles and people. The Prince of Wales must be punished.

Tuesday, 13 September

The decision to withdraw having been taken, Prince Edward wasted no more time. The baggage train set off first with a strong escort from the vanguard. The rest of the army followed, marching up out of the valley of the Indre and onto the plateau towards Ste-Maure-de-Touraine. By mid-morning his scouts were reporting that Jean was on the march too, the French army pouring south down the roads from Amboise. The prince steered his own army towards the next valley to the south, the Creuse.

The French followed a parallel course to the east. Jean probably expected Prince Edward to move up the valley of the Indre from Montbazon towards the great Plantagenet fortress of Loches. Accordingly, Jean made Loches his own destination. His vanguard reached the town after a punishing march of more than 20 miles, but he missed his quarry. The Anglo-Gascon force was keeping well to the west, and marching every bit as hard as the French. By evening Prince Edward's little army had reached the little town of La Haye (known today as Descartes) on the right bank of the Creuse.[13] The two armies were now about 20 miles apart. So far, Prince Edward had managed to elude King Jean, but he had not managed to shake off the French pursuit entirely.

Wednesday, 14 September

Early the next morning the Prince of Wales pulled his men out of La Haye, crossing the Creuse and climbing up into the hilly country to the southwest, dragging the heavily laden wagons up the slopes. By veering off to the right, he hoped to put distance between himself and the French.

He hoped in vain. Rousing his own army, Jean marched straight towards La Haye. His intention here is less clear; he must have known that the English would be marching away from La Haye. Perhaps he guessed that Edward would steer a more westerly course and was determined to stay in contact with him; he may even have hoped to follow the trail of the English and send his mounted men on ahead to force them to stop and give battle. At all events, after another march of about 20 miles, Jean arrived in La Haye that evening, about 12 hours after the English departed.

But by now, Jean's army was becoming badly strung out and losing its organisational shape. The baggage train and foot soldiers were falling behind, and the less well-mounted of the men-at-arms were straggling too. Bridges, such as the ones at Loches and La Haye, were choke points where only a few men could cross at a time. To give him his due, Jean refused to slacken the pursuit and ordered a further march the next day. He knew that Prince Edward had halted for the night at Châtellerault, 12 miles to the southwest. His plan was to move his own army around to the south of the prince, getting between him and his base in Bordeaux. Cut off from home, the prince would have no choice but to give battle.

Thursday, 15 September

Surprisingly, the Prince of Wales halted his army and remained at Châtellerault all that day, and the next. It is hard to tell if this was part of a cunning plan, or whether the prince had been affected by a highly unusual bout of indecision.

The prince was still in contact with the Duke of Lancaster, who had joined Knollys in the area around Angers, about 70 miles from the prince's position. Lancaster knew that the prince was retiring south, and attempted to join forces with him. His men tried to seize a river crossing near Angers, but the stubborn French garrison refused to budge and the attempt failed.[14] Prince Edward did not yet know this, however. The temptation to wait for Lancaster remained strong. Reinforcements from Lancaster's little force would bring his own army up to a strength where it might be possible to go into battle against the French with a reasonable expectation of winning.

Did the prince therefore wait at Châtellerault in hopes that Lancaster might have crossed the river and be on his way to join him? Or did he simply realise that he had no chance of outrunning the French, and decide that with or without Lancaster, he would give battle and hope for the best? That brings in the cunning plan scenario, which is that the prince halted at Châtellerault to rest his men and hope that Jean's heated pursuit would disorganise his army still further. His scouts would have told him that the French were becoming increasingly strung out along the roads to the east and southeast.[15] If Edward could cut off part of the French army and destroy it, he would have handed the French a stinging blow and shortened the odds when battle eventually came. So, he waited at Châtellerault and watched for his chance.

Thus the bulk of the Anglo-Gascon army remained camped around Châtellerault. Meanwhile Jean, determined to get in front of the prince and cut off his line of retreat, made his most ambitious march yet, 32 miles from La Haye southwest to Chauvigny on the banks of the Vienne. The river here is broad and deep, and Chauvigny's single bridge was the only crossing point upstream or downstream for some miles. And Chauvingy is only 14 miles east of Poitiers, a city which was strongly held by the French. Through that narrow gap the Prince of Wales would have to march if he was to continue south. Now, Jean was about to close that gap and block the prince's retreat with an immensely superior force. Victory seemed certain.

Friday, 16 September

But Jean had pushed his army hard – too hard. Some of the men had marched or ridden 70 miles in three days, and they and the horses were worn out. While Jean himself was in Chauvigny, most of his army was still straggling down the long roads behind him. His intention was to push on to Poitiers and use the city as a base, but if he crossed the Vienne with insufficient force, he would be opening himself up to attack by the English coming down from the north. He would risk suffering exactly the kind of defeat in detail that Prince Edward was hoping to inflict on him.

Chafing with impatience, Jean waited at Chauvigny while the rest of his weary army assembled. Eighteen miles to the north at Châtellerault the Prince of Wales waited too, resting his men. Aware of Jean's position, he guessed that the French would march tomorrow to Poitiers. He made his own plans accordingly.

Saturday, 17 September

His army assembled once more, Jean rode on with the vanguard to Poitiers, reaching it late morning. His army followed down the road from Chauvigny. The single bridge at Chauvigny acted as another chokepoint and it took a long time for the army to cross. Those who did cross seemed unaware of how near the enemy were. Carelessly, some men-at-arms had not even put on their armour as they rode. Instead of helms and bascinets, some wore hats with ostrich plumes. Riding in a long column down the road from Chauvigny to Poitiers, they were quite unready for battle.

Early that morning, the Prince of Wales marched from Châtellerault. To the south lay a large forest. The army plunged straight into this, counting on the woodlands to give them cover and conceal their approach from French scouts. By early afternoon they were approaching the road from Chauvigny to Poitiers.

In one respect the English were unlucky. When they reached the road, it was empty. A contingent of French men-at-arms had just passed by, heading west. The prince ordered a pursuit, and 200 English and Gascon men-at-arms led by Robert Ufford, the Earl of Suffolk, and Aimeri de Biron of Montferrand raced down the road after the unsuspecting French, quickly catching up with their rearguard. The French were startled and unprepared. There was a brief, violent collision before the French broke and fled, leaving many of their comrades stretched dead on the battlefield. In a few brief minutes the French lost more than 200 killed or captured. Prisoners included the notables Jean de Châlon, Count of Auxerre, Raoul de Joigny and Jean de Châtillon, the marshal of Burgundy. The local overlord, Louis de Chauvigny, Vicomte de Brosse, was among those who escaped.[16]

It was a sparkling little victory, but the prince had hoped for rather more. The aim had been to cut off, isolate and destroy an entire detachment, and that had not been achieved. And now, the element of surprise had been lost. The fugitives from the fight would spread the word, and if Jean moved quickly he could turn and trap the prince, whose own army was now in disarray. Some of his men were pursuing the survivors of the French force; others were still making their way through the woods. Recalling Suffolk and Montferrand and their men, the prince pushed on, passing the manor of Savigny and finally making camp in the woods northwest of the village of Nouaillé. Despite the recent rain there was no water to be found in the forest, and men and horses both passed an uncomfortable night.

Arriving in Poitiers, King Jean learned of the battle on the road. The casualties made little difference; he could shrug off the loss of 200 men. More

Abbaye de Nouaillé Maupertuis in 1699

important was the fact that the prince was now very close by; Nouaillé is only about 7 miles from Poitiers. Yet again, though, Jean was unable to take advantage of this. Much of his army was still crossing the narrow bridge at Chauvigny and making its way towards Poitiers. The last troops and wagons did not actually cross until late the following day, Sunday. Like the prince, he needed time to regroup.

The bluffs beside the river at Nouaillé Maupertuis

Sunday, 18 September

In urgent need of water, the prince shifted his army a few miles south through the woods to the little river Miosson. This river runs through Nouaillé, winding its way through a deep valley cut into the surrounding terrain. Nouaillé itself is surrounded by high hills. In places the banks of the Miosson are sheer cliffs, and under some of these cliffs springs bubble up from the ground, feeding the river.

West of Nouaillé there is a wooded hill, part of the forest known as the Fôret de Nouaillé. To the west of this hill is undulating ground, cut across by little valleys worn down by tributary streams leading down to the Miosson. Today much of the ground is covered by suburban residential housing, but in the 14th century the woods gave way to fields and vineyards with a few small hamlets in the distance. Just west of the hill, a track ran down to a ford known as the Gué de l'Omme, the Ford of the Elm (*omme* is a local dialect word for an elm tree), where the Miosson could be crossed. The horses were taken down to the river to drink at the ford, and water was carried up to the men on the high ground.

The Prince of Wales's intentions at this point have been subject to intense debate. We shall consider some of that debate later (see Appendix), but for the moment, let us consider his position. Lancaster was not coming to his aid. The French were pressing closely; Jean had displayed a furious if not always well-guided energy, and the prince's attempt to weaken the enemy by cutting off a detachment had failed. Although his army now had access to fresh water from the Miosson, they were running low on food. There had been no opportunity for pillaging the previous day, and the wait at Châtellerault had consumed most of the army's surplus food.

There was a good defensive position at the foot of the western side of the hill, above the Gué de l'Omme. A battle at such long odds would be risky, but probably less risky than attempting to retreat and getting caught on the open plain or at a river crossing by superior French forces. Conferring that afternoon, the captains agreed to gamble on a battle. As Geoffrey le Baker puts it, 'They advised the lord prince to choose a place for battle, and to put his army in order.'[17]

However, the lack of food was a serious issue. There was nothing much to forage in the forest, and few villages or settlements in the area to plunder. Some supplies could be had at the Benedictine abbey of St-Junien in Nouaillé, but they would not last for long. The English had to hope that King Jean would advance and attack them. If not, then shortage of food would force them to retreat once more.

For the moment, despite the shortage of food and the odds against the English, the decision was taken to stand and fight. However, today was Sunday and there was unlikely to be a battle. The old custom of the 'Truce of God', which forbade fighting on holy days, was more honoured in the breach than in the observance, but the presence of the two cardinals, Talleyrand and Capocci, in the French army was likely to be a restraining influence. So the English stood on the slopes of the Gué de l'Omme, waiting to see what the French would do. Surveying the position, the prince gave orders for pits to be dug and other obstacles to be placed in the vineyards immediately to the army's front, to hamper the approach of enemy cavalry. Trenches were dug and empty wagons and carts dragged forward for use as barricades. Methodically, the English made ready to fight.

For his part, Sunday or not, King Jean was also preparing for battle. His army marched out of Poitiers to within a few miles of the English position, and halted. His army began to make the usual preparations, checking armour and harnesses, sharpening weapons and also attending mass; the bishops of Sens and Châlons conducted divine service, blessing the army and ensuring the souls of those who died in battle tomorrow would be saved.

In the midst of all this bustle of preparation, Cardinal Talleyrand arrived from Poitiers and asked for an audience with the king. According to Froissart, Talleyrand argued that the king could get what he wanted without fighting. The Prince of Wales had his back to the wall; when battle came the powerful French army would roll over the English without difficulty. Surely the prince himself must realise this, and see reason. It was wrong and wicked to shed blood, said Talleyrand, when a peaceful arrangement could be negotiated. 'Permit me to go to the prince and remonstrate with him on the dangerous situation he is in,' he concluded.[18]

Talleyrand was being disingenuous here; he was still thinking of a larger negotiated peace between France and England, but Jean understood him to say that he was merely going to persuade the prince to surrender. Jean was intelligent enough to know that a battle would be risky, even with his superiority in numbers. Capturing the prince without a fight would give him a clear propaganda victory which he could exploit, as well as leverage against the prince's father, King Edward. He gave the cardinal leave to go, and promised to hold back from fighting until Talleyrand returned. With his bodyguard, including Robert of Durazzo and the Spanish Hospitaller Juan Fernández de Heredia, Talleyrand rode on towards the English camp.

The cardinal found the Prince of Wales to be in an unusually pliant mood too, much more so than at Montbazon. Talleyrand took this to mean that he was right; the prince knew his position was desperate and was willing to talk. For his part, the prince was probably more curious than anything else. Why, given the advantage of numbers he held, was Jean interested in talking terms? Was he after all reluctant to fight? If so, this would affect the prince's own decision, whether to stand or to retreat to find a foraging ground so he could feed his men. Another contemporary source, Chandos Herald, thinks the prince was happy to take advantage of peace talks to give his men some respite and rest, and this may well be true.[19]

To Talleyrand's delight, Prince Edward agreed to hold talks, and gave his consent to a truce. Talleyrand hurried back to King Jean, who had pitched his tent, a pavilion of vivid red silk, in the midst of the army. The cardinal reported that the English were ready to talk, and asked for the king's consent to a truce. The king refused at first; he was in bellicose mood once more, and had begun to suspect that Talleyrand might be playing some game of his own that would allow the prince to escape without surrendering or fighting. Members of his council, including Regnaud Chauveau, the firebrand Bishop of Châlons, spoke vehemently against a truce and urged the king to fight. But Talleyrand spoke again, soothing the king's suspicions. All would be well, he said; he himself would conduct the negotiations with the prince. King Jean agreed to a truce to last until the following morning, during which more detailed negotiations could take place.[20]

A truce was declared, to last until the following morning. Negotiating parties rode out to meet in the no-man's land between the two armies. The English were represented by Warwick the marshal and the Earl of Suffolk, along with Bartholomew Burghersh, John Chandos and James Audley; the French were led by Peter de la Fôret, the Archbishop of Rouen and Clermont the marshal, with the Comte de Tancarville and Geoffroi de Charny among their attendants.[21]

Talleyrand, chairing the discussions, now set out the peace plan he had been secretly devising. Its terms and conditions were not particularly favourable to the English. They should surrender all the towns and castles they had captured from the French over the last three years; they would pay an indemnity of around £60,000 for damage done to French property by the raids and *chevauchées*; and a marriage would be arranged between the Prince of Wales and one of King Jean's daughters (the eldest of whom was only 12 at the time). About the only thing the French would have to concede was the release of Charles of Navarre from prison.

On the English side Warwick, his tongue no doubt firmly wedged in his cheek, promised to think things over, but he warned the meeting that the prince had no power to make a binding agreement of this sort without the consent of King Edward. The French for their part were growing angry; they had been promised a negotiated surrender, not a vague discussion about a peace process that might or might not happen some time in the future. Geoffroi de Charny came forward with a proposal of his own: a trial by combat. Let each side send out a hundred knights, said Charny, to fight against each other, with victory going to the winners. Perhaps with a premonition of the battle and slaughter to come, Charny added: 'I think it will be best so, and that God will be gracious to us if the battle be avoided in which so many valiant men will be slain.'[22]

This was a typical chivalric gesture, but Warwick was in no mood for chivalry. What do you think you will gain by this? he asked Charny bluntly. You already have four times more men-at-arms than we do; if you believe in victory, come and fight us. We will be waiting for you. 'No other option do I know, no other will I accord,' said Warwick. 'May God support the right, where he sees it the stronger.'[23]

The meeting was becoming bad-tempered. In an incident that recalls one of those staring matches between pugilists at press conference on the eve of a boxing match, Jean de Clermont approached John Chandos. Both men had very similar coats of arms, and Clermont had taken offence at this. 'How long since you have taken it upon you to wear my arms?' he demanded.

'It is you who have mine,' said Chandos, rather childishly, 'for it is as much mine as yours.'

'I deny that,' snapped Clermont. 'And if it were not for the truce between us, I would soon show you that you have no right to wear it.'

'You will find me tomorrow in the field,' said Chandos, 'ready prepared to defend, and to prove by force of arms, that it is as much mine as yours.'[24] It was probably at this point that Warwick called his men away; there was nothing to be gained by further discussion now.

Both negotiating parties returned to their respective camps, Talleyrand riding to join the French. In the red silk pavilion, he presented the peace plan to King Jean. The king rejected the entire plan out of hand, and the Bishop of Châlons flew into a rage, denouncing the English as perfidious liars who could never be trusted, and pointing out that King Edward would never agree to the plan. The entire meeting had been a waste of time. The rest of the council agreed. Talleyrand pleaded with the king to at least extend the truce after the following morning; Jean refused.

Night fell over the forests and fields around Nouaillé. The French, well provisioned from Poitiers and their own supply train, dined well and continued to make ready for battle. The English remained in their camp, cold and hungry. The prince did not dare send out foraging parties into the wider countryside for fear that they might fall into French ambushes; he could not afford to lose a single man.

The day of confrontation had at last arrived. Talleyrand had done his best, and he had failed. Tomorrow, beyond doubt, there would be a battle.

CHAPTER 8

'No Break in War's Grim Madness'

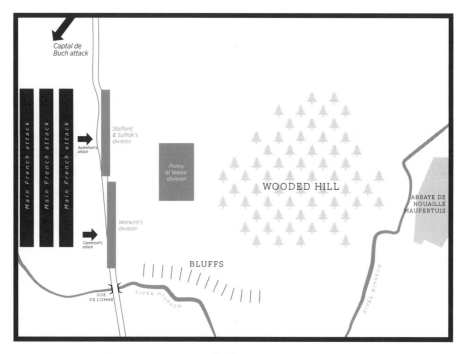

Battle of Poitiers

19 September, dawn

'The cardinal has betrayed us!'

Monday morning dawned cloudy and windy. The English army roused from the fields and hedgerows where it had slept, and made a meagre breakfast.

The shortage of food was still acute and most of the men had to make do with cold pottage, and probably not much of that. Horses were led down to the Miosson to be watered, and men began preparing their weapons and armour. The Prince of Wales and his senior commanders, who had snatched a few hours' sleep in the night, watched the fields to the north and west for signs of movement. It was then about six in the morning; in another hour, the truce negotiated by Cardinal Talleyrand would expire.

For the moment, there was little that Prince Edward could do but wait. His defensive position was chosen and prepared, his army as ready as it would ever be. Yesterday during the negotiations, he thought he had sensed that the French were reluctant to attack. They were willing to entertain negotiations, to discuss the idea of a longer truce. If the French king accepted Talleyrand's peace plan, then the English army was free to continue its march back to Bordeaux. But, it had been clear that some of the negotiators, especially the old warrior Geoffroi de Charny, disapproved of the truce. They wanted a fight. Well, if they wanted one, Prince Edward would give it to them. But for the moment the ball was in the French court.

Talleyrand returned just after sunrise, riding with his entourage down the road from La Cardinière. The English sentinels let him pass, and the cardinal rode on through the English camp. Here he saw men sharpening swords, donning their armour, checking the fletchings of arrows, harnessing horses, hitching wagons to teams. He was exhausted; he had been engaged in shuttle diplomacy between the French and English camps for the last 24 hours, and had slept hardly at all.

When the cardinal was brought before Prince Edward, his message was short and blunt. He had failed. The offer of peace had been withdrawn entirely. The Bishop of Châlons and the other hawks in the French council had prevailed, and King Jean was ready to fight. 'I cannot by any means pacify the king of France,' Talleyrand said bitterly. 'There must be a battle.'[1]

The prince received the news with outward calm. It had always been his intention to fight, he said steadily, 'and may God defend the right'.[2] At this point Talleyrand's sense of failure began to overwhelm him. He was a Frenchman by birth; but he had spent many years in England and knew the country and its people. Yes, the peace plan may have been designed in part to bolster his own reputation, but he had genuinely believed that peace was possible. Now he had failed, and people he knew and respected on both sides would die. His face streaked with tears, he mounted his horse and rode away towards Poitiers.

The English watched him go. They saw too that several men of his entourage, led by his nephew Robert of Durazzo and the Knight of St John, Heredia, turned their horses away from the cardinal and rode back to join the French army.[3] For the English, this was proof that Talleyrand had never been sincere in his desire to make peace. His own men were fighting for the French; the negotiations and offer of a truce had been a French trick. A murmur of anger ran through the ranks: 'The cardinal has betrayed us!'[4]

What the English soldiers did not know was that at that same moment, Talleyrand was being damned in very similar terms in the French army by Audrehem and Geoffroi de Charny. They believed that the cardinal's attempt to make peace had merely bought time for the English and allowed them to rest and prepare for the forthcoming battle.

The prince now gathered his commanders. The truce had expired; the waiting was over. What would the French do next? The bulk of the French army was still invisible to the northwest, concealed by the hedges and woods and rolling ground. The first step must be to reconnoitre the French lines. Another scouting party was sent out, but instead of sending the veteran Chandos or another experienced knight, the prince gave the task to two young men, Eustache d'Abrichecourt from Hainault and Petiton de Curton from Entre-deux-Mers in Gascony. Abrichecourt was a relatively junior member of the prince's household, though his elder brother Sanchet had been a founder member of the Order of the Garter and a member of the royal household until dying of the Black Death in 1349. It is likely that Abrichecourt begged to be given the post of scout in order to prove his knightly valour, and the prince, who had a soft spot for young men wanting to win reputations, accepted. Curton, whom we saw earlier in the thick of the action outside Romorantin, may well have been chosen for the same reason.

Abrichecourt and Curton trotted out from the English lines down the Poitiers road towards the French camp. They soon ran into trouble, in the form of a party of heavily armoured German men-at-arms from the contingent of the Count of Nassau-Weilburg. The sensible course of action would have been to circle around the Germans and try to get closer to the French army. Instead, a red mist descended over Abrichecourt. Without thinking about the consequences or counting the odds against him, he lowered his lance and spurred his horse into a charge. One of the Germans, a knight called Ludwig von Coucibras,[5] saw him coming, lowered his own lance and rode hard towards the oncoming Hainaulter.

The two knights met with a clash of steel, lances striking armoured bodies and throwing both men from the saddle. Coucibras, wounded in the shoulder, lay struggling and unable to get to his feet; Abrichecourt, less seriously hurt, scrambled up and rushed forward to take the other man captive. He then looked up to find himself surrounded by five more German men-at-arms, glowering at him through their visors and commanding him to drop his weapons. There was no genteel chivalry here; Abrichecourt was dragged ignominiously back to the French camp and tied to a cart so he could not escape, and his captors rode away to join their comrades.[6] Curton was also taken prisoner, either at the same time or shortly after.[7]

19 September, early morning

'You shall see me act like a true knight'

While waiting for the scouts to return, Prince Edward and his commanders deployed their own men. As they only had about 6,000 fighting men – casualties in battle, accidents and illness had worn the original force away to this number – arraying for battle did not take long.

The position had been chosen with care, and its choosing owed much to English military experience over the past two decades. The front of the English line formed up behind a dense hedgerow, running roughly from northeast to southwest. The hedge was several feet thick in places; the enemy could force their way through this, but only with difficulty.[8] The right-hand, northeastern end of the hedgerow was a little higher than the left, southwestern portion. There were also two gaps in the hedgerow, one in the eastern half of the line where the main road ran from Poitiers to Nouaillé, the other about 400 yards to the west where a rough track ran from the hamlet of La Cardiniére down to the Miosson, crossing the latter by the ford at the Gué de l'Omme. This western gap was blocked by overturned carts; the eastern gap, for reasons that are not entirely clear, was left open.[9]

In front of the hedgerow was a vineyard, the rows of vines running down the hill and roughly parallel to the English front; in order to attack, the French would have to force their way through these rows of vines.[10] Beyond the vineyard was pasture land, dotted with scrub. As already noted, gentle undulations in the ground meant that the two armies did not have each other in line of sight, despite their camps being little more than a mile apart. Among the vines were pitfalls and other obstacles dug by the army the previous day to further hamper the enemy's cavalry. It seems clear from these obstacles and the dispositions in general that the prince and his commanders expected an attack by massed mounted men-at-arms in the grand manner of Crécy.

The left, slightly lower flank of the line was guarded by a steep bank, below which were the marshes along the Miosson. It had rained recently, and the marshes were flooded and impassable, certainly to cavalry or heavily armoured foot soldiers. On the right, higher flank where the hedgerow ended, the English had dug a line of trenches to block the passage of warhorses and also made a barricade from more overturned wagons. Immediately to the rear of the main position was the Fôret de Nouaillé, a dense woodland stretching south and east up and over the hill towards the abbey and village. As at Crécy, the English plan was that if the French should break through the front line, the army would retreat and find cover in the woods where mounted French men-at-arms would find it difficult to pursue them.

The army was divided, as it had been throughout the campaign, into three divisions. The first was commanded by the marshal, Thomas Beauchamp, Earl of Warwick, with John de Vere, Earl of Oxford, as his able and efficient deputy. Reginald Cobham, that reliable old warhorse, was posted here too, and it seems likely that this division also included Ralph and Richard Stafford, and young Maurice de Berkeley, whose father had been at Crécy and died at the siege of Calais. This division held the left of the front line, from the marshes up past the point where the road to Gué de l'Homme passed through the hedgerow. It consisted of about a thousand men-at-arms, most dismounted and positioned behind the hedgerow, and perhaps 6 or 700 archers. Part of these were deployed on Warwick's left flank; the rest probably in line behind the men-at-arms, with a concentration around the hedgerow gap.[11] Warwick also had some of the army's thousand or so Gascon foot soldiers, lightly armoured and armed with spears; these were commanded by the Gascon nobleman Guilhem-Sans de Pommiers. Some of the other Gascon lords and knights were posted here too, including those hardened fighters Augier de Mussidan and Aimeri de Montferrand, and the lords of Duras and Rauzan.

On their right was the second division, led by the prince's friend and near contemporary, William Montacute, Earl of Salisbury, and the older and more experienced Robert Ufford, Earl of Suffolk. Ralph Bassett, John Willoughby and John Greystoke were among the knights and barons posted to this division, along with several knights from Flanders and Hainault, and Denys de Morbecque the French exile. This division was of about the same strength, a thousand dismounted men-at-arms, 6 or 700 archers and a few hundred Gascon spearmen. The archers of Salisbury and Suffolk's division were posted on higher ground slightly behind the line, enabling them to see – and shoot – over the men-at-arms to their front.

Behind these, acting as reserve, was the Prince of Wales's own division, of roughly the same strength as the other two. The prince commanded this division which also included his own household, his trusted advisors and servitors: John Chandos his confidante and friend, Bartholomew Burghersh,

Walter Wodelond the standard-bearer, James Audley the ever-valiant, Richard Stafford, Baldwin Botetourt, Alan Cheyne, John Kentwode the prince's esquire, John Wingfield, Baldwin Bereford, Roger de la Warre, Roger Cotesford, the brothers Edmund and Thomas Despenser, Frank Benhale who was a veteran of several campaigns, Richard Bembridge, old John Sully of Iddesleigh in Devon, Matthew Gurney the murderer, and Hugh Calveley who would later go on to win notoriety as the lieutenant of Robert Knollys in the free companies.[12]

Most of the men-at-arms dismounted, sending their horses back to the rear with grooms and pages holding their bridles. Two parties remained mounted for the moment. The first was the prince and his immediate household; the second was a party of 80 Gascon men-at-arms led by the Captal de Buch and including Bernard-Ezi d'Albret and his kinsmen, with around a hundred archers mounted on ponies. This was a change from previous tactics; King Edward had held back no such mounted reserve at Crécy or Halidon Hill, and it is not clear what prompted the prince to take this decision. Perhaps the Captal and some of his men were unused to fighting on foot and Edward decided they would do better to stay on horseback; or perhaps some tactical sixth sense told him that a mounted reserve might come in useful. Whatever the reason, this proved to be a stroke of genius.

The army stood ready along the hedgerows, watching the vineyard for signs of French movement, in foul mood. The men were hungry, tired and grumbling, still angry over the supposed treachery of Cardinal Talleyrand. They knew that their little army was badly outnumbered, and they knew too that the enemy's strength was growing steadily; yesterday alone, more than a thousand men-at-arms had ridden in from the north to join the French army.[13] Now, some of the English and Gascons questioned their leaders. Why had so many men been left behind in Gascony? Why weren't those men here now? By weakening the army for the defence of Gascony, the commanders had put all their lives at risk.[14]

These rumours reached the prince's ears, and shook his resolve. He was only 26, and this was his first major battle as a commander. He was about to face the full might of the chivalry of France. True, he had faced that chivalry before, and seen it destroyed in an evening at Crécy; but the English army at Crécy had been stronger and, crucially, had many more archers. Edward had fewer than 2,000 longbowmen, which did not seem like nearly enough to confront the 10,000 men-at-arms Jean had at his disposal. At Crécy the troops had also trusted their experienced leader, the prince's father King Edward III. But the young prince, though generally admired and respected for his personal courage and generosity, had yet to be tested in a full-scale battle. The raids and skirmishes of the summer and the previous autumn were not the same thing. The prince had to reassure his men that he was as good a commander as his father.

He did so by taking a leaf from his father's book. Just as King Edward had done before Crécy, the prince now toured the army, riding at the front of his household with Wodelond the standard-bearer behind him, the dragon banner of Wales streaming in the wind. As he passed down the ranks he spoke to every contingent in turn, paying special attention to the archers and Gascon foot soldiers, who were probably the loudest grumblers. No one wrote down his words at the time, and Geoffrey le Baker, writing a few years later, puts into his mouth a long and flowery speech which Baker himself admits he simply copied from Roman examples.[15] Froissart's version of the speech is simpler, and probably comes closer to the truth:

> Now, my gallant fellows, we are a small body when compared to the army of our enemies. Do not let us be cast down on that account, for victory does not always follow numbers, but where the Almighty God pleases to bestow it. If, through good fortune, the day shall be ours, we will gain the greatest honour and glory in this world: if the contrary should happen and we be slain, I have a father and beloved brethren alive, and you all have some relations or good friends, who will be sure to revenge our deaths. I therefore entreat of you to exert yourselves, and combat manfully; for, if it please God and St. George, you shall see me this day act like a true knight.[16]

The speech (if that is what the prince said) is a good one: the prince comes across as honest and sincere, realistic about the possibility of defeat and death, promising the troops that he will lead by example, and challenging them to follow him. Then, on a more practical note, the prince gave further orders. Everyone was to hold the line; no one was to leave his position to pursue the enemy unless ordered to do so by one of the senior commanders. Also, the prince ordered that no prisoners were to be taken. As at Crécy 10 years earlier, the army could not afford to spare men to guard captives. The prince may already have guessed that King Jean was giving a similar order to his own army.

The men were reassured, but the prince still had his private doubts. Time was passing, and his two scouts had not returned. There was no sign of the French moving into position. Had they indeed had second thoughts? Would they fail to attack? In that case, there was nothing to be gained by standing here; he may as well start withdrawing over the Miosson and continue his march south.[17] In the end Prince Edward decided to hedge his bets. The army would stay in position but the slow-moving baggage train, rich with plunder taken earlier in the campaign, should be sent over the ford to the far side of the river, ready to move on in case the retreat should resume. He ordered

Warwick to mount some of his men-at-arms and escort the wagons down to the Gué de l'Homme.

If creating a mounted reserve was a stroke of genius, then moving the baggage wagons was a serious mistake. The wagons contained not just plunder and army stores, but also the reserve stocks of arrows for the archers. Although the archers carried full quivers – typically, 48 arrows per man when a battle was expected – this would not be enough to see them through prolonged fighting.

'The banners were unfurled in the wind'

A mile away, the glistening red silk pavilion of the King of France rippled in the wind, his personal standard with the lilies of France floating overhead. As soon as morning mass had been said, the king called his senior officers to attend him. Present were the king's brother the Duc d'Orléans; the grand chamberlain Pierre, Duc de Bourbon, and his brother Jacques, the former constable; Brienne, the current constable, along with the two marshals, Audrehem and Clermont; and as many as 20 counts, barons and knights including veterans such as Geoffroi de Charny and Eustache de Ribemont, who had fought at Crécy and St-Venant, whose father had died there. The Count of Saarbrücken was there to represent the allied contingents. The Scottish leader William, Lord Douglas was present, and so was that wandering soldier of fortune Robert of Durazzo, about to ride to his last battlefield.[18]

The mood in the pavilion was raw. French scouts had seen the Prince of Wales's banner moving in the distance, and reported this back to headquarters.[19] Dispute erupted over what this movement might portend. Audrehem insisted that the English were retreating and that the French must advance at once lest the enemy should escape over the Miosson. Clermont and William Douglas argued that this was a false assumption, and that all the evidence suggested the English were preparing to make a stand. Voices were raised, and the tensions between the two factions started to boil over. Sensibly, someone then suggested a further reconnaissance of the English lines to ascertain the true picture, and Eustache de Ribemont, Jean de Landas and Guiscard de Beaujeu were dispatched to scout the English position.

Unlike the madcap young English scouts, the experienced Ribemont and his companions carried out their mission and returned quickly to the council. Their news was discouraging. The English were not retreating. Instead, they had taken up a very strong position behind the hedgerow, with plenty of obstacles to their front, dismounting their men-at-arms and posting archers on the flanks. 'It will be no easy matter to defeat them,' Ribemont concluded.[20]

Ribemont was widely respected, and the quarrelling marshals calmed down long enough to listen. The king then asked Ribemont how he would set about attacking the English. Ribemont, with a nod to William Douglas, explained his plan. The first task must be to neutralise the archers. Small parties of mounted men, heavily armoured and on barded horses to protect against arrows, should dash straight at these, scattering them or at least drawing the fire. Crossbowmen should advance in support of these mounted parties, giving what we would now call covering fire.

The rest of the French men-at-arms should then dismount and advance on foot. Their armour should be proof against English arrows except at very close range, and they would also find it easier to negotiate the pits and obstacles in front of the English position, and to batter down the hedge so as to engage the enemy. Douglas concurred with this advice; he may even have been the one to suggest fighting on foot in the first place. Scottish armies fighting on foot had scored victories over the English, notably at Bannockburn.[21]

At this point there was another outcry, and some of those present described these tactics as 'shocking madness' (in the later words of Geoffrey le Baker), and urged the king not to listen to Ribemont and Douglas. But Jean, even though he had not been present, was like many other Frenchmen scarred still by the appalling carnage at Crécy when the French men-at-arms and their horses had been cut down in their hundreds. He knew that the new tactics made sense. If the English archers could be neutralised, the French could advance without hindrance; and even if some of the archers remained in action, without their vulnerable horses the armoured French men-at-arms would present much more difficult targets.

And, once the French had crossed the killing ground in front of the English line, their greater numbers should more than offset the English advantage of terrain. Jean had 10,000 men-at-arms under his command, more than the entire English army, plus another 3–4,000 crossbowmen and foot soldiers.

Thus it was decided. Instead of the traditional three divisions, the French army would attack in four waves. The first of these would consist of two companies of mounted men-at-arms, each of about 200 men and led by the two marshals. Clermont and Audrehem went out and toured the army, picking men with the heaviest armour and barding, or horse armour, to protect the heads and chests of their mounts. (Only a few wealthy men could afford barding; most horses in the army remained unarmoured.) The Counts of Nassau-Weilberg, Nidau and Saarbrücken with their German and Swiss knights were among those selected for these companies.[22] To these chosen men would fall the dubious honour of attacking the English archers head on, and hoping that their armour was as strong as the armourers claimed it was.

The dismounted men-at-arms were then divided into three divisions. The first of these, probably of about 3,000 men, was nominally commanded by the king's younger brother, the Duc d'Orléans.[23] Real authority rested with the Constable of France, the Duke of Athens. Robert of Durazzo was with this division, as were William Douglas and his brother Archibald and their 200 Scottish followers, Pierre de Bourbon and his brother Jacques, and the counts of Alençon, Eu, Longueville, Dammartin and Sancerre. Many of the lesser knights came from Picardy or the Bourbonnais, or were local men from Poitou.

The second battalion was commanded by the 18-year-old Dauphin Charles, the king's eldest son, with a knight named Tristan de Maguelais carrying his personal standard. Again, the actual command of this division was vested in the Dauphin's guardians, Jean de Landas and Theobald de Bodenay and the lord of St-Venant. Two of the Dauphin's younger brothers, Louis and Jean, the Comte de Poitiers, were also posted here. We know very little else about the composition of this division, but it too probably numbered about 3,000 men. The final division, originally numbering around 2,000 men-at-arms and supported by more crossbowmen, was led by King Jean himself, accompanied by his youngest son, the 14-year-old Philippe.[24] Geoffroi de Charny, the veteran knight and symbol of chivalric virtue, was placed at the king's side. His task was to bear the great battle standard, the Oriflamme.

At first glance it was hard to find the king, not because he was inconspicuous in his fine armour, but because 19 other men wore identical armour and devices on their shields.[25] These men were decoys, whose purpose in times of danger was to lure the enemy away from the king – if necessary, at the cost of their own lives.

And now, writes Chandos Herald, 'The banners and pennants were unfurled in the wind, purple and gold and ermine; trumpets, drums, horns and bugles rang throughout the camp.' The movement of marching men, he says, made the ground shake.[26] The French nobles and knights had parted with their beloved warhorses, sent back to Poitiers for their own safety, but their banners and pennants and painted shields gleamed as brightly as ever in the fitful sunlight. They were a magnificent sight, and when King Jean reviewed his troops his confidence was high. Accompanied by Geoffroi de Charny, carrying the great blood-red and gold battle standard, the Oriflamme, he spoke to his men. The English would be crushed, he said, and no prisoners were to be taken save for the Prince of Wales himself. Whoever captured the prince should bring his prisoner directly to the king. Jean did not just want to defeat his enemy; he wanted to humiliate and destroy him.

This day would belong to France. The humiliation of Crécy was about to be avenged.

19 September, late morning

'By St-Denis, you are very bold!'

The sounds of horns and trumpets would have carried clearly to the English camp, alerting Prince Edward and his commanders to the impending attack. The English had done all they could do. Warwick and his horsemen were still escorting the vulnerable baggage train down to the river and across the ford at Gué de l'Homme. The rest of the army stood to, Salisbury and Suffolk's division and the rest of Warwick's in the forward line, the prince's division a little to the rear, with the mounted reserve standing by. They gripped their weapons and waited, trying to ignore the rumbling in their empty stomachs.

The prince himself took up a post on a low rise in ground behind the main line. This gave him a view down over the hedgerow and vineyard and the pastureland beyond. He and his household could hear the tramp of marching men, the thud of boots accompanied by an incessant rattle and clank of metal armour. They saw the first bright banners and pennants come into view, and then over the low hill to the northwest came two companies of mounted men, bright shields and surcoats and armour all gleaming with colour. The prince's heralds would have been able to pick out the coats of arms of the enemy, and name the nobles and knights riding towards the English lines. And then, behind the cavalry, there came long glittering ranks of men, thousands of men-at-arms on foot. Each man carried a lance, its butt cut off and shortened to about 5 feet, so that the great marching array bristled with spears.

In front of the prince's position, the English line rippled into motion. English and Gascon men-at-arms and foot soldiers presented their own spears, while the archers tossed blades of grass into the air to gauge the strength of the wind, then stood with bows strung and ready, facing the enemy. Messengers went racing away to find Warwick and bring his men back to the battlefield.

In the French vanguard, the two marshals were arguing once again. The plan depended on the mounted men receiving close support from Orléans's division behind them, but upon seeing the enemy Arnoul d'Audrehem lost patience and urged Clermont to move faster. He was still obsessed with the notion that the English were retreating. Hurry, he urged Clermont, if we do not attack now, we will lose them. 'You are in too much of a hurry,' Clermont responded grimly. 'Do not be so hasty; we shall get there in good time.' 'Your delay will make us lose them,' Audrehem retorted.

Something in Clermont snapped. 'By St-Denis, marshal, you are very bold,' he snarled, 'but not so bold. Your lance will never come near my horse's arse', meaning that Audrehem would never be able to catch up with him, and probably also implying something about his rival marshal's sexual proclivities. Then he spurred his horse to a gallop, yelling to his men to charge.[27] Audrehem did the same. Nothing mattered to these two now but to reach the English line before the other. Away thundered the 400 horsemen, Audrehem's men veering down the track towards Warwick's division, Clermont and his followers racing down the Nouaillé road through the vineyard; and at 250 yards from the English position they saw archers on a low ridge behind the hedgerow, bows raised and arrows nocked.

Then the archers began to shoot.

'Ghastly strokes of warcraft'

Clermont's task was to charge and disperse the English archers on the flank of Salisbury's division, but a direct attack on these was clearly impossible; between him and the archers were the vineyard, the hedgerow and a line of English foot soldiers. Salisbury and Suffolk had used the ground well, eschewing the old tactical deployment of posting the archers out on the wing and instead deploying them behind his main line where they could shoot over the heads of the men in front. Instead, Clermont made for the gap in the hedgerow where the Nouaillé road passed through, hoping to burst through this, penetrate the line of English men-at-arms and then attack the archers.

Riding at full speed, his men endured a hail of arrows – the deadly arithmetic is that, with 600 archers shooting as many as 15 arrows a minute, Clermont's cavalry were deluged with arrows at a rate of 50 *per second* – but the heavy armour of horses and men held out. They reached the gap in the hedgerow and poured through, Clermont leading.

Salisbury counter-attacked. Leading his own dismounted men-at-arms and Gascons, he flung himself on the foremost riders. There ensued one of those terrible hack-and-slash fights where both sides cut each other to pieces, neither giving nor asking for quarter. The English archers continued to shoot at Clermont's men as they struggled to force their way through the hedge, and now at very close range the cold chisel heads of the arrows began to bite through even the toughest armour and barding. Horses and men went down, crashing to earth; some of the dismounted men ran forward to join the fight but others staggered away to the rear, their battle done.

Orléans's division was close behind, and crossbowmen ran forward to shoot at the English archers; 'the bolts from the crossbowmen flew even more thickly and frequently,'[28] says the chronicler Geoffrey le Baker, but the longbowmen with their higher rate of fire shot the crossbowmen to pieces and drove them back, before resuming their steady picking off of the rearmost men of Clermont's company. Shattered by arrows, their ranks sadly thinned, the surviving French broke and fled, leaving Clermont and the leaders trapped inside the hedge. Salisbury's men cut them down without mercy. Clermont was dragged from his horse and fell to the ground; lying winded on his back, he asked for quarter. None was given, and the spears came down. 'There he fell,' says the chronicler John of Fordun, 'together with all who came with him, overcome by the archers and other ghastly strokes of warcraft.'[29]

Audrehem too was stymied; Warwick's archers were equally unassailable behind the hedgerow. An unusual caution gripped Audrehem; he held his men back from the line, and although Warwick's archers shot a hail of arrows at them, the range was greater and their heavy armour prevented them suffering serious casualties. Baker records how 'the arrows shot were either broken to pieces or deflected up to the heavens' when they hit the French and German armour.[30] But if the archers could not stop Audrehem's horsemen, neither could the latter find a way through the hedgerow to get at the archers. A standoff ensued, Audrehem and his men enduring with some courage the deluge of arrows falling on them, while up from behind, clanking and jingling as they marched, came the men-at-arms of Orléans's division.

Whether by design or by chance, probably the latter, Audrehem's division was now masking the advance of the right flank of Orléans's division. Warwick's archers could neither shoot down the cavalry nor target the oncoming infantry. John de Vere, Earl of Oxford, commanding the English division in Warwick's continued absence, spotted the problem and hit on a bold solution. Calling on the archers to follow him, he ran around the left-hand end of the hedgerow and along the top of the bank above the marshes of the Miosson until they were almost level with Audrehem's company. From here they could shoot at the flanks and rear of the French cavalry; and significantly, the horses were only armoured on their chests and heads, and not on the rear.

Oxford directed his archers to shoot at the hindquarters of the horses. The effect was swift and terrible. 'The horses, smarting under the pain of their wounds, would not advance but turned about and, by their unruliness, threw their masters, who could not manage them, nor could those that had fallen get up again for the confusion.'[31] Some of the men-at-arms were trampled to death by their own horses. Audrehem's company reeled back towards Orléans's division. Audrehem and some others who had lost their mounts joined with these and renewed their attack; the rest fled.[32]

The attack of the marshals had been a bloody failure. But a much sterner test for both sides was about to begin.

'More lethal than the others'

With the French crossbowmen dispersed, the English archers could concentrate on the marching men-at-arms. But these were a different proposition from cavalry with vulnerable mounts.[33] Out on the wings, the archers did indeed tear holes in the French ranks; by some accounts the archers were ordered to shoot at the heads of the oncoming French, in hopes of finding weak spots in their visors or at the neck. But the French centre held. Crashing through the rows of vines, Orléans and the constable and their men reached the hedgerow. Some poured through the gap along the Nouaillé road; others began forcing their way through weak points in the hedgerow to left and right.

Warwick had by this point returned from the Gué de l'Omme, and Oxford had withdrawn his archers to their original post, but in fact Warwick's division was not heavily pressed. Acting on his own initiative, Warwick ordered the company who had escorted the wagons to remain on horseback rather than joining the line, while he waited to see how the battle developed. It was on Salisbury's men that the hardest blow fell. It may be that the marching French had veered instinctively towards the higher ground; it may also be that Brienne, the Constable, decided to break through on the English right (the French left) and then wheel and roll up the English line, driving the enemy into the marshes of the Miosson; we shall never know. The two lines clashed, and the fighting began once more.

'There was no break now in war's grim madness,' writes Geoffrey le Baker.[34] Every account speaks of a long and exhausting combat in which both sides strained and struggled, the French hacking at the hedgerow and the English hacking at them while arrows never ceased to rain. The noise, of men shouting and screaming in their death throes and the terrible, unceasing clang of metal on metal, was deafening. Brienne the Constable was killed; Robert of Durazzo was cut down; William Douglas was badly wounded and many of his Scots followers were killed; but the armoured flood rolled on and Salisbury's men were driven back by weight of numbers. There was danger that the line would break, but the Earl of Suffolk saved the day. Running along the line, he exhorted his men to stand their ground and directed the fire of the archers towards the points of greatest danger. The English rallied, the wavering stopped, but the French outnumbered them by three to one and the pressure continued to build.

Watching from higher ground, the Prince of Wales saw the danger and gave fresh orders. His own division threw itself forward in a violent counter-attack led Sir James Audley and his four valiant esquires: Dutton of Dutton, Delves of Doddington, Fowlehurst of Crewe and Hawkhurst of Wainhill. Years later, men who watched their attack still spoke of it with breathless awe. Utterly fearless, heedless of the risk to his own life, Audley and his followers hurled themselves on the French, and the rest of the division followed their lead. The French, stunned by the sheer audacity of the charge, lost impetus. They still outnumbered the English by three to two, but the impetus of the counterattack and the sheer fighting fury of Audley and his men stopped their advance and drove them back.

Yet still the fighting went on, and on. There is general agreement that this was a terrible fight; one French chronicle referred to the combat as 'more amazing, harder and more lethal than the others', referring presumably to the earlier charge of the marshals.[35] 'Man fought frenziedly against man,' says Baker, 'each one striving to bring death to his opponent so that he himself might live.' Packed together in dense ranks, the men in the front of the combat had no choice but to kill or be killed. James Audley, in the thick of the fighting, was wounded in the body, head and face but fought steadily on.

Slowly at first, then with increasing speed, the French line began to disintegrate, hammered apart by arrows and the hard-fighting English men-at-arms. Audrehem, now in command, remained resolute, encouraging his men to renew the attack, but the men were losing heart. More and more men in the rear ranks, lashed by arrows, turned and began to retreat, first individually, then in small groups. The second division, under the command of the Dauphin, was now coming up behind the first, but many of the Dauphin's men, seeing the first division dissolving into wreckage, turned and retreated too.[36] After a long and bloody fight of at least an hour's duration, the French line sagged back. In the waspish words of Geoffrey le Baker, 'They wisely took that cautious step which the French, invincible in argument, are accustomed to call not a flight, but a retreat to a fair position.'[37]

Baker singles out the French quite unfairly; this form of words has been used by every army in history, from Troy to Afghanistan. What is more, the French had fought hard and boldly. What triggered the final collapse was the decision by the Dauphin's minders to get him and his two brothers, Louis and Jean, off the battlefield and away from danger. Protesting, the young men were hustled away from the front; and when their men saw them go they concluded, not without reason, that the day was lost. They fell back from the hedgerow and retreated.

Down the hill, Warwick saw that the moment had come. The French were defeated; three divisions, one on horse and two on foot, had attacked and been thrown back in turn. Now the pursuit could begin. The marshal ordered his men to pull aside the barricade covering the gap in the hedges on the Gué de l'Omme track, and then led his armoured horsemen in thundering column towards the retreating French. The retreat became a rout. The French fled before the lances and hooves of Warwick's men-at-arms, back through the vineyard and over the rolling ground, the English skewering or riding down the hindmost. Many, including the Dauphin and the young princes and their escort, made straight for the safety of Poitiers. William Douglas also fled the field; wounded, he could fight no more, but in any case his loyalties had always been to Douglas first, Scotland second and everyone else a long way third. Hard fighter though he was, the Scottish baron had no qualms about ensuring his own safety.

Nor did the English have it all their own way. Young Maurice de Berkeley, anxious to prove himself, spotted the Dauphin's banners and charged towards them, apparently intent on single-handedly capturing the heir to the French throne. Instead he found himself alone and unsupported, surrounded by French men-at-arms. Berkeley fought like a tiger, but his lance shattered, his sword broke in his hand and he fell from his saddle. A Picard esquire named Jean de Hellenes stabbed Berkeley so hard that the sword passed through both his thighs, and the young knight collapsed to the ground, unable to move. He might well have been killed out of hand, but Jean de Hellenes disobeyed orders and spared his life. Berkeley was dragged away with the retreating French, a prisoner.[38]

Behind them, Warwick halted his pursuit. He had doubtless seen Berkeley's impulsive charge, but there was nothing he could do to rescue his errant knight. He had just realised his mistake. There were not three divisions to the French army, but four. And the fourth, larger and more formidable than the others, with the lilies of France and the Oriflamme floating above its ranks, was advancing steadily towards the English lines.

19 September, midday

'Alas, we are beaten!'

The Prince of Wales and his household watched as King Jean's division rolled over the distant ridge and began to march towards them. Hearts sank. Fatalities in the English line were surprisingly low, but there were many wounded; these had been laid out behind the hedgerow and were being given such medical care as was possible. Those men who remained upright were battered, bleeding and exhausted from more than an hour of hard fighting. The archers had salvaged what arrows they could from the field in front of them, pulling some from the still living bodies of men they had shot earlier, but even so they had only a handful of arrows left; and the supply wagons with the reserve stocks were on the far side of the Miosson a mile away. The greatest weapon of the English army, the longbow, had been all but neutralised. This time there would be no continuous storm of arrows, only a swift shower; and then nothing.

The French division marching towards them was huge. King Jean may have started the day with two thousand men-at-arms, but many hundreds from the other two divisions had rallied to the Oriflamme and now he had perhaps 4,000 men under his command. There were more crossbowmen on the flanks too. The core of the division was fresh and unwearied, and the king himself led them. As the tramping, clanking men-at-arms drew closer, someone in the Prince of Wales's household cried out in fear: 'Alas, we are beaten!'[39]

'Miserable coward!' the prince snarled at him. 'Are you suggesting that I can be defeated while I am still alive?'[40] He rallied his exhausted and shocked men, but he realised that they were in no fit state to defend against this final assault. This time, the French would undoubtedly roll over them. The prince knew the tactical plan that had been used by the English to win battle after battle: Halidon Hill, Morlaix, Neville's Cross, Crécy. But those tactics would no longer work. He threw the plan away, and called instead for the last thing the French would expect: a counterattack.

There was not a moment to lose. The French were advancing in formation, crashing through the battered vineyard. Edward summoned the Captal de Buch and gave his orders. The Gascon was to take his 80 men-at-arms and a hundred archers around the flank of the French army, using the woods as a screen to shield them. When they were in position to attack the French rear, the banner of St George would be dipped. The prince then called his household and ordered them to mount, and he also sent orders to Warwick, freshly returned to the English lines, to keep his own mounted force ready. In addition to Buch's force, he had about 400 men mounted and ready to charge.[41] James Audley, weak and bleeding from his wounds, nonetheless mounted his horse and made ready, protected by his esquires.

Closer and closer came the French, and once again the arrows began to fly. The French crossbowmen moved forward, and, in the words of Geoffrey le Baker, the thick darkness of their bolts brought grim night to the battlefield; but once again their fire seems to have been remarkably ineffective. However, the English longbowmen were forced to expend precious arrows killing these pests and driving the survivors away. They turned their attention back to the advancing men-at-arms, but now bowman after bowman had empty quivers and the hail of arrows began to slacken. Triumphant, shouting their war cry of 'Montjoie St-Denis!' the French surged towards the hedgerow.

The English men-at-arms and Gascons fought desperately. The archers, out of arrows, seized whatever weapons they could find and threw themselves into the fray as well, unarmoured men using their greater agility to seize and drag down armoured knights and kill them. There are reports of spears being hurled through the air, suggesting some archers had picked up the lances of Frenchmen killed in the earlier fight and were throwing them back at the enemy. For the moment the French were held, but it was only a matter of time before their greater numbers began to tell.

A little behind the line the Prince of Wales sat on his horse, while fighting raged across the face of Salisbury and Suffolk's division below him. His eyes scanned the distant fields, waiting for the signal.

'Banners, advance!'

The Captal de Buch and his 180 men rode at first towards the rear of the English position, back towards the forest of Nouaillé. Their movement was seen by some of the English in the front line, who, unaware of the prince's intentions, thought the Gascons were fleeing the field. But as soon as he was out of sight of the French, Buch changed course. The ground around the battlefield undulates only very gently, but there was enough cover from woods and contours in the ground to allow his men to ride unseen. Hastily, knowing that every minute counted now, they made their way around the left flank of the French army. They heard the clamour of fighting break out as the king's division crashed into the English lines.

This was the most dangerous moment in the battle. If the Gascons got lost, came out in the wrong position or failed to find the battlefield at all, then the Prince of Wales's plan would fail, and very probably his army would be crushed. The prince was fortunate in his choice of the Captal de Buch as leader. Brave as a lion, highly experienced and utterly reliable, he was one of the few men who could have executed that difficult, high-speed flanking movement and bring his men to precisely the spot where they could do the most damage. Reaching the slope above the French camp, Buch wheeled his men and rode southeast towards the sounds of battle. Coming out onto the low ridge that Jean's men had crossed earlier, he saw the French directly ahead and gave the order to make the signal.[42]

The prince and his followers saw the movement: a fleck of white crossed with red, the banner of St George dipped. His own dragon standard dipped in response. The prince gave one more order: 'Banners, advance!'

Horns and drums sounded the charge. Down the gentle slope the English horsemen galloped, and Salisbury's men disengaged and parted to make way for them. James Audley once again led the way, the prince and his household close behind. They collided with the dismounted French men-at-arms and scattered them, armoured men skittled over by the onrushing horses. The French wavered before the assault; and then, with cries of 'Guienne! Guienne!' the Captal de Buch and his horsemen struck the French array from the rear. At the same time the archers who had accompanied the Captal began to shoot, using their limited supply of arrows to deadly effect as they shot the French men-at-arms down from behind.

The French fought hard at first. The prince and Warwick and their men did not have things all their own way; Audley was wounded again and fell from his saddle, and his esquires dragged him to cover, shielding him with their own bodies. Others fell. But Buch and his Gascons were hacking the French line apart from the rear, and the issue could not be long in doubt. Once again a steady trickle of men broke away from King Jean's division; once again, the trickle turned into a stream. Assailed from two sides, the king's division broke, and the dense ranks dissolved into a chaotic mass of men stumbling over the fields, encumbered by their armour, hoping desperately to outrun the English. They failed. The English horsemen rode over them, and the more lightly armoured English and Gascon foot soldiers pursued them like furies, and caught them.

19 September, early afternoon

'The blood of servants and the blood of kings'

Now the real slaughter began.

When the French broke for the final time, the English and Gascons left their positions behind the hedges and launched in pursuit. They probably did so without orders, but they recognised that this time the French really were defeated. Now the time had come, for those who were so minded, to take prisoners and make what profit they could; for others, crazed by battle, it was a time to kill.[43]

The walls of Poitiers were the first objective for the fleeing French. If they could reach the city and shut the gates behind them, they could keep out the English. Astonishingly, quite a few of them, on foot and encumbered by

80–100 pounds of armour, managed to run the 4 miles to Poitiers in advance of the English. It is probable that the English horsemen were impeded by the sheer numbers of fugitives in their way, and could not fight their way through to reach the gates in time.

But when the first French fugitives reached Poitiers they found to their horror that the people of the city, fearing that the English might break in, had already slammed and bolted the gates. Some of the fleeing men, those that could, ran on past the city. Others were caught in the open ground outside the walls when the English horsemen arrived. For them, there was no escape. Most were slaughtered on the causeway outside the town, the Seigneur de Pons and Guiscard d'Angle among them; a few, such as the Vicomte de Rochechouart and the seigneurs of Partenay, Saintonge and Montendre – the better-armed and better-armoured and therefore most likely to be rich – were taken prisoner.[44]

Other English horsemen overran the French camp, and among other things they set free young Eustache d'Abrichecourt, untying him from his cart. Abrichecourt lost no time in finding a sword and joining in the fray. For although the king's division had collapsed, there was still hard fighting in the fields later known as the Champs d'Alexandre, overlooking the Moisson. Here most of the third French division had been corralled, cut off from Poitiers by the marauding horsemen, hemmed in by the rest of the English army.

The battle turned now into a series of savage little combats, many of them man-to-man as the French fought to get away. Some managed to do so. The French knight Edouard de Roucy, retreating from the field, was challenged by an English pursuer to turn and fight. Roucy did so, hitting his enemy with a blow on the helmet that stunned him and knocked him to the ground. Putting his sword point to the Englishman's throat, Roucy presented him with a simple choice: surrender or die. The Englishman surrendered, and the audacious Roucy managed to get himself and his captive away safely from the field.[45]

Most French knights and nobles were less fortunate. Scattered, separated from their fellows, they were set upon by Englishmen hunting in packs. The lightly armed and unarmoured English archers were terrible foes; alone, they could not match an armoured man-at-arms, but in groups of three or four they could drag their man down and capture or dispatch him. The fighting was savage. 'Banners tottered and bearers fell,' writes Baker. He continues his gory account:

> Some Frenchmen trod on their own poured-out entrails, others spat out teeth, many were fixed to the ground [i.e., impaled], and others who were standing were missing their arms, which had been cut off. Dying men rolled about in the blood of others or moaned at their weights which had fallen on them, and as their proud souls left their feeble bodies, they

uttered dreadful groans. The blood of servants and the blood of kings ran together in one current and, empurpling the streams of the neighbourhood, fed the fishes on rare nectar.[46]

Somewhere in that melee, the Constable's brother, Pierre de Bourbon, was killed. So too were Guiscard de Beaujeu and Jean de Landas, two of the knights who had ridden out to scout that morning, and the Bishop of Châlons, his ecclesiastical dignity offering no protection.

Some were taken prisoner. The counts of Vaudemont, Genville and Vendôme were among those permitted to lay down their arms. The marshal, Arnoul d'Audrehem, was probably captured here too. Others, badly wounded and unable to fight, were also granted mercy; the Archpriest, Arnault de Cervolles, was one of these, and so was the Seigneur de Pompadour, ancestor of the later mistress of Louis XV. As greedy as they were deadly, some of the English did not even stay to guard their prisoners but simply accepted their surrender and rushed off to find more. The Comte de Dammartin was taken prisoner in the rout by a Gascon esquire. This is his story in his own words:

> He called on me to surrender, and I did so at once. I gave him my word so that he would protect me. He said that I should be quite safe and need have no fear. Then he tried to take off my bascinet [helmet]. When I begged him to leave it, he answered that he could not properly protect me unless he took it off. So he took it off, and my gauntlets as well. As he did so, another man came up and cut the strap of my sword [i.e., the belt holding the scabbard] so that it fell to the ground. I told the squire to take the sword, for I should prefer him to have it than anyone else. The esquire once more demanded my fealty that I would be his faithful prisoner whatever the result of the day might be, and I gave it to him in such wise that he should save me. He said I should be quite safe and have no fear. Then he made me mount his horse and handed me over to the keeping of a man of his, and thus he left me.
>
> But as soon as he had gone, this man abandoned me and made off. Then another Gascon came up and demanded my pledge [to surrender]. I answered that I was already a prisoner, but all the same I gave him my word, simply in order that he would protect me. He took an escutcheon from my coat armour and then abandoned me like the last man. I shouted after him that since he was deserting me, I would pledge myself to anyone else who might come up and be willing to protect me. 'Protect yourself, if you can', he shouted back. Another man, who belonged to Sir John Blaunkminster, then appeared and demanded my pledge. I answered that I had already been captured by two people, but I gave him my word so that he would protect me. This man stayed with me, guarded men, and eventually brought me to the Earl of Salisbury.[47]

There is perhaps a bleak humour to Dammartin's account, but there is horror too; in his words we get an echo of the feelings of a man alone, unarmed and helpless on a bloody battlefield, surrounded by men who did not care if he lived or died, while others swept the field killing indiscriminately. One wonders how many others, abandoned like Dammartin, did not survive.

Here and there, little groups of men held out. One hard-fighting little knot of men included Eustache de Ribemont, along with Guillaume de Montagu, Louis de Melval and Pierre de Buffiere. They fought desperately, and Ribemont and Montagu and the Seigneur de la Tour were killed before the English accepted the surrender of the others. Charles d'Artois and another small company fought for some time before finally surrendering to the Captal de Buch. Another group of knights led by Gris Mouton, Philippe de Chambly, and Baudrin de la House fought to the end, but were overwhelmed by weight of numbers and killed.

19 September, mid-afternoon

'My lord, my lord, surrender yourself!'

When the king's division broke up, the Prince of Wales and his household rode across the field, cutting down anyone who got in their path. 'So raged the boar of Cornwall,' says Geoffrey le Baker, 'glad to find no path, but those by bloodshed won.'[48] His exact movements are unclear; he may have joined Warwick in the pursuit to Poitiers, or he may have stayed to direct the mopping up on the Champs d'Alexandre. It is probable that he tried to find the king, although the 19 decoys would have made this a difficult task. It is not recorded how many, if any, of the 19 survived.

Around mid-afternoon, on the advice of Chandos, the prince called a halt to the pursuit. Trumpets began recalling the men to their banners. It was clear that the victory had been immense and complete. Thousands of French lay dead or dying on the field, and hundreds more were being shepherded away as prisoners. The only cloud on the otherwise bright face of the prince's happiness was that he did not know what had happened to his adversary, King Jean. He questioned the men around him, asking if they knew anything, and as they talked the prince became aware of a commotion some distance away towards the river, men shouting and yelling in anger. Irritated, Prince Edward asked Warwick and Reginald Cobham to find out what was happening. The two men rode away to investigate, followed by their men-at-arms. What they found was the last act of the drama being played out.

King Jean of France had fought on for a long time, even though his cause had been lost hours ago. Surrounded by his household, including his 14-year-old son Philippe and Geoffroi de Charny, the standard bearer with the Oriflamme, he continued to resist after most of the rest of his men were dead or prisoners. Even English chroniclers are full of admiration for his conduct; if one-quarter

Monument erected on the part of the site of the Battle of Poitiers. (*Photo courtesy of Michael Jecks*)

of his own army had fought so well, one said, the French might have prevailed that day He personally killed or wounded several of his opponents, and was so dangerous that for a time they fell back before his sword.

But Jean's men were surrounded and outnumbered, and falling one by one. Some were pulled down and killed, and others, like Jacques de Bourbon, seized and dragged away as prisoners.[49] Jean de Rochechouart, a survivor of Crécy, fought beside the king until he was killed. Charny, encumbered with the Oriflamme, fought to the end but to no avail; the man whom many regarded as the epitome of chivalry was cut down and died with the standard still in his hands.[50]

It is probable that those he was fighting did not know who he was; to them, he was just another Frenchman to be captured or killed. It was Denys de Morbecque, the exile from Artois in English service, who finally recognised the king. Pushing through the ranks of attackers, he called out to Jean: 'My lord, my lord, surrender yourself!' 'Who are you?' Jean asked. Morbecque identified himself. Jean hesitated; proud man that he was, if he was going to surrender to anyone, he wanted it to be his royal opponent the Prince of Wales. Morbecque pointed out that time was running out; if Jean did not surrender, his enemies would overwhelm him and kill him and his son. Though no source mentions this, it would be astonishing if concern for his young son did not influence Jean's decision. He offered Morbecque his surrender, and handed over his sword. The young prince Philippe surrendered to John Kentwode, one of the Prince of Wales's esquires who had presumably become separated from his master in the fighting, and to a knight named Sir Edward Wauncey.

The other assailants then realised who he was, and there was an undignified scrum as several Gascons fought to get hold of the king, manhandling and trying to drag him away. Morbecque, furious, asserted his rights and a quarrel ensued. Jean tried to calm tempers: 'My lords, my lords, I am well able to enrich you all.'[51] His captors ignored him and were on the verge of coming to blows when Warwick and Reginald Cobham arrived on the scene. At their command the quarrelling Gascons fell back and Warwick dismounted and strode forward. He recognised the king at once and bowed. 'My lord,' he said quietly, 'I have come to conduct you to the Prince of Wales.'[52]

It was then about four o'clock in the afternoon. The King of France, who had started the day in triumphant mood, was a prisoner in the hands of his enemies.

CHAPTER 9

'Marvellous to Behold'

As the sounds of combat began to die away, replaced by the groans and cries of the wounded, the Prince of Wales recalled his army. The dragon standard was hung high in the branches of a tree so that it could be seen from a distance, and trumpets and drums began to play, summoning the army to return.[1] The prince's own servants arrived a little later with his baggage and pitched his pavilion. Like King Jean's pavilion, the prince's tent was also faced with red silk. Wine was brought to the prince and his household, and more was served out to the other knights and nobles who began coming in, dragging their prisoners with them.

It was then that Warwick and Cobham arrived with their men, escorting King Jean and his son. Battered, bruised and bloody, the king faced the prince with as much dignity as he could muster. The prince could have been triumphant, gloating over his captive, but he was not. He knew very well how close the day had gone, the knife-edge margin between victory and defeat. Jean's fate – a helpless captive, his army wrecked – could easily have been his own. He bowed deeply to the king, giving him the respect he deserved, then called for a cup of wine and presented it to the king with his own hands.

Outside, the aftermath of battle had begun. The army, writes Geoffrey le Baker, 'gave its attention to healing the wounded, providing rest for the weary, guarding safe the captives and feeding the famished'.[2] Food was taken from the abandoned French camp, which also yielded a great deal of loot. Other men went looking for comrades who had gone missing in action:

> Then they realised that there were missing from their company men who had left them in search of the honour a knight should win, and persons full of pity were sent to search for them, and to bring them back to the army dead or alive. And so all of these, sick at heart for the perils of friends that were missing, hurriedly ran to the battlefield bemoaning their fate. There, amid the piles of the dead, they found men scarcely breathing … who had poured out large quantities of their own blood.[3]

Centuries later, the Duke of Wellington would remark that 'nothing except a battle lost can be half so melancholy as a battle won.'

Many of the wounded being carried in were French, but there were quite a few English as well . At one point a little hush fell and all turned to watch as Sir James Audley's esquires carried their master into the pavilion. The prince rose at once and knelt over the fallen hero, who had lost so much blood that his body was cold; he was unconscious and seemed very near death. The prince knelt over the body and kissed him, whereupon Audley roused a little and opened his eyes. Prince Edward told him the news; the battle was won. Audley closed his eyes again. The prince remained kneeling beside him for a while, oblivious to the others in the room, forgetting his great victory while he wept for his friend. No greater testament to the strength of the bond between the prince and his captains can be found. Band of brothers, indeed.[4]

Audley was carried away to his own tent to be tended by his men (he made a full recovery and continued in the prince's service for many years). The prince then turned to King Jean and apologised for his behaviour. He ordered a table laid and food to be brought for the king and the other high-ranking prisoners, including Jacques de Bourbon and the counts of Tancarville and Dammartin. The prince himself would not sit in the presence of the king and insisted on serving Jean and his son with his own hands, as a mark of respect for the courage both had shown that day. At one point Prince Edward offered Jean a few words of consolation; what had happened today, he said, was the fortunes of war. Jean could console himself that he had not turned fugitive, but stayed and fought to the end. Gloomily, Jean agreed.

The following day the army shifted a few miles southwest and established a new camp away from the blood-soaked earth of the battlefield. On the field itself, the grim work of stock-taking began. Just as at Crécy 10 years earlier, Reginald Cobham was given the task of identifying the dead, assisted by the army's heralds who could recognise the coats of arms of both friend and foe. The task took most of the day. Exactly how many French were killed is not known, but the historian H. J. Hewitt reckons around 2,000 men-at-arms were killed and around 800 others, mostly crossbowmen.[5] The Duc de Bourbon, the grand chamberlain of France, was dead. So was Gautier de Brienne, the Duke of Athens; he had schemed for years to become Constable of France, but he only enjoyed the office for a few months. Jean de Clermont the marshal was dead, as was the fire-breathing Bishop of Châlons; he would revile the English no more. The wise old knight Eustache de Ribemont was dead. The flower of chivalry, Geoffroi de Charny, had ridden to his last battle.

Philippe de Chambly, Gris Mouton, was dead along with his brother Pierre. Louis de Chauvigny, Vicomte de Brosse, who had survived the ambush two days earlier, was dead. His son André, who had so gallantly defended the keep at Argenton back in August, had died with him. Jean de Rochechouart, whose town had offered Edward resistance early in the campaign, had been fortunate to survive the battle of Crécy. At Poitiers, his luck ran out.

Many of the noble dead were taken to Poitiers where a garrison under the lord of Roye was holding the city. Roye's men had arrived too late for the battle but they had encountered the retreating wreckage of the army at Chauvigny, where the Dauphin Charles and his officers were trying to restore order. As Roye's force was about the only organised body of French troops available, the Dauphin had ordered him to hurry to Poitiers and defend the town. It was a sensible precaution, but it proved unnecessary; exhausted and laden with prisoners and loot, the English never considered an attack on the city.[6] Now, under a flag of truce, the bodies of the dead were carried into the city. A hundred at least were buried in the convent of the Dominican Order, and as many more in the convent of the Franciscans; both convents recorded the names of those who died.[7] Others were buried in other churches around the city. The poorer men-at-arms, the commoners and the Genoese were buried in mass graves.

Then there were the prisoners. As well as the king and his son, there were many men of high rank: Jacques de Bourbon; Guillaume de Melun, the Archbishop of Sens; Marshal d'Audrehem; and according to Geoffrey le Baker, the counts of Ponthieu, Eu, Longueville, Tancarville, Ventadour, Sancerre, Vaudemont, Vendôme and Dammartin. Captured also were two of the German leaders, the counts of Saarbrucken and Nassau-Weilberg. Nidau, the Swiss commander, had managed to escape the field, as had the Castilian Enrique de Trastámara. His fellow Spaniard, Juan Fernández de Heredia, had not been so lucky; he too was a prisoner. Arnaut de Cervolles, the Archpriest, had also been taken.

Hundreds of others had been captured too. One historian has estimated the total number of prisoners at 3,000, including 1,400 knights.[8] If so, when added to the death toll, this meant the French army had lost around 5,000 men-at-arms killed or captured, half the number who had assembled at Chartres and a quarter of the entire army. Even without the capture of the king, this was a disaster for French arms far greater even than Crécy.

Dealing with the prisoners occupied much of the next two days. The Prince of Wales took the more important captives, including those mentioned above, into his own custody for safe-keeping, to ensure there could be no attempts at rescue or escape. There then ensued a prolonged period of negotiation and trading. First, the ransoms for the prisoners had to be fixed. This was an interesting process, for the captors had to try to assess how much each man was worth, and in most cases they could only really do this by guesswork – looking at their harness and baggage, how many servants and horses they had and so on, and then trying to come up with a figure. If the ransom was too high, the prisoner would not be able to afford to pay it; in which case the captor was still responsible for him, and would have to feed and lodge the prisoner at his own expense until someone came forward to pay the ransom. That could take months, even years. On the other hand, if the price was set too low, the prisoner could pay it easily and go free, but the captor would lose out. For their part, the prisoners were only too ready to talk down the value of their estates and goods, and eager to explain how burdened with debt they were. (This latter was probably true in many cases; equipping a knight to go to war, with weapons, armour, horses and servants, was a highly expensive business, and many mortgaged their estates to do so.)

Ransom prices therefore ranged from a few pounds to several thousands. Guillaume-Sans de Pommier was paid £5,000 for the ransom of the Comte d'Eu, taken at Poitiers, while the Comte de Auxerre, taken during the fighting two days before the battle, was ransomed for the equivalent of £3,297.[9]

Those who had taken prisoners and wanted ready money could sell their captives at a discount to the prince or the wealthier knights and barons. With deeper pockets, these men could afford the leisure of long negotiations, and to maintain their prisoners until ransoms could be paid. Another common practice for poorer prisoners who could only pay small ransoms was to let them go on parole. The prisoner was allowed to return home, promising to raise the ransom money and forward it to the captor at the first opportunity. Surprisingly, it seems that most did so. Of course, if they reneged on a promise to pay and were captured again, things might not go particularly well for them, so prompt payment of the ransom was in part a matter of self-interest.[10] During the days that followed the battle, a large number of prisoners were released on parole. So too were some of the more seriously wounded French knights and nobles, including Jean d'Artois, the Comte d'Eu. Only those who were both wealthy and healthy remained in custody.

And finally, there was the loot to sort out and value. The entire French camp and baggage train had been taken, including the personal effects of the king, princes, nobles and knights. Apart from the headline pieces such as King Jean's personal illuminated bible (purchased eventually by the Earl of

Salisbury) and a silver *nef*, a salt cellar in the shape of a ship that graced the royal dining table, there were jewels, money, fine clothes, weapons, armour, and horses. The value of the loot taken far outweighed the costs of outfitting for the campaign. For men who went to war to get rich, this was equivalent to breaking the bank.

In the midst of all this trading and haggling, Cardinal Talleyrand and the remainder of his bodyguard came riding back to the English camp. The cardinal had come, he said, to apologise; he had genuinely wanted to make peace before the battle, but the intransigence of the king and some of his advisors had prevented his doing so.[11] The prince accused him of betraying the English by buying time for the French army to bring up more men and increase its strength. Talleyrand protested his innocence. His intention was still to make peace, he said, and he pointed out that with King Jean now a prisoner in English hands, a real opportunity existed to bring the war to a close. The prince saw the sense of this, and relented. Talleyrand may also have spoken to Jean and gained his consent to act as mediator. At the same time, the prince released the body of the cardinal's nephew, Robert of Durazzo, which had been found lying beneath a tree, and ordered it taken to Poitiers so Talleyrand could make arrangements for burial.

Return to Bordeaux

On 22 September the army marched again, accompanied by a baggage train with wagons groaning with the weight of plunder, and the remaining prisoners. There is no need to describe the march in great detail. The army avoided the route by which it had travelled north, for there was still a need to find fodder and food and the eastern route had been stripped bare. Instead, the army moved further west, camping for the night of the 22nd at Couhé, south of Poitiers. The arson and destruction had stopped, for there was no longer any point in wasting French lands – France would need all the money it had to pay the forthcoming ransoms – but foraging for food continued.

On the 23rd the army marched to Ruffec, following the road south towards Angoulême, and on the 24th crossed the river Charentes and halted at Mouton. Veering around to the east of Angoulême, they marched to La Rochefoucauld on the 25th and Villebois on the 26th. A long march through hilly country to St-Aulaye followed on the 27th, but after that the army was back in friendly territory and the march proceeded in leisurely fashion, to St-Antonin in the valley of the Isle and then reaching the Dordogne near St-Emilion on the 30th. There was a short wait at Libourne while preparations were made for a ceremonial entry into the city, and then on 2 October the prince and his household, including King Jean and the French nobles, marched into Bordeaux.

They received a hero's welcome. 'Nobly were they received and welcomed by all the people,' writes Chandos Herald. 'With crosses and processions, singing their orisons, all the members of the collegial churches at Bordeaux came to meet them, and the ladies and the damsels, old and young, and the serving-maids. At Bordeaux was such joy made that it was marvellous to behold.'[12] For once, Chandos Herald is probably not exaggerating. The prince went to lodge in part of the abbey of St-André, where he was showered with gifts including a tame lioness, which he kept as a pet. Apartments were also prepared at St-André for King Jean, and he and his son were unwilling guests at a series of feasts and celebrations that lasted through much of the rest of the winter.

Bordeaux for a time resembled one of those frontier towns during the gold rush era of the 19th century. Knights, esquires and common soldiers, suddenly made rich beyond dreams of avarice through ransoms and plunder, rushed to spend their money. The prince bought most of the remaining ransoms of the notables from their captors, adding to the flow of gold and silver. Froissart says that the men spent their money 'foolishly', which means that they gambled some of it away and spent the rest on wine, women and song, not necessarily in that order.[13]

Inevitably, quarrels broke out among the victors, especially over ransoms. The most bitter dispute concerned Denys de Morbecque. His capture of King Jean was challenged by a Gascon squire, Bernard de Trouttes, who claimed that the king had surrendered to him. Despite Jean's own statement that he had yielded to Morbecque, Trouttes persisted with his claim. The dispute escalated until the two men challenged each other to trial by combat. At this point Prince Edward stepped in and placed both men under arrest. Morbecque's claim was eventually proven.

Couriers had rushed ahead of the army to Bordeaux, giving the news there and then taking ship for home. By early October two of the prince's friends, Nele Loring and Roger Cotesford, were in London, handing over letters from the prince, Burghersh and other notables with the expedition. One of the prince's attendants, Geoffrey Hamlyn, followed soon after with the armour and bascinet King Jean had worn at Poitiers as proof of his capture. The atmosphere in England when the news became known was a mixture of joy and astonishment, even shock. England had been hoping for a victory, perhaps even expecting one, but nothing on this scale could ever have been dreamed of. Never before in all their years of warfare had an English army captured a king of France on the battlefield. Stunned, the English court did not at first know how to take advantage of their victory.

One man did know. On hearing the news of the victory at Poitiers, the Duke of Lancaster realised the prince no longer needed his assistance. He knew too that there would be a power vacuum in France, and he proceeded to take advantage of it. Marching swiftly into Brittany, Lancaster joined forces with the pro-English claimant to the Duchy of Brittany, Jean de Montfort, and began mopping up French-held castles and strongholds. Charles of Blois, the French-backed candidate taken prisoner nine years earlier at La Roche-Derrien, had finally been released a few months before. But without support from France, he could do nothing to stop Lancaster from taking the town of Lannion and then settling down to besiege Rennes. That city was strongly garrisoned and its captain was a Breton knight whom the English would get to know very well in the years to come: Bertrand du Guesclin. Despite Lancaster and Montfort's best efforts, the city held out against all assaults, and Lancaster's expedition ground to a halt.

France lies bleeding

If England was stunned, France was in a state of catatonic shock. Authority in the French state now rested on the shoulders of the young Dauphin Charles. His advisors hurried the Dauphin back to Paris. As a first step to dealing with the national emergency, the Estates-General was called upon to assemble. The government, including the Dauphin and the chancellor, Pierre de la Fôret, believed that the first priority was to get the king home. No ransom demand had yet been received, but one would not be long in coming. New taxes would be necessary to pay the king's ransom.

The Estates-General, which first met on 17 October, had other ideas. Their representatives, a body known as the Council of Eighty, expressed their anger at how the war had been conducted. They accused the king's ministers of corruption and incompetence. Arrogantly summoning the Dauphin to appear before them, the Eighty issued three demands. First, most of the government ministers must be dismissed immediately from their posts. Second, a commission of 20 men representing the nobility, the clergy and the towns should be appointed to 'advise' the Dauphin while he governed in lieu of his father; in reality, they would have pretty much complete control over him. Third, Charles of Navarre should be released from prison. This last condition was added by Navarre's supporters among the Eighty, and it is quite probable that a plot was brewing to overthrow Jean and replace him with Charles.

In return, said the Council of Eighty, the Estates-General would authorise and collect taxes to pay for a new army of 30,000 men, enough to sweep the English out of France. The Dauphin's advisors were sceptical. The last tax proposed by the Estates-General had been a complete failure, and they saw no reason why this one would be any different. With some of the more hostile elements in the Council of Eighty now openly calling for Jean to be dethroned and replaced by either his son or Charles of Navarre, the Dauphin refused the Council's proposals. On 2 November he suspended the Estates-General.[14]

Meanwhile, the peace process was stuttering into life. Cardinals Talleyrand and Capocci were instructed by the pope to re-start the negotiations. Both men travelled to Bordeaux, where they asked for an audience with Prince Edward. The prince kept them waiting for a fortnight. Froissart thinks this was because the prince still did not trust Talleyrand; however, they seemed to have patched things up after Poitiers, and it is equally possible that the prince was simply too busy giving parties.[15] The main reason for the delay, however, was that the prince and his officers were still waiting for instructions from London. While they waited, Capocci and Talleyrand quarrelled and the Roman cardinal withdrew to Paris in a huff. He then attempted to start his own peace process independently of Talleyrand, and wrote a series of letters to Prince Edward offering to mediate. All these letters were ignored. Talleyrand too withdrew after a time, having had only one inconclusive meeting with the prince.

The Holy Roman Emperor, Charles IV, also offered to intercede and called a peace conference at Metz, inviting both sides to send representatives. King Jean had been his brother-in-law, and now the emperor also offered to lend the French government money to help with its financial crisis. His nephew the Dauphin rushed to Metz, taking Cardinal Talleyrand with him as mediator, but Edward III declined to send an envoy. Without an English presence nothing could be achieved, and the conference fizzled out.

Edward was still trying to decide what he could get. As well as Jean's ransom, there was also a golden chance to end the war at a stroke. But how far could he press his demands? Edward still claimed to be the rightful King of France; but could he persuade the French nobles to set Jean aside in favour of himself? It seemed unlikely. If they wanted an alternative to Jean, they were likely to pick Charles of Navarre. Until he could decide on his best strategy, Edward was in no hurry to make peace. Not until November did he send instructions to Bordeaux, along with the experienced lawyer William Lynne, Dean of Chichester, to act as negotiator.[16]

The Dauphin returned to Paris to find fresh emergencies cropping up everywhere. In Normandy, Lancaster and Philippe of Navarre were raiding and pillaging at will, almost up to the walls of Paris. The French did score one success late in 1356 when they defeated a force of Norman rebels, in the process killing one of the French crown's most determined foes, the Norman baron Godefroi d'Harcourt. But for the most part, the French were on the defensive. Paris itself was in a state of near revolt, and its powerful Provost of Merchants, Étienne Marcel, was demanding that the Estates-General be recalled. The Dauphin had very little choice but to comply. He surrendered to the Estates-General's demands and dismissed most of his ministers and financial officials. Charles of Navarre, however, remained in prison.

On 3 March 1357 the Estates-General promulgated the Great Ordinance, which effectively allowed it to form a new government. Étienne Marcel suddenly became the most powerful man in France.[17] But alas, the new reforming government was no more competent than the old. So inexperienced were the new officials in charge of the treasury that they asked for some of their dismissed predecessors to be recalled so they could explain how things worked.

Late in January 1357, a team led by the earls of Warwick and Suffolk and including William Lynne as the chief negotiator met with a group of French officials near Bordeaux. The negotiations fell apart when the Estates-General dismissed several members of the negotiating team and did not replace them. The others gave up and returned to Paris. Exasperated, the captive king appointed his own negotiating team and in March 1357 began talks with his captors in Bordeaux. The Estates-General insisted these negotiations were not valid, on the basis that it and only it had the right to conduct negotiations.

On 23 March 1357, Jean's negotiators agreed a two-year truce covering all of France, to expire at Easter 1359. Two of the prisoners, the Archbishop of Sens and the Comte de Tancarville, were sent to Paris to proclaim the news. He also instructed that the session of the Estates-General should be suspended and its members sent home. Jean no doubt thought that his own release was now imminent and that he would soon return to Paris to pick up the reins of power. If so, he was badly mistaken. Paris was on the verge of revolt. Just as it would later do in 1789, the Estates-General refused to suspend its session. Tancarville and the archbishop were abused and shouted down. The Dauphin, who was now fully in Marcel's power, was compelled to issue a decree – of dubious legality – countermanding the king's orders and rejecting the truce. How exactly the Estates-General thought it could carry on the fight with no money and no army is not at all clear.

Meanwhile the raiding and burning went on. Central control in France was breaking down, and more and more French knights and regional nobles were throwing off their allegiance to France and joining the English. Some joined in the raids against their neighbours. Even worse, increasing numbers of soldiers from both sides, sometimes working together, were leaving the service of their overlords altogether and setting up private armies. These were the dreaded *routiers*, the Free Companies, who burned, robbed and murdered for profit alone. Already there were a number of these operating in Normandy and Brittany, and more were appearing in the Languedoc. France desperately needed to find a negotiated peace so it could deal with its internal problems; but between the intransigence of the Estates-General and King Edward's own delaying tactics, there was no sign of peace on the horizon. Geoffrey le Baker ends his chronicle with the ominous words, 'For two years afterwards, no such wished-for peace was signed.'[18]

Triumphant homecoming

Late in April 1357, the Prince of Wales and his household set sail for home, bearing with them the captive king and his son Philippe. Landing in early May, they made a triumphal procession across the country before arriving in London to another ceremonial welcome. King Jean was installed in the Savoy Palace, the home of the Duke of Lancaster. Although he was closely guarded, the king lived a comfortable life, even going hunting in the forests outside London. King Edward and Queen Philippa showed him great respect and treated him courteously. At first Londoners gathered around the Savoy to gawk at the spectacle of the captive king, but they quickly lost interest.

Even before the return home, the Prince of Wales had been handing out rewards to his followers. For his courage, James Audley was given an annuity of 500 marks, which he promptly passed on to the esquires who had supported him on the battlefield and rescued him when he fell. The prince, hearing of this, gave Sir James a new annuity, this time of 600 marks. Many others received lavish awards as well. The historian H. J. Hewitt has compiled a lengthy list of awards and recipients.[19] Some of the awards went to prominent figures. John Chandos received two annuities, one of £40 and another of 600 gold crowns to be drawn from the town of Marmande in Gascony, as well as income from a manor in Lincolnshire. Roger Cotesford received an annuity of 40 marks, and Nele Loring an annuity of £83 6s 8d. Alan Cheyne, who had been in the prince's entourage at Poitiers, likewise received 40 marks.[20] Richard Leominster, the Dominican friar who had accompanied the prince, received an annuity of

20 marks. But the humbler of station were rewarded too. The clerk William Blackwater received a gift of £20, and a servant, John Palington, was given a gift of land. Richard Dokeseye, the prince's baker, received an annuity of 10 marks out of the revenues of the prince's mills and bake oven at Macclesfield.[21]

There are plenty of records too of archers from Cheshire and Wales receiving rewards, sometimes money, sometimes rights to hunt, fish or gather wood. John Bilkington was given five oak trees from the prince's park at Bickleigh. John Harding similarly received four oaks 'for the repair of his houses', and William Holford received 20 acres of land. John Overton received the right of pasturage on the prince's land for 24 'great beasts', probably cattle or oxen, and pasturage rights were also given to David Wodehull.[22] John Stockton received the right of turbary – the cutting of peat – also at Bickleigh.[23]

Sometimes the reward took the form of a pardon for past misdeeds. Robert Astell, probably an archer, was pardoned for killing John Coo of Knutsford, on account of 'good service in Gascony and the great part he played in the battle of Poitiers'.[24] Others, including John Overton and Thomas Frodesham, received general pardons 'for all felonies and trespasses'.[25]

The festivities that marked the prince's return to England were even greater than those in Bordeaux. Chandos Herald maintains that the court passed the next four years in hunting, jousting, feasting and hawking, 'just as in the reign of Arthur', and adds enthusiastically, 'there was … many a lady, many a damsel, right amorous, sprightly and fair'. Apart from his obsession with damsels, Chandos Herald's observation is interesting for another reason. Throughout most of his reign, King Edward had consciously modelled his own life and his court on that of King Arthur, as described in the romances of the poet Chrétien de Troyes and others. The Order of the Garter was consciously modelled on Arthur's Round Table. Here was a perfect chance to show himself off as a latter-day Arthur, a victorious king who had elevated England to new heights. We can take it for granted that many of the celebrations had an Arthurian theme.

The king would have been wise to do less celebrating and more negotiating. Unless he was careful, the advantage won by his victory at Poiters would slip away. Yet still he delayed. In June 1357 Cardinals Talleyrand and Capocci arrived in London, the latter still smarting from a rebuke given by the pope for failing to support Talleyrand the previous year. With them came the Archbishop of Sens and a team of French negotiators. Still the English delayed. English diplomats were preoccupied with another treaty, settling the war with Scotland, a considerably less important affair. Not until September 1357, a year after the battle, did negotiations begin in earnest.

In November 1357 events took another turn for the worse. The Picard nobleman Jean de Picquigny had originally been a Valois loyalist and had fought at Crécy, but he had later fallen out badly with King Jean and joined the Navarre faction. Now he decided to take matters into his own hands. Gathering 30 of his followers at Amiens, he attacked the castle of Arleux, where Charles of Navarre was then being held. The guards were overwhelmed and Charles was released. Charles the Bad was back in the game, complicating matters for everyone still further.

If Charles was rusty from his prison cell, he showed no sign of it. Gathering his friends and supporters, he rode to Paris to demand justice for himself and his followers. His men terrorised the Dauphin's household and he himself harangued the Estates-General, where he had many supporters. He demanded 40,000 gold *écus* as a compensation for wrongs done to him, restoration of all his lands and castles, a free pardon for his followers and, in addition, that the Duchy of Normandy and County of Champagne should be handed over to him. Étienne Marcel, seeing the tide of sentiment flowing in Charles's direction, agreed to his demands. The Dauphin, showing more strength than anyone had guessed he possessed, stubbornly held out.

Charles was clearly setting himself up to seize the throne for himself, and this finally galvanised the English negotiators into action. Restless, mercurial, ambitious to a fault, Charles had been an unreliable ally; they did not want to see him become a powerful enemy. Better by far that Jean should return to his throne. In December, agreement was reached. Jean would pay a ransom of 4 million *écus*, or about £670,000. Around £100,000 was to be paid before Jean was allowed to leave England, with the rest to follow in instalments. Edward would receive full sovereignty over Gascony, which he would no longer hold as a vassal of France. The counties of Saintonge, Poitou, Angoulême and Périgord and the whole of the Limousin, the Agenais and Quercy were to be ceded to him, along with Bigorre in the Pyrenees and other territories in Normandy and the north. The question of Edward's claim to the French throne was quietly set to one side.

The agreement cut the ground from under Charles of Navarre's feet. Jean would soon be home, and the English were now ready to bring the war to an end. In an act of pure spite, he opened the gates of every prison in Paris, letting the criminals out into the streets to do what damage they wished, and then gathered his men and rode out of Paris. Back in Normandy, he mustered his forces and prepared to plunge France into a state of civil war, unless he could get his own way.

The road to Bretigny

But Charles underestimated the impact of the peace proposals. For one thing, the peace terms had to be ratified by the English Parliament, and this took time. For another, the first £100,000 had to be raised, and given the chaos in France and the unwillingness of the Estates-General to cooperate, that might never happen. Many, including Marcel, did not want to see Jean return.

Marcel was now the master of Paris, the Dauphin his prisoner in all but name. The Estates-General was pushed to one side. The real power in Paris now was the people of the capital, who followed Marcel enthusiastically. Almost without anyone noticing, he had worked a revolution in Paris that had propelled him into power. But the Provost of Merchants was now playing a very dangerous game. He was still in touch with Charles of Navarre, but had never officially lent his weight to the campaign to promote Charles to the throne of France. He was a revolutionary of a different sort, like Cola di Rienzo in Rome or Simone Boccanegra in Genoa. His covert aim seems to have been nothing less than the proclamation of a republic, with himself at its head. As long as Marcel remained in power, it was unlikely that King Jean would ever come home. It remained to be seen, however, whether he could control Charles of Navarre.

Marcel intended to use Charles as a kind of military protector of the revolution, in much the same way that the Directory would try to use Napoleon in 1795. To this end, he invited Charles back to Paris early in 1358. Charles returned, renewing his demands for compensation and lands. The Dauphin agreed, but then in another surprising show of strength, he suddenly left Paris in March 1358 and set up a base at Compiègne 50 miles north of the capital. Here he set about raising an army. He had no money to speak of, but there were plenty who hated Marcel and Charles of Navarre and were willing to support him.

A new force now entered the scene. The thousands of knights and nobles captured at Poitiers had to raise funds for their ransoms somehow, and many chose to do so by exacting money from the peasants on their estates. On top of the clumsy, fumbling attempts by the Estates-General to increase taxes, these exactions were a crushing burden on the poor. Their hardship and misery gradually turned to rage. Anger over the fact that the king still languished in a foreign prison added fuel to the fire, as did the activities of the *routiers* and Free Companies. The peasants reckoned, correctly, that it was the duty of the knights and nobles to protect them. Where were they, and why were they not doing so?

Violence first flared near the village of St-Leu in Picardy at the end of May 1358, and spread rapidly across northern France. The revolt became known as the Jacquerie, after 'Jacques Bonhomme', a derisive nickname applied to peasants by the other classes. The houses of the nobility were the primary targets, after which the rebels turned against other officials of the state such as tax collectors. Lurid tales of murder, rape, the slaughter of women and children, even of cannibalism, began to circulate. Most of these were probably invented, but it is likely that there was some fire beneath the smoke. Certainly a number of notables and their families were killed during the few months that the Jacquerie lasted; how many will never be known.[26]

As the revolt spread, some towns and cities began opening their doors to the rebels, hoping to appease them. In Paris, Étienne Marcel saw the Jacquerie as a popular revolt like the one he had fostered in Paris. Perhaps they, rather than Charles of Navarre and his army, could become the guardians of the revolution. But much the same thought had occurred to Charles, who had his own ideas about who should have power in France. He marched against the Jacquerie, and on 10 June 1358 he crushed the main rebel force at Mello in Picardy. The rebels scattered, and now it was the turn of the nobility to exact vengeance. For several months thereafter, bands of men-at-arms roamed the plains of northern France, butchering peasants at random. As many as 20,000 may have died.[27]

As the Jacquerie collapsed, the Dauphin advanced. By mid-summer his army, about 12,000 men, had moved down to Vincennes, just east of Paris. On 31 July Étienne Marcel was assassinated in Paris, probably at the Dauphin's instigation, and in the days that followed many of his followers were murdered as well. Charles of Navarre fled the city and began plundering the western suburbs, allowing the Dauphin to march in and take control of the city.

The terms of the Treaty of London were finally ratified in England, and the draft treaty was sent to France for similar ratification. The Dauphin and the Estates-General were horrified by the terms. In the aftermath of Marcel's downfall the young prince had worked hard to conciliate the Estates-General – who were themselves shocked by Marcel's naked ambition and the violence of the Jacquerie – and the two were now working together. They realised that the ransom could never be paid, and the territorial concessions involved handing over more than a third of France to the English. The Estates-General refused to accept the Treaty of London, and the Dauphin concurred.

That meant the war would resume. In reality it had never stopped; Brittany was specifically excluded from the terms of the truce arranged in 1357, and the war there had continued for some time. Charles and Philippe of Navarre continued to raid and pillage, and the Free Companies were growing stronger. Now, Edward III prepared to take a hand. The objective of the campaign this time was to force France to its knees and compel it to sign a treaty at sword's point.

In the summer of 1359 an army of 10,000 men was raised, and a fleet of 1,100 ships to transport it and its horses and supplies.[28] On 28 October this force marched out of Calais before dividing into three columns, one led by Lancaster, one by the Prince of Wales and one by the king himself. Forewarned, the Dauphin had made his preparations. All civilians were taken into the safety of walled towns, which were heavily garrisoned. All foodstuffs and supplies that might be of use to the enemy were likewise taken away or burned and destroyed, leaving the country bare. The English would find nothing with which to sustain themselves. No one was to attempt to hinder the enemy's passage. Let them advance, said the orders, until they are deep in the countryside and begin to starve.

The English advanced through pouring rain. As the Dauphin had intended, they suffered almost at once from shortages of food. Some men deserted, probably to join the *routiers*; some of the Flemish and German mercenaries simply went home. Early in December the three columns converged on the walled city of Reims and began to lay siege to it. But Reims was vigorously defended by an able captain, Gautier de Châtillon, and its storerooms were well stocked with provisions. When the English set up mangonels to throw stones at the walls, the French replied with catapults of their own, smashing the enemy siege machines. Attempts to storm the walls were beaten back. On 11 January 1360 the siege was abandoned.

Instead of retreating, King Edward and the Prince of Wales led their men south on a long and destructive *chevauchée* into Burgundy. The French retaliated by raiding the coast of Kent and Sussex and burning the town of Winchelsea. By March, the English army was moving north again, and by the end of the month they were camped outside Paris. This was a demonstration, to compel the Estates-General to see reason. Ironically, both Edward and Jean of France were now on the same side; both wanted the treaty, and both wanted to compel the Estates-General to sign it. Even as Edward was camped outside the walls, officials loyal to Jean like the Archbishop of Sens were inside the city, using their influence to win over the Estates.

But Edward's army was now suffering terribly from lack of supplies. He was forced to withdraw to Chartres and set up a new base there, relieving the pressure on the capital. Reluctantly, he offered to renegotiate the Treaty of London. The Estates-General accepted. Over the course of 1–3 May, negotiators met at the village of Bretigny, near Chartres, and came to a new agreement.

Jean's ransom was reduced from 4 million *écus* to 3 million, and he would be released immediately so that he could take over the reins of government and arrange the repayment.[29] Edward cut his territorial demands by about half. On 14 June 1360, Jean ratified the Treaty of Bretigny, and on 8 July he arrived back at Calais, on his way home after nearly four years as a captive.

That was not the end of the story. Jean had been released on a promise that the ransom would be paid, and he intended to honour that promise. His second son, Prince Louis, was sent to London as a hostage to ensure that he did so. Back in Paris, Jean quickly made peace with Charles of Navarre, pardoning him and restoring his lands, and devoted himself to raising the ransom. The effort of raising even 3 million *écus* in impoverished and exhausted war-ravaged France took longer than the king expected. Then, in June 1363 the hostage, Prince Louis, escaped and returned to France.

No one quite expected what happened next. Jean was furious with his son, and proclaimed himself to be dishonoured. The only way to restore his honour, he said, was to return to captivity himself. Aghast, his councillors tried to dissuade him, but as ever with Jean, once his mind was made up there was no shaking him. Early in 1364 he returned to London where his English captors, equally surprised, lauded his honourable behaviour and held a feast to celebrate.

It was the last act. In April 1364, Jean fell ill and died at the Savoy Palace in London. His death, in the end, was as futile as his life had been.

Things fall apart

The peace that was no peace after the Treaty of Bretigny lasted for nine years. During that time England and France continued to fight proxy wars. The first involved Charles of Navarre. Even before Jean's death he had revived his territorial demands, this time laying claim to the Duchy of Burgundy. Jean refused; Burgundy was intended for his youngest son, Philippe.

When Jean refused, Charles was on the march again, bringing troops north from Navarre to invade French territory and scorch their way across to the frontiers of Burgundy, adding to the general destruction and misery that much of France was now enduring. The end of war had meant unemployment for thousands of soldiers, and many of these now turned to freelancing. The ranks of the *routiers* and Free Companies swelled. Some companies, like those of Arnaut de Cervolles, the Archpriest, and the combined bands of Robert Knollys and Hugh Calveley, numbered thousands of men and were as powerful as many armies of the day. No district of France was immune to them, not even

Avignon, the seat of the papacy. Even strong cities had to pay ransoms to make them go away. The countryside in many areas was reduced to a wasteland.

But the Dauphin, deputing for his father once again after Jean's quixotic return to London, was equal to the task. To his father's stubbornness he brought a refreshing streak of common sense and a high intelligence. Realising that the best way of stopping the *routiers* was to deny them opportunities for plunder, he spent money on fortifying his towns and cities to make them into safe havens. People, livestock and possessions were evacuated to these fortified places as soon as the *routiers* approached. It did not save everyone, everywhere, but it preserved a little of France's strength for the time when rebuilding would be possible. Meanwhile, his garrisons blunted Charles of Navarre's attacks and drove the latter back from the borders of Burgundy.

A new French captain now enters the scene. A simple knight from a humble background, Bertrand du Guesclin had entered royal service and risen to prominence through his military skill. We saw him earlier, successfully defending Rennes against Henry of Lancaster. In the spring of 1364 he led French troops against Charles of Navarre's army in Normandy, which was being supported by an Anglo-Gascon force led by the Captal de Buch. At the battle of Cocherel on 16 May, Guesclin smashed the Navarrese army, capturing the Captal. That was not the end of Charles the Bad's endeavours in Normandy, but thereafter he was increasingly on the defensive.

In 1366 another proxy war broke out in Spain. Enrique de Trastámara, the illegitimate son of the late King Alfonso of Castille, launched an attack on his brother, the current king, Pedro I, known as the Cruel. Enrique was strongly supported by France, and a French royal force under Bertrand du Guesclin was sent to join him. Charles V of France, as the Dauphin now was, had come up with a novel way of getting rid of most of the Free Companies; he paid them to join Guesclin's expedition, and serve Enrique. The Companies agreed. One of the most dangerous leaders, Arnaud de Cervolles, was murdered that year by his own men and his company had begun to break up. Others were simply running out of places to plunder in France, and thought Spain might offer welcome opportunities.

Pedro the Cruel took refuge in Bordeaux and applied to Prince Edward for assistance. The prince, who had married his cousin Joan of Kent a few years earlier and was living in happy luxury as English viceroy in Gascony, agreed on the condition that Pedro would defray the expenses of the campaign. An Anglo-Gascon force with a few more Free Companies attached marched over the Pyrenees and defeated Enrique's army, led by Guesclin, at the battle of Nájera. The battle was a particularly bloody one, but dysentery and other camp diseases killed more men than died in the fighting. Most of the *routiers* perished of one cause or another, thus ridding France, and the world, of their presence. Prince Edward himself fell ill, and never fully recovered his health.

The expedition against Enrique was not an official one; no English tax money had been spent, and the Prince of Wales had financed the expedition himself. When Pedro refused to honour his promise to pay Prince Edward's expenses, Edward abandoned the expedition and returned home. With Guesclin's support, Enrique regained the throne, tracking down his brother and murdering him a few years later. Pedro was not greatly mourned. Meanwhile, back in Bordeaux, Edward tried to recoup his losses and repay his debts by levying swingeing new taxes on his Gascon subjects. As a result, even his friends began to turn against him. By 1368 many Gascon nobles, led by his old comrades the Albret brothers, were in open revolt. They switched their allegiance to the French.

Suddenly the English position in Gascony, which had looked so strong after the Treaty of Bretigny, was undermined. In 1369 Charles V repudiated the treaty and opened the war again. There followed several years of fairly fruitless campaigning, with a great deal of destruction but few real military gains, but Charles bided his time. With Guesclin, who in 1370 was appointed Constable of France, he rebuilt his army. And English power was weakening. Edward III was now an old man, too feeble to take the field. The health of the Prince of Wales was deteriorating steadily. In 1370 he led his army one last time, driving back the encroaching French from the borders of Gascony, a campaign which included the bloody sack of the city of Limoges. He never led an army into battle again.

Many of the other commanders were dead now too, the band of brothers broken up and gone. One of the deaths the prince felt most keenly was that of John Chandos, mortally wounded in a skirmish at Lussac only a few miles from the battlefield of Poitiers on the last day of December, 1369. He died the following day. Unusually, and rather movingly, later generations of French residents of Lussac erected a memorial to their great enemy. When we visited this in 2008, someone had left fresh flowers at the foot of the memorial.

By 1372 Prince Edward's health was so bad that he left Gascony and returned to England. He died at Westminster Palace in 1376 and is buried in Canterbury Cathedral. A year later his father followed him to the grave. England had lost its two great captains. Prince Edward's son was crowned King Richard II, but he was still a minor. The regents and nobles began quarrelling among themselves, and England's slow slide into civil war began.

It had all been for nothing. Twenty years after Poitiers, the Prince of Wales was dead, England was weakening steadily, and the power of France was rising. A chance had been lost. A lasting peace imposed after Poitiers could have brought an end to the war and spared France the horrors of the Free Companies and Jacquerie, and also put an end to Charles of Navarre. As so often in the Hundred Years War, England had been superb at managing the business of war. But it had fumbled the peace. The conflict would drag on for nearly another hundred years until the final dismal, bloody end at Castillon on the Dordogne.

However, let us end this book on a happier note. Charles the Bad, who bears direct or indirect responsibility for so much of the violence and death we have recorded in this book, never really recovered from the defeat at Cocherel. By the early 1370s he had been driven out of his Norman lands altogether and retreated to his kingdom in the Pyrenees, penniless, bankrupt and ill. He suffered increasingly from a form of paralysis of the limbs. In 1387, a physician recommended that his body be wrapped tightly in a cloth soaked in brandy. As his attendants were sewing up the alcohol-impregnated shroud, one of them accidentally set fire to the cloth with a candle. Alcohol and cloth both burned like a torch. His body covered in burns, Charles lived in agony for another fortnight before he finally expired. It was a fitting end for a bad man.

Appendix: Reconstructing Poitiers

Reconstructing the events of any medieval battle brings with it certain challenges, and Poitiers is no exception. The evidence for what happened, where, when and to whom is fragmentary and often contradictory. This should come as no surprise. Reconstructing *any* battle is difficult, because eyewitness accounts of what happened will often differ. The extreme levels of stress that combat imposes on soldiers plays tricks with both perception and memory. Time and space themselves become distorted. People remember things that did not actually happen, and forget many things that did happen.

At least with a modern battle, there is a plethora of different accounts and administrative records, copies of orders, recordings of radio transmissions and so on, which give the researcher a broad evidence base through which to sift. For medieval battles, even big ones like Poitiers, this is not so. The administrative records of the English crown, like the *Register of the Black Prince*, provide background information that can help us establish certain facts. There are a few eyewitness accounts in letters home – the Prince of Wales, Bartholomew Burghersh and others – but these letters are disappointingly brief and, we must remember, were intended for public consumption as propaganda. On the French side, the survival of administrative records has been very poor. Eyewitness accounts such as that of the Comte de Dammartin which we quoted in Chapter 8 are rare as hen's teeth and, when they do occur, are usually found copied into other documents.

That leaves us with the chroniclers. Many chronicles make reference to the battle and the events before and after. Of these, the two best known are the chronicles of Jean Froissart and Geoffrey le Baker.

Froissart was probably in his late teens when the battle was fought and did not take part in the battle. He wrote his chronicle many years later, and for his description of Poitiers relied heavily on a French chronicler, Jean le Bel, although he did have access to some eyewitnesses as well. But his account of the battle is confused and muddy, and it is not always clear that he is describing events in the order they really happened. There is a great deal that is illogical in terms of military probability. But Froissart was not trying to reconstruct the battle. He loved grand scenes that displayed the virtues of chivalry for all to see. To this end, he puts flowery speeches into the mouths of his characters, sometimes even in the heat of battle. We have quoted from a few of these speeches, where we think there is a reasonable chance that they actually were delivered; others are obviously his idea of what people might have said, or should have said, in the circumstances.

Historians have damned Froissart for his inaccuracies, but everyone uses him; for any historian of the 14th century, there simply is no choice but to cite Froissart from time to time, crossing one's fingers as one does so. Fortunately, there is another source for the battle of Poitiers against which Froissart can be checked. The chronicle of Geoffrey le Baker contains the most detailed account of the battle, and it seems clear too that Baker really is trying to reconstruct what happened. He seems to have had access to both eyewitnesses and some official records of the campaign. He too invents flowery speeches, like the Prince of Wales's soliloquy to his men on the morning of the battle, but he tells us quite plainly that he *is* inventing, and why. Like all historians, Baker got things wrong, but when researching our previous book, *The Road to Crécy*, we were impressed by the number of things he also got right.

Even so, there are holes in Baker's account that need to be filled. Chandos Herald, gossipy and cheerful with a keen eye for damsels, recounts a few incidents, and several other chroniclers like Baker who had access to official documents – Robert of Avesbury and the authors of the *Anonimalle Chronicle* and *Eulogium Historiarum*, for example – can help with details too.

But gaps still remain. There are contradictions and confusions between accounts. Was Maurice de Berkeley captured during the final pursuit and chase, or midway through the battle? The latter seems on balance more likely, so we have gone with that. Did William Douglas serve with Clermont's mounted contingent, as Froissart suggests, or with the men-at-arms on foot, as other sources seem to think? Given that Douglas supposedly advised King Jean to dismount most of his army and fight on foot, it seems unlikely that he would then volunteer to join the mounted contingent. Did the Duc d'Orléans or the Dauphin command the first division of the French army? We know that the Dauphin was hustled away from the battle by his guardians, so the second division, which saw little fighting, would seem to make more sense. All these judgements are based on the evidence as we see it, but we accept that the truth cannot be known absolutely and our judgements are to some extent acts of faith.

There are several puzzling aspects about the battle which historians have long debated, and doubtless will continue to debate. Here, we set out what we believe happened, and our reasons for this belief.

The battlefield

The battlefield of Poitiers is now largely covered in suburban housing, and only the area down by the river Miosson, around the Gué de l'Omme, has survived in anything like its original condition. The terrain has changed, the forests have shrunk and the vineyards have gone.

In the 19th century there was not even a consensus on where the battle took place. That has now been largely resolved, and most historians agree that it took place west of Nouaillé, on the far side of the wooded hill that rises above the town. It seems clear that the left flank of the line was close to the Miosson; recall the English archers running along the top of the bank to shoot into the flank of the advancing French. That flank was probably a little west of the Gué de l'Omme itself, as it seems reasonable that the baggage train moved behind the Anglo-Gascon front line when it went down to the river that morning.

The hedgerow behind which the front line sheltered has long since gone, but surviving accounts of the battle describe the hedgerow, the gaps in it, and the vineyard. Our account suggests that the rows of vines ran parallel to the English line. Vineyards are usually planted to run down the slope instead of across it, as this makes for better drainage.

Accounts of the English disposition vary. We have chosen to largely follow Baker, on the grounds that he had access to better sources, both official records and eyewitnesses. The division on the left was clearly commanded by Warwick. There is a notion that Salisbury commanded the division on the right; this is possible, but it would seem odd to set the young and comparatively inexperienced Salisbury over a seasoned veteran like Suffolk, even if the former was a close friend of the Prince of Wales. During the campaign of 1355, Salisbury and Suffolk had been joint commanders of a division, and we opted for the same arrangement here.

Battle formation

The standard tactical formation of English armies of the period was for each division to form a row of foot soldiers, including dismounted men-at-arms, the row being three to four men deep in the centre, and then the archers on the wings in wedge formations which contemporary sources describe as a 'herce', or harrow. Debate has long raged about what exactly this herce formation looked like. Fortunately, we don't have to get into that discussion because we don't think the herce formation was used at Poitiers.

Why not? One reason is the nature of the ground. A wedge formation, of whatever shape, is useful in open fields, such as at Crécy and Neville's Cross. But in this rather tangled landscape of hedgerows and vineyards, the effectiveness of the wedge would have been lost. Also, in the battles just mentioned, the English were positioned on the forward slope of a hill. That meant the men at the rear of the wedge could still see and aim at the enemy. This was not the case at Poitiers where the English do not seem to have enjoyed an advantage of elevation (though the Prince of Wales and his household are described as being on a hill, perhaps the lower slopes of the afore-mentioned hill west of Nouaillé). Finally, there is the relatively small number of archers the prince had at his disposal, no more than 2,000. The wedges would have been relatively small.

Our argument is that the prince broke with existing tactical doctrine – as he did several times that day – and put his archers into the line alongside the men-at-arms. This would allow them to shoot at the enemy at very close range, giving their arrows a better chance of penetrating French armour. It seems clear that during the hand-to-hand fighting, the archers were engaging with the enemy alongside the English and Gascon men-at-arms, something they would not have done if they were in their wedge formations at the ends of the line of battle. It should be noted that other commanders, including Thomas Dagworth and Walter Bentley, did not always use the wedge formation either.

What were the prince's intentions on the morning of the battle?

Historians have puzzled over whether the prince meant to give battle. The trigger to the debate is the decision to send the baggage train, escorted by some of Warwick's men, over the Gué de l'Omme before the French came into sight. It has been argued that this was the first move of a planned withdrawal. The prince had lost his nerve and decided the risks of battle were too great, and he would retreat. The arrival of the French army forced him to change his mind; it was too late to retreat, and he would have to stand and fight.

We concede this is entirely possible, but we would point out several pieces of evidence against such a conclusion. First, if the prince had wanted to retreat, he could easily have done so on Sunday. Instead, he chose to hold on to his position even though his army was short of food. That suggests he liked the position and thought he could fight and win a battle there. He also spent a good deal of time on Sunday improving the position, digging pits and throwing up barricades. Second, the prince told Cardinal Talleyrand that he intended to fight.

Of course, the prince might have changed his mind; he would not be the first commander to do so. But we think the vital issue was the supply problem. The prince needed the French to attack, and that may have been one of the reasons he was angry with Talleyrand. Without the cardinal's interference, King Jean might have been moved to ignore the Truce of God and attack on Sunday, and that would have suited the prince down to the ground. But by Monday morning, the food shortage was becoming acute. If Jean did not attack, hunger would force the English to retreat. Despite Talleyrand's assurance that the French would attack, as time passed the prince may well have become worried that *they* had lost their nerve and were holding back. So, the movement of the baggage train may well have presaged a retreat, but not for the reasons hitherto supposed.

What happened to the French second division?

Contemporary accounts are unanimous that, after the failure of the marshals' attack and the breaking of the French first division, the second division retreated without striking a blow. Much is made of the right of independent withdrawal, and there is no doubt that some French men-at-arms, thinking the battle was lost, did choose to exercise this right and departed the battle. But it seems inconceivable that an entire division of several thousand men-at-arms – led by the king's son and heir, and before the eyes of the king himself – would choose to exercise that right simultaneously.

Others have suggested that the commanders of the second division mistook or misread signals and thought they had been ordered to retreat. This is possible, and with the Constable and marshals dead or captured, it is not clear who was now giving orders in the French army at all. Less likely is the notion that the second division, watching the first division break, believed the battle was lost. The whole point of this formation, as every man-at-arms would have known, is that if the first division was forced to retire, the second would take up the assault.

There is a simpler solution, and this is the one we have adopted. The first division's attack on the English line lasted for some time, and the second division would have had plenty of time to come up close behind. When the first division broke, the press of men forced the second division back too. Although some men probably were carried away from the battlefield, it seems clear that quite a few rallied around the third division and joined it when it advanced. We know the third division was originally the same size as the other two, yet it is spoken of as being much larger when it advanced. This could only be true if men from the other two divisions joined it.

The Captal de Buch's ride

One of the most famous incidents of the battle is the Captal de Buch's intervention, riding around the left flank of the French army with his mounted force and attacking the French from the rear. There has been much debate over where the Captal actually went, sparked off by the chroniclers' accounts which state that the Captal went behind a 'hill' for concealment. Historians have looked in vain for a hill on the French left flank, and found none. Various theories have been advanced, including one which suggests that the Captal actually went the other direction, around the French *right* flank. This is a highly complicated manoeuvre which would have involved crossing the Miosson twice, and indeed the knowledge that the Miosson actually could be crossed further along, in the right place to bring the Captal's force against the French rear.

Again, this seems far too complicated. Let us stop worrying about the 'hill'. The reference to a hill could easily be a misunderstanding or exaggeration on the part of the chroniclers. A man on horseback presents a silhouette no more than 8 or 9 feet in height. That means even a relatively modest fold in the ground will be enough to hide him from sight. Recall too that the attention of the French was fixed on the enemy to their front. If the Captal's men faded into the trees behind the English position, they could easily have circled around the French lines using trees and low undulations in the ground for cover, and come out behind the French third division. This is a safer and easier manoeuvre than crossing the river, and much more likely to succeed.

Casualties

As usual in medieval battles, we have lists of names of the important people who died, but little or no information about the others. The figures we have given for the French – 3,000 men-at-arms captured and 2,000 killed, plus around 800 others killed as well – are generally accepted and seem realistic. Despite the severity of the hand-to-hand fighting along the hedgerow, the majority of the dead are likely to have been killed during the rout that followed the breaking of the king's division. Very few of those men would have got away.

English casualties are a mystery. No personage of note was killed; James Audley was the most high-profile wounded man. It would be logical to assume a death toll of several hundred, plus an equal number of wounded, nearly all in the fighting along the hedgerow. Once the rout began, despite the severity of some of the individual combats, English and Gascon losses would have been slight.

Notes

Chapter 1

1 M. Livingstone and M. Witzel, *The Road to Crécy: The English Invasion of France, 1346*, London: Longman, 2005, p. 275. The figure of 10,000 includes non-combatants such as servants, grooms and drivers.

2 Livingstone and Witzel, *The Road to Crécy*, pp. 291–2.

3 Although aid did come, from another division of the army; it is possible that the king already knew this, hence his insouciance to Sir Thomas Norwich. Livingstone and Witzel, *The Road to Crécy*.

4 *The Chronicle of Geoffrey le Baker*, p. 74.

5 *Chronique de Jean le Bel*, p. 103.

6 The English royal secretary Michel de Northburgh recorded 1,542 dead French knights and nobles on the field at Crécy; most of the rest of the dead would have been Genoese crossbowmen. An unknown number of French and allies were also killed during the sortie the following morning. English losses were slight, as few as three knights and a couple of hundred other ranks. See also Livingstone and Witzel, pp. 315–16.

7 J. Sumption, *The Hundred Years War: Trial by Battle*, p. 356, estimates the size of this army at 15,000–20,000.

8 Following the battle of Agincourt in 1415 and the ensuing peace settlement, England occupied a large portion of modern France, but the English continued to face bitter resistance and were unable to fully pacify the country or rule it for long.

9 One of Philippe IV's childless sons had ruled briefly as Philippe VI.

10 Livingstone and Witzel, *The Road to Crécy*.

11 J. Sumption, *The Hundred Years War*, vol. 1, *Trial by Battle*, London: Faber & Faber, 1990.

12 Livingstone and Witzel, *The Road to Crécy*.

13 The scene is described in detail, albeit at second or third hand, by Jean Froissart, *Chroniques*, vol. 2, pp. 177–80.

14 D. Lenoir, *Prevues généalogiques at historiques de la maison d'Harcourt*, Paris, 1907.

15 A. R. Bridbury, *England and the Salt Trade in the Later Middle Ages*, Oxford: Clarendon, 1955; L. F. Saltzman, *English Trade in the Middle Ages*, Oxford: Clarendon, 1931.

16 The canonisation was quickly revoked after lobbying from his political rivals, but in 1904 Charles was finally beatified, the next level below sainthood.

17 W. M. Ormrod, *The Reign of Edward III: Crown and Political Society in England, 1327–1377*, London: Guild, 1990.

18 Livingstone and Witzel, *The Road to Crécy*.

19 J. Mumby, R. Barber and R. Brown, *Edward III's Round Table at Windsor*, Woodbridge: The Boydell Press, 2007.

20 R. Barber, *Edward, Prince of Wales and Aquitaine: A Biography of the Black Prince*, pp. 84–5, discusses the controversy of the actual date of foundation and the reasons for assigning this particular date. See also Barber, *Edward III and the Triumph of England: The Battle of Crécy and the Order of the Garter*. Ormrod, *The Reign of Edward III*, makes the point that Edward also made many references to St George and was one of the first English kings to popularise his cult.

21 Barber, *Edward, Prince of Wales and Aquitaine*, p. 84.

22 Ibid., p. 89.

23 Ibid., pp. 88–9.

24 J. Hatcher, *The Black Death*, London: Phoenix, 2008, p. 37.

25 Quoted in Hatcher, *The Black Death*, p. 55.

26 Hatcher, *The Black Death*, p. 87.

27 Ibid.

28 This has long been a historian's rule of thumb, but much evidence supports it. For example. John Hatcher, *The Black Death*, reports that harvest yields in 1349 and 1350 were only about 30–40 per cent of the long-term average, which would be consisted with a drop in manpower of about a third.

29 Froissart, *Chroniques*, vol. 2, pp. 239–40.

30 Ibid., p. 243.

31 Ibid., p. 246.

32 R. W. Kaeuper and E. Kennedy, *The Book of Chivalry of Geoffroi de Charny: Text, Context and Translation*, Philadelphia: University of Philadelphia Press, 1996.

33 Bramborough's name is sometimes also given as Richmond, or John.

34 Froissart, *Chroniques*, vol. 2, p. 240.

35 Ibid.

36 For the fate of the Genoese contingent at Crécy, see Livingstone and Witzel, *The Road to Crécy*.

37 Froissart, *Chroniques*, vol. 2, p. 258.

38 He is sometimes referred to as Jean I, but that title is more usually accorded to Jean the son of Louis X who was born posthumously and 'reigned' from his birth until his death five days later. As the infant was never crowned, it could be argued that he was never actually king.

39 H. J. Hewitt, *The Black Prince's Expedition*, Manchester: Manchester University Press, 1958, p. 3; Barber, *Edward, Prince of Wales and Aquitaine*, p. 113.

Chapter 2

1 A. Pellisier, *Innocent VI le reformateur, deuxième pape Limousin (1352–1362)*, Tulle: F. Layotte, 1961.

2 For an account of Rienzo's career and his negotiations with Innocent, see A. L. Collins, *Greater Than Emperor: Cola di Rienzo and the World of Fourteenth-Century Rome*, Ann Arbor: University of Michigan Press, 2002.

3 The best account of the course of the negotiations is probably that of Sumption in *The Hundred Years War*, vol. 2, pp. 139–41.

4 John of Fordun, *Chronica Gentis Scotorum*, ed. W. F. Skene, *John of Fordun's Chronicle of the Scottish Nation*, Edinburgh: Edmonston and Douglas, 1872.

5 Quoted in Barber, *Edward Prince of Wales and Aquitaine*, p. 113.

6 Barber, p. 33.

7 Barber, p. 22.

8   S. McGlynn, *By Sword and Fire: Cruelty and Atrocity in Medieval Warfare*, London: Weidenfeld & Nicolson, 1978.

9   Barber, p. 16.

10 Ibid., p. 22.

11 D. Green, *Edward the Black Prince: Power in Medieval Europe*, Harlow: Longman, 2007; see also J. Harvey, *The Black Prince and His Age*, London: B. T. Batsford, 1976.

12 *The Register of Walter de Stapledon, Bishop of Exeter, 1307–1326*, ed. F. C. Hingeston-Randolph, London, 1892.

13 I. Mortimer, *The Perfect King: The Life of Edward III, Father of the English Nation*, London: Vintage, 2008.

14 W. M. Ormrod, 'Ufford, Robert, first Earl of Suffolk', *Oxford Dictionary of National Biography*, 2004.

15 N. H. Nicholas, *The Controversy Between Sir Richard Scrope and Sir Robert Grosvenor in the Court of Chivalry, AD MCCCLXXXV-MCCCXC*, London, 1832.

16 It is sometimes claimed that Hawkwood fought at Crécy as well as Poitiers, but the evidence for this is less certain. There is no evidence to support the legend that he was knighted on the battlefield after Poitiers. See W. Caferro, *John Hawkwood: An English Mercenary in Fourteenth-Century Italy*, Baltimore: Johns Hopkins University Press, 2006.

17 A. E. Prince, 'The Strength of English Armies in the Reign of Edward III', *English Historical Review* 46, 1951, pp. 355–66.

18 Hewitt, *The Black Prince's Expedition*, p. 20.

19 Hewitt, p. 17; *Register of Edward the Black Prince*, vol. 3, pp. 198–205.

20 *Register of Edward the Black Prince*, vol. 3, pp. 199–200.

21 PRO E101/169.

22 *Register of Edward the Black Prince*, vol. 3, p. 205.

23 Sumption, *The Hundred Years War*, vol. 2, p. 147.

24 N. Saul, *Scenes From Provincial Life: Knightly Familes in Sussex, 1280–1400*; Saul, *Knights and Esquires: The Gloucestershire Gentry in the Fourteenth Century*.

25 R. E. Oakeshott, *The Sword in the Age of Chivalry*, London, 1961, pp. 13–14.

26 For information on medieval horses, especially war horses, see A. Ayton, *Knights and Warhorses: Military Service and the English Aristocracy under Edward III*, Woodbridge: Boydell and Brewer; A. Hyland, *The Horse in the Middle Ages*, Stroud: Sutton, 1999.

27 Hewitt, *The Black Prince's Expedition*, p. 32.

28 *Register of Edward the Black Prince*, vol. 3, pp. 206–7.

29 Ibid., p. 204.

30 E. Burke, *The History of Archery*, London: Heinemann, 1958; C. J. Longman and H. Walrond, *Archery*, London: Longmans, Green & Co, 1884, especially Chapter 7; R. Hardy, *Longbow*; T. Foy, *A Guide to Archery*, London: Pelham Books, 1980.

31 Livingstone and Witzel, *The Road to Crécy*.

32 *Register of Edward the Black Prince*, vol. 3, p. 204.

33 Ibid., p. 212.

34 Barber, *Edward Prince of Wales and Aquitaine*, pp. 114–15.

35 *Register of Edward the Black Prince*, vol. 3, p. 214.

36 Ibid., pp. 214–16.

37 Hewitt, *The Black Prince's Expedition*, makes a fair attempt at reconstructing the flotilla and discovering the names and ports of origin of each ship. The detail concerning Clerk comes from Barber, *Edward Prince of Wales and Aquitaine*.

Chapter 3

1 Sumption, *The Hundred Years War*, vol. 2, p. 162.

2 Sumption, p. 164, believes that the French were unclear about English intentions and believed the main invasion force would land in Calais and attack Picardy. This seems surprising, given the obvious advantages to England that control of Normandy would give. French intelligence concerning English strategic intentions was usually fairly accurate.

3 See R. Cazelles, *Société politique, noblesse et couronne sous Jean le Bon et Charles V*, Geneva: Librairie Droz, 1982; P. Contamine (ed.), *La noblesse au moyen age*, Paris: Fayard, 1976.

4 See particularly J. R. Strayer, *The Reign of Philip the Fair*, Ann Arbor: University of Michigan Press, 1980.

5 J. B. Henneman, *Royal Taxation in Fourteenth-Century France: The Development of War Financing, 1322–1356*, Princeton: Princeton University Press, 1971.

6 P. Contamine, 'The Norman "Nation" and the French "Nation" in the Fourteenth and Fifteenth Centuries', in D. Bates and A. Curry (eds), *England and Normandy in the Middle Ages*, London: The Hambledon Press, 1994. The essays in this volume are very useful for a better understanding of contemporary Normandy.

7 N. Vincent, 'The Magna Carta (1215) and the *Charte aux Normands* (1315): Some Anglo-Norman Connections and Correspondences', *The Jersey and Guernsey Law Review*, vol. 2, 2015, pp. 189–97.

8 For biographies of the Dauphin, who later became King Charles V of France, see J. Quillet, *Charles V, le Roi lettré*, Paris: Perrin, 2002, and F. Autrand, *Charles V le Sage*, Paris: Fayard 1992.

9 Sumption, *The Hundred Years War*, vol. 2, p. 195.

10 *The Chronicle of Geoffrey le Baker*, p. 108.

11 Froissart, *Chroniques*, vol. 2, p. 279.

12 Sumption, *The Hundred Years War*, vol. 2, p. 68.

13 J. Deviosse, *Jean le Bon*, Paris: Fayard, 1985; Cazelles, *Société politique, noblesse et couronne sous Jean le Bon et Charles V*.

14 D. J. D. Boulton, *The Knights of the Crown: The Monarchical Orders of Knighthood in Later Medieval Europe, 1325–1520*, Woodbridge: Boydell, 2000.

15 *The Chronicle of Geoffrey le Baker*, p. 101.

16 Barber, *Edward, Prince of Wales and Aquitaine*, p. 103. Other accounts say the number of Knights of the Star who died at Mauron may have been as high as 90.

17 Deviosse, *Jean le Bon*.

18 Froissart, *Chroniques*, quoted in Sumption, *The Hundred Years War*, vol. 2, p. 68.

19 Kaeuper and Kennedy, *The Book of Chivalry of Geoffroi de Charny*. See also M. Keen, *Chivalry*, London: Yale University Press, 1984, for an assessment of Charny and his ideas.

20 A good biography of Gautier de Brienne is still lacking. D. M. Nicol, *The Despotate of Epirus, 1267–1470: A Contribution to the History of Greece in the Middle Ages*, Cambridge: Cambridge University Press, and W. Miller, *The Latins in the Levant: A History of Frankish Greece, 1204–1566*, New York: E.P. Dutton, 1908 are the best sources for his early life and career.

21 P. Contamine, *Guerre, État et Société à la Fin du Moyen Âge*, Paris: Mouton, 1972.

22 Livingstone and Witzel, *The Road to Crécy*.

23 Keen, *Chivalry*.

24 An account of his career can be found in Contamine, *War in the Middle Ages*.

25 C. L. Kingsford, 'Knollys, Robert', *Dictionary of National Biography*; P. Contamine, *War in the Middle Ages*.

26 F. de Bernardy, *Princes of Monaco*, London, 1961, p. 17.

27 According to some accounts Doria was killed at Crécy, but there is also evidence that he survived the battle; Livingstone and Witzel, *The Road to Crécy*.

28 R. Payne-Galway, *The Book of the Crossbow*, London, 1995.

29 F. Bilson, *Crossbows*, Newton Abbot: David & Charles, 1974.

30 Livingstone and Witzel, *The Road to Crécy*.

31 *The Chronicle of Geoffrey le Baker*, pp. 98–9, 108.

32 Froissart, *Chroniques*, vol. 2, p. 251.

33 Sumption, *The Hundred Years War*, vol. 2, p. 167.

34 Froissart, *Chroniques*, vol. 2, p. 282.

Chapter 4

1 *The Chronicle of Geoffrey le Baker*, p. 110; *Register of the Black Prince*; Hewitt, *The Black Prince's Expedition*, p. 40.

2 Today known as Castillon-la-Bataille, after the final battle of the Hundred Years War which was fought nearby in 1453.

3 David Green, *The Battle of Poitiers, 1356*, Stroud: The History Press, 2008, pp. 130–2, gives a useful potted biography of the Captal.

4 Keen, *Chivalry*; see also T. Jones, *Chaucer's Knight: The Portrait of a Medieval Mercenary*, London: Eyre Methuen, 1980.

5 For biographies of Gaston, see R. Vernier, *Lord of the Pyrenees: Gaston Fébus, Count of Foix (1331–1391)*, Woodbridge: Boydell, 2008; S. Lagabrielle, *Gaston Fébus: Prince Soleil 1331–1391*, Paris: Grand Palais, 2011.

6 N. P. Zacour, 'Talleyrand: The Cardinal of Périgord (1301–1364)', *Transactions of the American Philosophical Society* n.s. 50 (7), 1960, pp. 54–60; D. Wood, *Clement VI: The Pontificate and Ideas of an Avignon Pope*, Cambridge: Cambridge University Press, 1989.

7 *The Chronicle of Geoffrey le Baker*, p. 110. Baker is the principal primary source for the events that follow; other chroniclers, even Froissart and Jean le Bel, barely mention the events of the autumn and winter of 1355. Hewitt, *The Black Prince's Expedition*, reconstructs the campaign, and any gaps in his narrative are filled by the meticulous work of Hoskins, *In the Steps of the Black Prince*.

8 Hewitt, pp. 49–50.

9 *The Chronicle of Geoffrey le Baker*, p. 111.

10 Ibid.

11 Ibid.

12 Ibid.

13 Three other founding members, Sanchet d'Abrichecourt, Hugh Courtenay and Thomas Wale, had predeceased Lisle, but all had died of natural causes, Abrichecourt and Courtenay most likely of the Black Death.

14 Baker makes no reference to an attack, but one French historian reckons several assaults on the town were made; see S. Dejean, 'L'incursion du Prince Noir en Agenais et en Touloussain (1355)', in *La Guerre au Moyen Age*, Toulouse: Académie Touloussaine d'Histoire et d'Arts Militaires, 1994, pp. 36–53.

15 *The Chronicle of Geoffrey le Baker*, p. 112.

16 Ibid.

17 Ibid.

18 J. H. Mundy, *Society and Government at Toulouse in the Age of the Cathars*, Toronto: Pontifical

Institute of Medieval Studies, 1997; see also L. Ariste and L. Braud, *Histoire Populaire de Toulouse*, Toulouse: Midi Republicain, 1898.

19 M. Cowper, *Cathar Castles: Fortresses of the Albigensian Crusade 1209–1300*, Oxford: Osprey; J. Catalo, 'Pôle de pouvoir et entrée de ville: le château Narbonnais de Toulouse', 4e Congrès International d'Archéologie Médiévale et Moderne, Paris, 3–8 septembre 2007, http://medieval-europe-paris-2007.univ-paris1.fr/J.%20Catalo.pdf.

20 J. Sumption, *The Albigensian Crusade*, London: Faber, 1978; J. R. Strayer, *The Albigensian Crusades*, Ann Arbor: University of Michigan Press, 1993.

21 Froissart believes that the people of Toulouse were ready to fight, but Armagnac refused to call them up, thinking they would not be able to stand up to the experienced English troops; Froissart, *Oeuvres*, 5, 343.

22 Hoskins, *In the Steps of the Black Prince*, p. 55.

23 *The Chronicle of Geoffrey le Baker*, p. 113.

24 Froissart, *Oeuvres*, 5, 346

25 *The Chronicle of Geoffrey le Baker*, p. 112.

26 Hoskins, *In the Steps of the Black Prince*, p. 59.

27 Cowper, *Cathar Castles*; F. de Lannoy, *La Cité de Carcassonne*, Bayeux: Heimdal, 2004; J. Poux, *La Cité de Carcassonne*, Toulouse: Privat, 1923.

28 *The Chronicle of Geoffrey le Baker*, p. 114.

29 J. Michaud and A. Cabanis (eds), *Histoire de Narbonne*, Toulouse: Privat, 2004.

30 *The Chronicle of Geoffrey le Baker*, p. 115.

31 Ibid., p. 116.

32 Ibid., p. 118.

33 G. Minois, *Poitiers*, Paris: Tallandier, 2014, p. 76.

34 Hewitt, *The Black Prince's Expedition*, pp. 73–4.

Chapter 5

1 Chandos Herald, *Life of the Black Prince*, pp. 9–10.

2 His first name is also sometimes given as Philippe.

3 M. J. Depoin, *La maison de Chambly sous les Capétiens directs*, Paris: Imprimerie National, 1915, pp. 150–51.

4 Sumption, *The Hundred Years War*, vol. 2, pp. 192–3.

5 Chandos Herald, *Life of the Black Prince*; Sumption, *The Hundred Years War*, vol. 2, p. 190; Hewitt, *The Black Prince's Expedition*, p. 88.

6 Sumption, *The Hundred Years War*, vol. 2, p. 190.

7 John Wingfield, writing from Bordeaux around this time, thought that Jean d'Armagnac himself was inside the city of Agen, but given what we know about Armagnac's movements during this winter, that seems unlikely.

8 Chronicle of Robert of Avesbury, p. 46.

9 The text of several of these letters is preserved in the chronicle of Robert of Avesbury.

10 John of Fordun, *Chronicle*, pp. 374–5.

11 Froissart, *Chroniques*, vol. 2, pp. 285–8; Sumption, *The Hundred Years War*, vol. 2, pp. 196–8.

12 Froissart, *Chroniques*, vol. 2, pp. 288, 291.

13 Minois, *Poitiers*, pp. 90–1.

14 R. Cazelles, 'Le parti navarrais jusqu'a la mort d'Étienne Marcel', *Bulletin philologique et historique do Comité des Travaux Historiques et Scientifiques*, 1960, pp. 839–69.

15 Froissart, *Chroniques*, vol. 2, pp. 296–7; Sumption, *The Hundred Years War*, vol. 2, pp. 205–7.

16 Minois, *Poitiers*, p. 97.

17 Sumption, *The Hundred Years War*, vol. 2, p. 210.

18 *Register of Edward the Black Prince*, vol. 3, p. 224.

19 Ibid., pp. 223–4.

20 Sumption, *The Hundred Years War*, vol. 2, p. 211.

21 Minois, *Poitiers*, p. 100.

22 Sumption, *The Hundred Years War*, vol. 2, pp. 219–20. See also K. Fowler, *The King's Lieutenant: Henry of Grosmont, First Duke of Lancaster 1310–1361*, New York: Barnes & Noble, 1969.

23 Froissart, *Chroniques*, vol. 2, pp. 291–2.

24 Ibid.

25 Minois, *Poitiers*, p. 106.

26 Froissart, *Chroniques* translation, vol. 2, p. 292. Froissart says two months, but other sources speak of the siege being lifted on 20 August (see Chapter 6); Froissart is perhaps referring also to the earlier siege, lifted by Lancaster, and adding the two together.

27 Livingstone and Witzel, *The Road to Crécy*; A. Ayton and P. Preston, *The Battle of Crécy, 1346*, Woodbridge: Boydell, 2005.

28 For example, see J. M. Tourneur-Aumont, *La bataille de Poitiers (1356) et la construction de France*, Paris: Sceaux, 1940; Hewitt, *The Black Prince's Expedition*; Sumption, *The Hundred Years War*, vol. 2, *Trial by Fire*. For a contrary point of view, that the prince actually had a clear strategic goal in mind, see Hoskins, *In the Steps of the Black Prince*; Minois, *Poitiers*; C. J. Rogers, *War Cruel and Sharp: English Strategy under Edward III, 1327–1360*, Woodbridge: Boydell, 2000; Barber, *Edward Prince of Wales and Aquitaine*.

29 *The Chronicle of Geoffrey le Baker*, pp. 119–20; chronicle of Robert of Avesbury, p. 50; Sumption, *The Hundred Years War*, vol. 2, p. 225. It is possible that this was a bluff, designed to distract the French still further and keep them focused on the north, for this third expedition never actually set out.

30 This is the view taken by Barber, *Edward Prince of Wales and Aquitaine*.

31 Hoskins, *In the Steps of the Black Prince*, pp. 127–8.

32 Minois, *Poitiers*, p. 111.

33 *The Chronicle of Geoffrey le Baker*, p. 120.

34 This is the generally agreed modern estimate – Sumption in *The Hundred Yeard War*, vol. 2, suggests 6–7,000 – and tallies quite closely with the contemporary estimate of Froissart, who says the prince had 2,000 men-at-arms and 6,000 archers; Froissart, *Chroniques*, vol. 2, p. 294. Baker gives slightly different figures; 4,000 men-at-arms, 2,000 archers and 1,000 other foot soldiers. His estimate is likely to be closer to correct. *The Chronicle of Geoffrey le Baker*, p. 122.

35 *Anonimalle Chronicle*, p. 35.

Chapter 6

1 Minois, *Poitiers*, p. 113; Hoskins, *In the Steps of the Black Prince*, p. 129.

2 Hoskins, *In the Steps of the Black Prince*, pp. 130–33.

3 A. Grézillier, *Histoire de Rochechouart, des origines à la Révolution*, Paris: Dupanier, 1977.

4 *The Chronicle of Geoffrey le Baker*, p. 120.

5 Ibid.

6 *Anonimalle Chronicle, 1331–1381*, ed. V. H. Galbraith, Manchester, 1970. Once again, Peter Hoskins has done some excellent detective work, filling in the gaps in the *Anonimalle* account.

7   Livingstone and Witzel, *The Road to Crécy*, p. 221.
8   Hoskins, *In the Steps of the Black Prince*, and Fowler, *The King's Lieutenant*, both suggest Aimery was killed later in the summer, but he seems to have still been alive in 1365. It is possible that he is being confused with Jean de Rochechouart.
9   S. L. Field, 'Marie of St.-Pol and Her Books', *English Historical Review* 125, 2010, pp. 255–78.
10 Hoskins, *In the Steps of the Black Prince*, p. 141, unpicks the complicated ownership of Le Dorat.
11 *Eulogium Historiarum*, p. 217.
12 Froissart, *Chroniques*, vol. 2, p. 294.
13 Minois, *Poitiers*, p. 116.
14 This incident is described by Hoskins, *In the Steps of the Black Prince*, pp. 143–4, after the work of a local historian; we have not been able to trace the source. There is no André listed among the offspring of Louis de Chauvigny, but he may have been an illegitimate son, in which case he would not necessarily appear in genealogies.
15 Hoskins believes this force consisted of the other two divisions, the vanguard and rearguard; *In the Steps of the Black Prince*, p. 45. This would make Warwick the obvious commander.
16 Froissart, *Chroniques*, vol. 2, p. 295.
17 *The Chronicle of Geoffrey le Baker*, pp. 119–20.
18 Froissart, *Chroniques*, vol. 2, p. 295.
19 Ibid., p. 296.
20 *The Chronicle of Geoffrey le Baker*, pp. 119–20; *Eulogium*, p. 219. Once again, accounts of the affray are confused. The *Eulogium* believes the English were heavily outnumbered, but this is unlikely. Baker asserts that the French were all killed or captured, but we know this is untrue, as Gris Mouton himself escaped the battlefield. This skirmish is usually said to have taken place the following day, 28 August, but we find this hard to match with the distances and routes travelled; it seems to us far more likely that the skirmish happened on the 27th.
21 Froissart, *Chroniques*, vol. 2, p. 295.
22 Chandos Herald reckoned the French force at about 10,000, but he is probably only counting the men-at-arms; *Life of the Black Prince*, p. 10.
23 Froissart, *Chroniques*, vol. 2, p. 297.
24 Ibid.
25 Ibid., pp. 298–9.
26 Ibid., p. 299. Some histories give the date of the army's arrival at Romorantin as 30 August.
27 Froissart, *Chroniques*, vol. 2, pp. 299–300.
28 *The Chronicle of Geoffrey le Baker*, p. 121.
29 *Eulogium Historiarum*, p. 217.
30 Minois, *Poitiers*, p. 120.

Chapter 7

1   Minois, *Poitiers*, p. 121.
2   E. Giraudet, *Histoire de la ville de Tours*, Tours, 1873, vol. 1, p. 146.
3   A. Luttrell, 'Juan Fernandez de Heredia's History of Greece', *Byzantine and Modern Greek Studies* 34(1), 2010, pp. 30–37.
4   *The Chronicle of Geoffrey le Baker*, p. 122.
5   Ibid.
6   Barber, *Edward, Prince of Wales and Aquitaine*, p. 136; Hewitt, *The Black Prince's Expedition*, p. 107. Both Barber and Hewitt are convinced that linking up with Lancaster was the prince's

primary objective, and it has been suggested that he intended to march north into Normandy. But to do so would have denuded Gascony not only of the prince and his men, but of a large force of Gascon men-at-arms and left the province virtually defenceless. That the prince contemplated some sort of joint action with Lancaster is entirely likely, but not a full-scale march north.

7   *Eulogium Historiarum*, p. 251.
8   Froissart, *Chroniques*, vol. 2, p. 301.
9   *Eulogium Historiarum*, p. 221.
10 *The Chronicle of Geoffrey le Baker*, p. 122.
11 Minois, *Poitiers*, p. 122.
12 *Eulogium Historiarum*, p. 221.
13 René Descartes, the 17th-century philosopher, was born there; the town was renamed in his honour in the 19th century.
14 P. H. Morice, *Memoirs pour servir de preuves a l'histoire ecclesiastique et civile de Bretagne*, Paris, 1742; Hoskins, *In the Steps of the Black Prince*, p. 160.
15 Hoskins believes that the prince's intelligence service had let him down and during his stay in Châtellerault he did not know for certain where the French were. This seems unlikely, given the distance between the two forces. If Edward knew where the Duke of Lancaster was, he must surely have known where the French were.
16 Froissart suggests that the English force led the French into an ambush prepared by the English main body, while Baker maintains that the scouting party fought the French alone; we have followed Baker's account on the grounds that he was using more contemporary sources and is usually – not always – more reliable. Froissart also says that Louis de Chauvigny was taken prisoner, but he is mistaken; other sources indicate that Chauvigny was killed at Poitiers two days later. Froissart, *Chroniques*, vol. 2, pp. 304–5; *The Chronicle of Geoffrey le Baker*, p. 122; *Eulogium Historiarum*, p. 222.
17 *The Chronicle of Geoffrey le Baker*, p. 122.
18 Froissart, *Chroniques*, vol. 2, pp. 312–13.
19 Chandos Herald, *Life of the Black Prince*, p. 12.
20 Ibid.; Froissart, *Chroniques*, vol. 2, pp. 313–14.
21 Chandos Herald, *Life of the Black Prince*, p. 12. Chandos Herald also names Boucicaut as among those who attended, but this is clearly a mistake; Boucicaut had been captured at Romorantin earlier in the month, and was still a prisoner.
22 Ibid.
23 Ibid.
24 Froissart, *Chroniques*, vol. 2, pp. 314–15.

Chapter 8

1   Froissart, *Chroniques*, vol. 2, p. 316.
2   Ibid.
3   Heredia is known in some sources simply as 'the castellan of Amposta', one of several official posts he held.
4   Chandos Herald, *Life of the Black Prince*, p. 13. The Herald is sympathetic to Talleyrand, and believes both sides were unjust in their criticism.
5   In other redactions, Froissart also refers to him as Louis de Recombes; his real identity has proved impossible to identify.

6 Froissart, *Chroniques*, p. 321.

7 Chandos Herald, *Life of the Black Prince*, p. 14.

8 Hoskins, *In the Steps of the Black Prince*, pp. 184–7.

9 There is considerable debate over the exact disposition and position of the English army; see the subsequent chapter on 'Reconstructing Poitiers'.

10 A reasonable assumption; vines are often (though not always) planted in rows up and down slopes so as to make better use of drainage.

11 Many sources insist that the English archers were deployed in the traditional wedge or herce formation, but there are problems with this; see the chapter on 'Reconstructing Poitiers'.

12 Froissart, *Chroniques*, vol. 2, p. 319 gives a lengthy list of English knights, but it is not clear which division some of them served in.

13 Alternatively, this may be a reference to the Dauphin's Normans arriving from Tours.

14 *The Chronicle of Geoffrey le Baker*, p. 124.

15 Baker lards his description of Poitiers with frequent paraphrases from and allusions to Lucan's *Pharsalia*. This traditions of invented grand speeches by commanders on the eve of battle goes back to Thucydides.

16 Froissart, *Oeuvres*, vol. 5, p. 376.

17 Chandos Herald seems convinced that this plan was adopted, stating that Edward gave orders for the army to withdraw south and that Warwick's vanguard had crossed the Miosson by the time the French attacked (Chandos Herald, *Life of the Black Prince*, p. 16). This view has been followed by some modern historians as well (Sumption, Hoskins). But the Herald's account is full of contradictions, and there are several good reasons for believing that this never happened; see the subsequent chapter on 'Reconstructing Poitiers'.

18 Froissart gives 21 names and adds 'and many more'. Large committees seldom make good decisions; Froissart, *Chroniques*, vol. 2, p. 307.

19 *The Chronicle of Geoffrey le Baker*, p. 126.

20 Froissart, *Chroniques*, vol. 2, p. 309.

21 *The Chronicle of Geoffrey le Baker*, p. 124, maintains that the original idea came from Douglas; it seems quite likely that Ribemont and Douglas had discussed the idea privately beforehand.

22 German armourers led the way in developing new techniques in plate armour for both men and horses, and it stands to reason that many of the Germans would have been more heavily armoured than their French counterparts.

23 Chandos Herald, *Life of the Black Prince*, p. 13, who puts the overall number at 4,000.

24 This is the generally accepted deployment, though Chandos Herald, p. 13, transposes the divisions of Orléans and the Dauphin. Baker places Douglas and his Scots with the marshals and their cavalry, but given that it had in part been Douglas's idea to fight on foot, this too seems unlikely.

25 Froissart, *Oeuvres*, vol. 5, p. 376. This may seem rather cowardly, but the practice was not uncommon. Other senior French nobles at Poitiers and other battles also used decoys.

26 Chandos Herald, *Life of the Black Prince*, p. 13.

27 Ibid., p. 15, rephrased slightly; the rather gentle translation loses the fairly obvious innuendo.

28 *The Chronicle of Geoffrey le Baker*, p. 127.

29 Quoted in Teutsch, *Victory at Poitiers*, p. 104.

30 *The Chronicle of Geoffrey le Baker*, p. 127.

31 Froissart, *Chroniques*, vol. 2, pp. 321–2.

32 According to both Froissart and Baker, Audrehem was captured during this first attack, but this seems unlikely given that the English were not at this point taking prisoners (as witnessed

by the death of Clermont). If we accept that Audrehem was defeated by Sir James Audley, then he was probably captured during the final pursuit (see below).

33 'Chronique Valois', quoted in Teutsch, *Victory at Poitiers*, pp. 108–9.

34 *The Chronicle of Geoffrey le Baker*, p. 127.

35 Chronique des Quatre Premiers Valois, quoted in Teutsch, *Victory at Poitiers*, p. 109.

36 Some sources indicate that Orléans and his entire division retreated without striking a blow; this seems unlikely, as we will discuss in the chapter on 'Reconstructing Poitiers'.

37 *The Chronicle of Geoffrey le Baker*, p. 128.

38 Froissart, *Chroniques*, vol. 2, pp. 333–4, is under the impression that Berkeley was captured during the final pursuit, but Baker is specific about his intent to attack the Dauphin. It is possible that Froissart is confusing two incidents, and Jean de Hellenes captured someone else.

39 *The Chronicle of Geoffrey le Baker*, p. 129.

40 Ibid.

41 The figure given by Baker, p. 129, but 'four hundred' is a number commonly used by chroniclers; the real number may have been less.

42 Nearly every source mentions the Captal de Buch's famous ride, even if there is still great debate as to exactly what course he followed; Teutsch and Hoskins believe that he rode around the *right* flank of the French, to the west (see the later chapter on 'Reconstructing Poitiers'). Whatever the truth, this was a remarkably bold and audacious movement, and one that could have easily gone wrong.

43 There is no indication that the prince ever rescinded his order to take no prisoners, but the changed circumstances would clearly have made taking prisoners permissible.

44 *The Chronicle of Geoffrey le Baker*, pp. 131–2.

45 Froissart, *Chroniques*, vol. 2, pp. 332–3.

46 Ibid., p. 131.

47 *Register of the Black Prince*, quoted in Sumption.

48 *The Chronicle of Geoffrey le Baker*, p. 131, paraphrasing from the *Aeneid*.

49 Green, *The Battle of Poitiers*, says that Bourbon was captured by the Captal de Buch, but it is possible that the Captal acquired his prisoner from another man who captured him; prisoners often changed hands after the battle was over.

50 Froissart says that Charny was killed by Reginald Cobham, which is unlikely in the extreme; Cobham knew Charny well, and would doubtless have persuaded him to surrender. It is much more likely that the chivalrous Charny met his end at the hands of low-born Gascons and English archers.

51 Froissart, *Chroniques*, vol. 2, p. 339.

52 Ibid.

Chapter 9

1 Froissart, *Chroniques*, vol. 2, p. 338.

2 *The Chronicle of Geoffrey le Baker*, p. 132.

3 Ibid.

4 This is the scene as reported by Baker, *The Chronicle of Geoffrey le Baker*, p. 132. Many others reported this famous scene as well. Some, like Froissart, *Chroniques*, vol. 2, pp. 340–1, add long rhetorical speeches by both Audley and the prince. In reality, Audley was far too badly wounded to sustain much conversation at all.

5 Hewitt, *The Black Prince's Expedition*, p. 137.

6 Froissart; *Chroniques*, vol. 2, p. 351.

7 These can be found in the published archives of Poitou, but are also included as footnotes in the Johnes edition of Froissart; *Chroniques*, vol. 2, pp. 347–50.

8 Sumption, *The Hundred Years War*, vol. 2, p. 247.

9 C. Given-Wilson and F. Briac, 'Edward III's Prisoners of War: The Battle of Poitiers and Its Context', *English Historical Review*, September 2001, pp. 802–33.

10 Keen, *Chivalry*; Given-Wilson and Briac, 'Edward III's Prisoners of War'; A. J. Kosto, *Hostages in the Middle Ages*, Oxford: Oxford University Press, 2012.

11 *The Chronicle of Geoffrey le Baker*, p. 132.

12 Chandos Herald, *Life of the Black Prince*, p. 19.

13 Froissart, *Chroniques*, vol. 2, p. 352.

14 For a more detailed account of the negotiations see *Grand Chronique de France*, pp. 83–9; Sumption, *The Hundred Years War*, vol. 2, pp. 257–60.

15 Froissart, *Chroniques*, vol. 2, p. 355.

16 Hewitt, *The Black Prince's Expedition*, p. 145.

17 R. Cazelles, *Étienne Marcel*, Paris: Taillandier, 2006.

18 *The Chronicle of Geoffrey le Baker*, p. 134.

19 Hewitt, *The Black Prince's Expedition*, pp. 160–2.

20 Ibid., p. 237.

21 Ibid., p. 234.

22 Ibid., pp. 231, 238.

23 Ibid., p. 238.

24 Ibid., p. 237.

25 Ibid.

26 M. Dommanget, *La Jacquerie*, Paris: Maspero, 1971; S. Luce, *Histoire de la Jacquerie d'après des documents inédits*, Paris: A. Durand, 1859.

27 Ibid.

28 Sumption, *The Hundred Years War*, vol. 2, p. 425.

29 Kosto, *Hostages in the Middle Ages*, pp. 11–12.

Bibliography

Primary sources

Adae Murimuth Contiuato Chronicarum, ed. E. M. Thompson, London, 1889.

Anonimalle Chronicle, 1331–1381, ed. V. H. Galbraith, Manchester, 1970.

Chandos Herald, *Life of the Black Prince*, trans. M. K. Pope and E. C. Lodge, Cambridge, Ont: In Parentheses Publications, 2000.

Chronicon Galfridi le Baker de Swynebroke, trans. D. Preest, *The Chronicle of Geoffrey le Baker*, Woodbridge: Boydell, 2012.

Chronique de Jean le Bel, eds J. Viard and E. Déprez, Paris, 1905.

Chronique des Quatre Premiers Valois (1327–1393), ed. S. Luce, Paris, 1862.

Chronique Nomande du XIVe Siécle, eds A. and E. Molinier, Paris, 1882.

Eulogium Historiarum, ed. F. S. Haydon, London, 1863.

Froissart, J., *Chroniques*, ed. T. Johnes, *Chronicles of England, France and Spain and adjoining counties*, London, 1896.

Froissart, J., *Oeuvres*, ed. Kervyn de Lettenhove, *Oeuvres de Froissart*, Brussels, 1868.

John of Fordun, *Chronica Gentis Scotorum*, ed. W. F. Skene, *John of Fordun's Chronicle of the Scottish Nation*, Edinburgh: Edmonston and Douglas, 1872.

PRO E101/169.

Register of Edward the Black Prince, ed. M. C. B. Dawes, London: HMSO, 1930–33, 4 vols.

Robertus de Avesbury de gestis mirabilis Regis Edwardi Tertii, ed. E. M. Thompson, Rolls Series, 1889.

The Register of Walter de Stapledon, Bishop of Exeter, 1307–1326, ed. F. C. Hingeston-Randolph, London, 1892.

Secondary sources

Allmand, C., *The Hundred Years War: England and France at War, c. 1300–c.1450*, Cambridge: Cambridge University Press, 1988.

Ariste, L. and Braud, L, *Histoire Populaire de Toulouse*, Toulouse: Midi Republicain, 1898.

Autrand, F., *Charles V le Sage*, Paris: Fayard, 1992.

Ayton, A., *Knights and Warhorses: Military Service and the English Aristocracy under Edward III*, Woodbridge: Boydell and Brewer, 1994.

Ayton, A. and Preston, P., *The Battle of Crécy, 1346*, Woodbridge: Boydell and Brewer, 2005.

Barber, R., *Edward, Prince of Wales and Aquitaine: A Biography of the Black Prince*, London: Allen Lane, 1978.

Barber, R. (ed.), *The Life and Campaigns of the Black Prince*, Woodbridge: Boydell and Brewer, 1986.

Barber, R., *Edward III and the Triumph of England: The Battle of Crécy and the Order of the Garter*, London: Allen Lane, 2013.

Bernardy F. de, *Princes of Monaco*, London: Arthur Barker, 1961.

Bilson, F., *Crossbows*, Newton Abbot: David & Charles, 1974.

Boitani, P. and Torti, A. (eds), *Literature in Fourteenth-Century England*, Cambridge: D. S. Brewer, 1983.

Boulton, D. J. D., *The Knights of the Crown: The Monarchical Orders of Knighthood in Later Medieval Europe, 1325–1520*, Woodbridge: Boydell and Brewer, 2000.

Boutell, C., *Arms and Armour in Antiquity and the Middle Ages*, London: Reeves & Turner, 1907; repr. Conshohocken, PA: Combined Books, 1996.

Bridbury, A. R., *England and the Salt Trade in the Later Middle Ages*, Oxford: Clarendon, 1955.

Burke, E., *The History of Archery*, London: Heinemann, 1958.

Burne, A. H., *The Crécy War: A Military History of the Hundred Years War from 1337 to the Peace of Bretigny, 1360*, London: Eyre and Spottiswood, 1955; repr. London: Wordsworth, 1999.

Caferro, W., *John Hawkwood: An English Mercenary in Fourteenth-Century Italy*, Baltimore: Johns Hopkins University Press, 2006.

Catalo, J., 'Pôle de pouvoir et entrée de ville: le château Narbonnais de Toulouse', 4e Congrès International d'Archéologie Médiévale et Moderne, Paris, 3–8 septembre 2007, http://medieval-europe-paris-2007.univ-paris1.fr/J.%20Catalo.pdf.

Cazelles, R., 'Le parti navarrais jusqu'a la mort d'Étienne Marcel', *Bulletin philologique et historique do Comité des Travaux Historiques et Scientifiques*, 1960, pp. 839–69.

Cazelles, R., *Société politique, noblesse et couronne sous Jean le Bon et Charles V*, Geneva: Librairie Droz, 1982.

Cazellese, R., *Étienne Marcel*, Paris: Tallandier, 2006.

Collins, A. L., *Greater Than Emperor: Cola di Rienzo and the World of Fourteenth-Century Rome*, Ann Arbor: University of Michigan Press, 2002.

Contamine, P., *Guerre, État et Société à la Fin du Moyen Âge*, Paris: Mouton, 1972.

Contamine, P. (ed.), *La noblesse au moyen age*, Paris: Fayard, 1976.

Contamine, P. (ed.), *Histoire Militaire de la France*, vol. 1, *Des origines á 1715*, Paris, 1992.

Contamine, P., 'The Norman "Nation" and the French "Nation" in the Fourteenth and Fifteenth Centuries', in D. Bates and A. Curry (eds), *England and Normandy in the Middle Ages*, London: The Hambledon Press, 1994.

Cowper, M., *Cathar Castles: Fortresses of the Albigensian Crusade 1209–1300*, Oxford: Osprey, 2006.

Curry, A. and Hughes, H. (eds) *Arms, Armies and Fortifications in the Hundred Years War*, Woodbridge: Boydell and Brewer, 1994.

Dejean, S., 'L'incursion du Prince Noir en Agenais et en Touloussain (1355)', in *La Guerre au Moyen Age*, Toulouse: Académie Touloussaine d'Histoire et d'Arts Militaires, 1994, pp. 36–53.

Denifle, P. H., *La Guerre de Cent Ans et la Désolaton des Églises, Monastères et Hopitaux en France*, Paris, 1899; repr. Brussels: Impression Anastaltique, 1965.

Depoin, M. J., *La maison de Chambly sous les Capétiens directs*, Paris: Imprimerie National, 1915.

Deviosse, J., *Jean le Bon*, Paris: Fayard, 1985.

Dommanget, M., *La Jacquerie*, Paris: Maspero, 1971.

Estancelin, L., *Histoire des Comtes d'Eu*, Paris: Chez Delaunay, 1821.

Field, S. L., 'Marie of St.-Pol and Her Books', *English Historical Review* 125, 2010, pp. 255–78.

Fowler, K., *The King's Lieutenant: Henry of Grosmont, First Duke of Lancaster 1310–1361*, New York: Barnes & Noble, 1969.

Fowler, K. (ed.), *The Hundred Years War*, London: Macmillan, 1971.

Foy, T., *A Guide to Archery*, London: Pelham Books, 1980.

Giraudet, E., *Histoire de la ville de Tours*, Tours, 1873.

Given-Wilson, C., *The Royal Household and the King's Affinity*, Princeton: Princeton University Press, 1986.

Given-Wilson, C. and Briac, F., 'Edward III's Prisoners of War: The Battle of Poitiers and Its Context', *English Historical Review* 116, September 2001, pp. 802–33.

Green, D., *Edward the Black Prince: Power in Medieval Europe*, Harlow: Longman, 2007.

Grézillier, A., *Histoire de Rochechouart, des origines à la Révolution*, Paris: Dupanier, 1977.

Hardy, R., *Longbow: A Social and Military History*, Cambridge: Patrick Stephens, 1976.

Harvey, J., *The Black Prince and His Age*, London: B. T. Batsford, 1976.

Hatcher, J., *The Black Death*, London: Phoenix, 2008.

Henneman, J. B., *Royal Taxation in Fourteenth-Century France: The Development of War Financing, 1322–1356*, Princeton: Princeton University Press, 1971.

Hewitt, H. J., *The Black Prince's Expedition*, Manchester University Press, 1958; repr. Barnsley: Pen and Sword, 2010.

Hyland, A., *The Horse in the Middle Ages*, Stroud: Sutton, 1999.

Kaeuper. R. W. and Kennedy, E., *The Book of Chivalry of Geoffroi de Charny: Text, Context and Translation*, Philadelphia: University of Pennsylvania Press, 1996.

Keen, M., *Chivalry*, London: Yale University Press, 1984.

Kingsford, C. L., 'Knollys, Robert', *Oxford Dictionary of National Biography*.

Kosto, A. J., *Hostages in the Middle Ages*, Oxford: Oxford University Press, 2012.

Lagabrielle, S., *Gaston Fébus: Prince Soleil 1331–1391*, Paris: Grand Palais, 2011.

Lannoy, F. de, *La Cité de Carcassonne*, Bayeux: Heimdal, 2004.

Lenoir, D., *Prevues généalogiques at historiques de la maison d'Harcourt*, Paris, 1907.

Livingstone, M. and Witzel, M, *The Road to Crécy: The English Invasion of France, 1346*, London: Longman, 2005.

Longman, C. J. and Walrond, H., *Archery*, London: Longmans, Green & Co, 1884.

Longman, W., *The History of the Life and Times of Edward the Third*, London: Longmans, Green & Co, 1869.

Luce, S., *Histoire de la Jacquerie d'après des documents inédits*, Paris: A. Durand, 1859.

Luttrell, A., 'Juan Fernandez de Heredia's History of Greece', *Byzantine and Modern Greek Studies* 34 (1), 2010.

McGlynn, S., *By Sword and Fire: Cruelty and Atrocity in Medieval Warfare*, London: Weidenfeld & Nicolson, 1978.

McHardy, A. K., 'Some Reflections on Edward III's Use of Propaganda', in J. Bothwell (ed.), *The Age of Edward III*, York: York Medieval Press, 2001, pp. 171–92.

Michaud, J. and Cabanis, A. (eds), *Histoire de Narbonne*, Toulouse: Privat, 2004.

Miller, W., *The Latins in the Levant: A History of Frankish Greece (1204–1566)*, New York: E.P. Dutton, 1908.

Minois, G., *Poitiers, 19 Septembre 1356*, Paris: Tallandier.

Moisant, J., *Le Prince Noir en Aquitaine*, Paris, 1894.

Morice, P. H., *Memoirs pour servir a preuves a l'histoire ecclesiastique et civile de Bretagne*, Paris, 1742.

Mortimer, I., *The Perfect King: The Life of Edward III, Father of the English Nation*, London: Vintage, 2008.

Mumby, J., Barber, R. and Brown, R., *Edward III's Round Table at Windsor*, Woodbridge: Boydell and Brewer, 2007.

Mundy, J. H., *Society and Government at Toulouse in the Age of the Cathars*, Toronto: Pontifical Institute of Medieval Studies, 1997.

Nicholas, N. H., *The Controversy Between Sir Richard Scrope and Sir Robert Grosvenor in the Court of Chivalry, AD MCCCLXXXV-MCCCXC*, London, 1832.

Nicol, D. M., *The Despotate of Epirus, 1267–1470: A Contribution to the History of Greece in the Middle Ages*, Cambridge: Cambridge University Press, 2010.

Nicolle, D., *French Armies of the Hundred Years War*, London: Osprey, 2000.

Noble, P., 'The Perversion of an Ideal', in C. Harper-Bill and R. Harvey (eds), *Medieval Knighthood*, vol. 4, Woobridge: Boydell and Brewer, 1992, pp. 177–86.

Oakeshott, R. E., *The Sword in the Age of Chivalry*, London: Lutterworth, 1961.

Oakeshott, R. E., *The Knight and His Horse*, London: Lutterworth, 1962.

Oman, C., *History of the Art of War in the Middle Ages*, London: Methuen, 1924.

Ormrod, W. M., *The Reign of Edward III: Crown and Political Society in England, 1327–1377*, London: Guild, 1990.

Ormrod, W. M., 'Ufford, Robert, first Earl of Suffolk', *Oxford Dictionary of National Biography*, 2004.

Packe, M., *King Edward III*, London: Routledge & Kegan Paul, 1983.

Payne-Galway, R., *The Book of the Crossbow*, London: Constable, 1995.

Pellisier, A., *Innocent VI le reformateur, deuxième pape Limousin (1352–1362)*, Tulle: F. Layotte, 1961.

Poux, J., *La Cité de Carcassonne*, Toulouse: Privat, 1923.

Powicke, M., *Military Obligation in Medieval England*, Oxford: Clarendon, 1962.

Prestwich, M., *The Three Edwards: War and State in England 1272–1377*, London, 1980.

Prestwich, M., *Armies and Warfare in the Middle Ages: The English Experience*, New Haven, CN: Yale University Press, 1996.

Prince, A. E., 'The Strength of English Armies in the Reign of Edward III', *English Historical Review* 46, 1951, pp. 355–66.

Quillet, J., *Charles V, le Roi lettré*, Paris: Perrin, 2002.

Rogers, C. J., *War Cruel and Sharp: English Strategy under Edward III, 1327–1360*, Woodbridge: Boydell and Brewer, 2000.

Rogers, C. J. (ed.), *The Wars of Edward III*, Woodbridge: Boydell and Brewer, 1999.

Saul, N., *Knights and Esquires: The Gloucestershire Gentry in the Fourteenth Century*, Oxford: Oxford University Press, 1981.

Saul, N., *Scenes From Provincial Life: Knightly Familes in Sussex, 1280–1400*, Oxford: Oxford University Press, 1986.

Saltzman, L. F., *English Trade in the Middle Ages*, Oxford: Clarendon, 1931.

Strayer, J. R., *The Reign of Philip the Fair*, Ann Arbor: University of Michigan Press, 1980.

Strayer, J. R., *The Albigensian Crusades*, Ann Arbor: University of Michigan Press, 1993.

Sumption, J., *The Albigensian Crusade*, London: Faber, 1978.

Sumption, J., *The Hundred Years War*, vol. 1, *Trial by Battle*, London: Faber & Faber, 1990.

Sumption, J., *The Hundred Years War*, vol. 2, *Trial by Fire*, London: Faber & Faber, 1999.

Teutsch, C., *Victory at Poitiers: The Black Prince and the Medieval Art of War*, Barnsley: Pen & Sword, 2010.

Tourneur-Aumont, J. M., *La bataille de Poitiers (1356) et la construction de France*, Paris: Sceaux, 1940.

Tuck, A., *Crown and Nobility 1272–1461*, Oxford: Oxford University Press, 1985.

Vernier, R., *Lord of the Pyrenees: Gaston Fébus, Count of Foix (1331–1391)*, Woodbridge: Boydell and Brewer, 2008.

Vincent, N., 'The Magna Carta (1215) and the *Charte aux Normands* (1315): Some Anglo-Norman Connections and Correspondences', *The Jersey and Guernsey Law Review*, vol. 2, 2015, pp. 189–97.

Vivent, J., *La Guerre de Cent Ans*, Paris: Flammarion, 1954.

Wood, D., *Clement VI: The Pontificate and Ideas of an Avignon Pope*, Cambridge: Cambridge University Press, 1989.

Zacour, N. P., 'Talleyrand: The Cardinal of Périgord (1301–1364)', *Transactions of the American Philosophical Society* n. s. 50 (7), 1960, pp. 54–60.